**The Early
Childhood Educator
at Work**

The Early Childhood Educator at Work

MILLIE ALMY
University of California
Berkeley

McGraw-Hill Book Company
New York   St. Louis   San Francisco   Düsseldorf   Johannesburg
Kuala Lumpur   London   Mexico   Montreal   New Delhi   Panama   Paris
São Paulo   Singapore   Sydney   Tokyo   Toronto

The Early Childhood Educator at Work

Copyright © 1975 by McGraw-Hill, Inc. All rights reserved. Printed in
the United States of America. No part of this publication may be
reproduced, stored in a retrieval system, or transmitted, in any form or by
any means, electronic, mechanical, photocopying, recording, or otherwise,
without the prior written permission of the publisher.

34567890 DODO 79876

This book was set in Times Roman by Compucomp Corporation. The
editors were Stephen D. Dragin, Thomas H. Quinn, and Phyllis T. Dulan;
the cover was designed by Pencils Portfolio, Inc.; the production
supervisor was Thomas J. LoPinto.

R. R. Donnelley & Sons Company was
printer and binder.

Library of Congress Cataloging in Publication Data

Almy, Millie Corinne, date
  The early childhood educator at work.

  Includes bibliographical references.
  1. Education, Primary. 2. Education, Preschool.
I. Title.
LB1507.A4   372.21   74-8858
ISBN 0-07-001126-5
ISBN 0-07-001125-7 (pbk.)

Contents

Preface

This book deals with the expanding field of early childhood education and care. It looks to the emergence of a new professional role—that of the early childhood educator. In this role a person competent in teaching children under the age of seven facilitates in a variety of ways the development and learning of young children.

Much that is done intuitively by those who enjoy working with young children effectively furthers the child's development. Nevertheless, full realization of the potentialities in early childhood is contingent on a wider range of supporting knowledge and skills than the typical early childhood teacher has. A clearer differentiation of teaching and supporting roles seems essential if early childhood programs are to build on accumulating research related to child development and learning.

This book is addressed to students and experienced teachers who either will come to fill the role of early childhood educator or will be working with other individuals who have that role. It should also be useful to those who are involved in training teachers and other workers in early childhood education and care and to administrators and others who are interested in understanding the scope of the field.

The organization of the book may best be described as spiral. Initially, to give the reader a sense of the diversity in early childhood education, I describe several programs in operation during the late sixties and early seventies. The following chapter introduces the role of the early childhood educator, comparing it to the more traditional role of the early childhood teacher. Chapters 3, 4, and 5 return again to the field of early childhood education, examining it from different perspectives. Chapter 3 considers some persistent issues whose resolution influences the work of both the teacher and the early childhood educator. Chapter 4, concerned with the analysis of early childhood programs, suggests some dimensions for comparing the kinds of programs that were initially described in Chapter 1. Chapter 5 examines the settings in which such programs may occur.

Chapter 6 moves back to the role of the early childhood educator. It deals with teaching, regarded as the core function of the role. In Chapter 7 provisioning for development and learning is looked at both as something the teacher does and as something for which she needs the support of the early childhood educator.

The following two chapters are directed to the ways the teacher and the early childhood educator work with other adults. Chapter 8 focuses on working with parents, and Chapter 9 deals with the functions of training and supervision and also includes some functions such as advocacy and negotiation that bear less directly on the child and teaching.

In Chapter 10 the focus returns to the child, as we consider how the teacher is to assess his development and learning and how the early childhood educator supports the teacher in these efforts.

Chapter 11, like the beginning chapters of the book, considers the broad field of early childhood education and the research that is needed to sustain it. It sees the early childhood educator taking an active and essential part in such research.

The concluding chapter represents a personal view in two senses. I use it to reiterate some of my own favorite themes and also to say a word for the early childhood educator as a person.

The book is not intended as either a survey of the field or a "how-to-do-it" manual. It is more concerned with issues than with providing a comprehensive view of the entire area. The student or the teacher who reads it cannot expect to be equipped thereby to function in the role that I have described. Nevertheless, if they are stimulated to reflect on the scope of the role and the complexities involved in the field, and to pursue some of the work of other authors that I have cited, the book will have served its intended purpose.

Although I take full responsibility for the presentation of both the field of early childhood education and the role of the early childhood educator, many people have contributed to my formulation. I began thinking about the book while I was at Teachers College, Columbia University. The framework for the role of the early childhood educator was worked out in discussion with the other faculty members of the Program in Early Childhood Education, Professors Patrick C. Lee and Joseph Stevens. Some of the conceptions were challenged and refined in a faculty seminar including among others, Professors Mary Alice White, Arno Bellack, Bruce Joyce, and Jonas Soltis. Sessions with Professors Ann Boehm Kaplan and Richard Weinberg were also productive in shaping my thinking. Professor Bellack gave specific and helpful counsel in the initial stages of the writing.

Although my move to the University of California at Berkeley somewhat delayed the completion of the book, it also enhanced it. My work brought me the stimulation of working with new colleagues and put me in closer touch with classrooms, with student teachers, and with the politics of day care.

I owe special gratitude to my graduate students, who have in many ways enlarged my horizons. Three of them, Nancy Gropper at Teachers College, and Enid Elliott and Celia Genishi at the University of California, have assisted me with bibliographical matters. Celia Genishi's cheerful willingness, over a period of two years, to track down the most elusive reference, coupled with her insight and good judgment, contributed greatly to the final completion of the book.

My thanks go also to Grace O'Connell for her expeditious typing of the manuscript.

The book was read in manuscript by Professor Lilian G. Katz, Professor Jane B. Raph, Bertha Addison, and Celia Genishi. Their comments and suggestions were of inestimable help to me.

Finally, I wish to acknowledge with appreciation the publishers and individuals who gave me permission to reproduce copyrighted materials.

Millie Almy

The Early
Childhood Educator
at Work

Chapter 1

The Scope of Early Childhood Education: An Introduction

We have a chance to build a truly creative program of early childhood development for all children. But we could also squander this opportunity and institutionalize, by default, an elaborate system of baby sitting for the poor. [1]

The decade of the 1960s, heralded as a period of renaissance for early childhood education, turned into the decade of the seventies with some marks of accomplishment, some continuing promises, and more than a few problems. The attention of many people, including the Congress and the President of the United States, had been turned to the early years. Some of the possibilities of so governing the young child's encounters with his environment as to markedly improve his basic intelligence [2] had been explored and found to be both difficult and expensive. Nonetheless an increasing number of parents, in

---

[1] Walter F. Mondale, "Day Care: Education or Custody?" *The National Elementary Principal,* 51(1): 81, 82 (September 1971).
[2] J. McV. Hunt, *Intelligence and Experience* (New York: Ronald Press, 1961), p. 363.

all segments of society and for a variety of reasons, wanted, and in many instances desperately needed, to have their own efforts at child care and education augmented.

The scope of current efforts to expand on and support the parental function is difficult to appraise. The period of years encompassed by early childhood has not been precisely defined. Although fairly adequate statistics are available for programs operated under the aegis of the public schools and of established social agencies, many programs have no association with any institution traditionally involved in child care and education—nor is it always clear which of several governmental agencies properly has jurisdiction over them.

A point sometimes at issue is the distinction to be made between early childhood care and early childhood education. Although it seems obvious that certain kinds of care may be miseducative and that education cannot proceed effectively unless the young child also receives adequate care, the distinction, as Senator Mondale implies, may serve as a deterrent to the development of effective programs.

The present volume, although recognizing that different individuals may carry different degrees of responsibility for care and for education, takes the position that *programs* ought not to be differentiated on that basis.

EARLY CHILDHOOD EDUCATION IN THIS BOOK

This book is directed toward the education of young children and encompasses the variety of teaching strategies and curricula available and the support needed to sustain them. Its principal focus is on group settings that are deliberately intended to affect the learning and development of children. The age range is from infancy to the age of seven. This broad age range permits a longitudinal view of development and learning. From a practical point of view it avoids the isolation of the kindergarten from the first grade and takes into account current research and experimental programs for children under the age of three.

Day care is included within the focus in the belief that only rarely will a day care program consider its function to be solely custodial. Although the principal focus is on group settings, the discussion includes programs that do not conform to the usual notions of day care centers, nursery schools, and kindergartens, including those that are home-based.

The diversity of programs encompassed in early childhood education reflects new knowledge of the early years and a variety of attempts to apply that knowledge effectively. Such application requires an understanding of early child development and learning and of the caretaking and instructional skills that facilitate development. This book looks to the emergence of a new professional person identified as an "early childhood educator." This person would have not only the understanding and skills required for teaching young children, but also the knowledge and skills necessary to collaborate with others in the planning and implementation of programs for young children. Some of these programs may follow traditional lines. Others may differ radically from those now in operation.

SOME PROGRAMS DESCRIBED

Whenever a college or university offers professional training in early childhood education it receives many inquiries, not only from prospective students, but also from the surrounding schools and agencies that provide services for young children. Some seek to employ teachers, some offer opportunities for student participation, some want information or assistance related to various aspects of their work. Many of them are agreeable to being visited. Brief descriptions of some of the kinds of schools and centers that I have visited while involved in graduate early childhood education programs on both coasts may serve to illustrate the expansion of the field, its diversity, and the difficulty of defining its scope. Since some of the descriptions are drawn from recollection rather than from records, it seems appropriate not to identify any of the schools or centers. The names given them here are fictitious.

Certain staff members in the programs to be described carry on the functions of the early childhood educator. In some programs they have had appropriate training for those functions, in others they are learning as they go.

The Lakeview Center for Infant Day Care

Housed in a large metropolitan church center which also has a weekday nursery school, this program operating on an 8 A.M. to 5 P.M. schedule provides care for the infants of unwed mothers who are enrolled in work training programs or employed. The program has interdisciplinary sponsorship involving the public schools, the Department of Health, the Department of Social Services, and a hospital mental health clinic. The director holds a master's degree in early childhood education. The rest of the full-time staff were selected for their mothering abilities and are being trained by the director as the program proceeds. A number of students from public health, pediatrics, social service, and psychology departments participate on a part-time basis.

University Student Child Care Centers

These centers grew out of the cooperative efforts of student mothers unable to make satisfactory arrangements for the care of their children while attending classes or studying. The centers operate from 8 A.M. to 5 P.M. and include children from six months to five years of age, with about half of them under the age of two years. Different children are cared for at different hours of the day, corresponding to the university class schedule, so that the total number of children served is considerably larger than those in attendance at any particular hour. The staff includes a head teacher with training and experience in early childhood education whose major responsibility is to "plan and implement the educational program," teachers licensed for work in children's centers, who may also be students, and teacher aides, most of whom are students. Parents are required to participate either with the children or by contributing related services. Recently the staff has been expanded to include a social worker to assist with problems of concern to the parents. A major part of the head teacher's work is devoted to the training of the staff members including the parent participants.

The Barrett Avenue Day Care Center and Community School

Now operated separately but sharing similar philosophies and serving the same neighborhood, both of these programs for children from two to eight owe their existence primarily to the efforts of a militant Black woman who established an illegal day care center, secured some private support, and after a long series of confrontations with agencies having jurisdiction over such centers, obtained temporary licensing and funding. The day care center is open from 8 A.M. to 6 P.M. and does not at present have facilities for the care of infants, though the need for their care is as great as that for those over two. The school's hours are from 9 A.M. to 3 P.M. The school, somewhat more than the center, serves an economically diverse group of parents. The curriculum in both the center and the school is quite similar, emphasizing the spontaneous interests of both children and teachers. Both programs have placed greater importance on securing staff with empathy for the background and aspirations of the parents than they have on college degrees and certification to teach.

The Masters School

Started in the late 1950s by two mothers who had received Montessori[3] training, this suburban school initially operated in the classic Montessori fashion. In recent years it has expanded to include children ages three through nine. The Montessori program has also been extensively modified. A wide

---

[3] Further discussion of Montessori and other programs mentioned here will be found in Chapter 6.

variety of equipment supplements the Montessori materials, and a "responsive environment" booth of the kind originally developed by Omar K. Moore is available for the use of the younger groups. The fives, sixes, and sevens participate in a British Infant School program. The Montessori-trained teachers continue in administrative capacity, but strict Montessori training is no longer a requirement for the staff. For example, one teacher was trained in England in Infant School methods; another holds a degree in architecture and has had no professional preparation for teaching.

The Children's Wonder Center

This widely advertised center is one of a commercially operated chain. Its program, designed by psychologists, is intended to provide intellectual stimulation and challenge for two- to six-year-olds. Parents make arrangements to bring their child once a week for two hours on a month-to-month basis. The child's interests and skills are assessed as he plays, and prescriptions for the appropriate toys and games are given. The center is equipped with various electronic devices, including a programmed typewriter and closed-circuit TV. For many children the two hours at the center each week provide their only opportunity for play in a group setting. Other children also participate in informal play groups and some are also enrolled in nursery schools or kindergartens. The staff members are designated as "learning assistants." Individuals who have not had specific training in early childhood education are preferred to those who have had such training.

Hill City Early Childhood Center

This center is a school within a school. Located in an innercity elementary school, its enrollment begins with children as young as three and includes those in the second grade. The center has its own director and a staff of teachers who meet requirements for city certification, plus teaching aides who are drawn from the community. The nearby university provides training. It also collaborates in the design of the curriculum, which involves a large proportion of programmed instruction. All staff members, but especially the director and head teachers, are concerned, in somewhat the same way as the staff at the Children's Wonder Center, with assessment. Each child proceeds at his own pace, although under considerable supervision, through a series of tasks intended to ensure that he acquires the skills and knowledge essential to successful coping with the elementary school program. When he finishes his tasks the preschooler participates in play.

The New Life Center

The parents of the children in this center are all members of a large commune. Their motives for joining the commune were varied, but all who continue in it are dedicated to a simple life style that involves honesty and commitment to each other. The children live in quarters apart from their parents. They are cared for by members of the commune whose concern for the children is reflected in the interesting and stimulating environment they provide for the groups of infants, toddlers, and older children. Their goals for the children focus on their cognitive development and on learning to care for one another.

The Open Doorway School

An integral part of a city school system, this school offers a coordinated and comprehensive program for 150 three- to eight-year-olds. Its parents include a mixture of socioeconomic and ethnic backgrounds. Many are enrolled because they need the day care service, others because they value the kind of integration of home and school that Open Doorway is attempting to provide. In many ways this school is trying to establish a long-term developmental way of looking at children. It is accordingly working with mixed age groups and experimenting with new kinds of evaluation.

The director of this center holds a master's degree in early childhood education and maintains a regular teaching schedule for a few hours each week, so that she knows what is going on with the children. She also trains other staff members, confers with parents, occasionally participates in proposal writing, and fulfills an advocacy role through frequent contacts with state legislators.

The East Side Houses Family Day Care Program

This program provides, in a sense, a series of miniature day care programs. A "receiving mother," who has children of her own, takes daytime responsibility for additional children whose mothers are employed. The receiving mother is licensed by the Department of Social Services to care for a specific number of children. A social worker at East Side Houses assists in the arrangements made by the "sending mother" and also provides some supervision to the receiving mother. From time to time receiving mothers meet together with the supervisor and specialists in early childhood education and such related fields as nutrition and pediatrics. Topics they have been particularly interested in include discipline and the provision of toys.

The Parent Development Program

This program is sponsored by a research center that has concerned itself with the early education of disadvantaged children for nearly a decade. Each week at a regularly scheduled time a parent worker visits each of the homes of a selected group of parents. She brings with her simple materials likely to catch the interest of infants and toddlers, enlisting the mother's assistance in using the materials with her children, reviewing with her their progress since her last visit, and planning their activities for the week to come. Now employed by the research center, most of the parent workers were themselves parent participants only a year or so ago.

The staff in this program includes, in addition to the parent workers, individuals trained in child development and early childhood education. They have been responsible for the initial planning of material and equipment to interest the children. Some are also involved in research related to the program.

More Traditional Programs

The reader will augment the above descriptions with the centers and schools he has observed. He will add those that may be more familiar: the traditional kindergarten, first and second grades as found in public, parochial, and independent schools across the United States; nursery schools and prekindergartens, sometimes associated with other schools, sometimes operated independently by individuals, universities, and colleges, or by high school home economics programs; early childhood programs in community centers, parks departments, mental health clinics and hospitals; day care centers, sometimes termed "day nurseries," with as diverse sponsorship as nursery schools and kindergartens.

The reader will also have noted that certain TV programs, of which "Sesame Street" (reported to be watched at least twice a week by some 8 million children) is a noteworthy example, are intended to serve educational functions for young children. Such programs, and unfortunately a variety of others not particularly intended for child audiences, may also be used to supplement or in some instances even to supplant the caretaking role of the adults. Informal investigations of day care across the United States have turned up many instances of children being put down in front of the TV set for long periods of the day. Although this practice seems more likely to occur where the center is operating illegally or with insufficient staff or equipment, it is not limited to such situations. For example, one center, housed in a large metropolitan church, relied almost entirely on the TV set to occupy the children, despite the availability of a park playground on the next block.

Numbers of Children in the United States Involved in Programs

The uncertain lines between programs that primarily provide day care and programs that primarily provide education, the numbers of research and demonstration programs that have come into existence under the aegis of different agencies, and the numbers of programs that are operating either illicitly or under temporary permits, make it difficult to estimate the number of children actually involved.

As far as day care is concerned, the U.S. Department of Labor Statistics shows that in March 1972, 32.9 million women were either working or seeking work, and of these women, 12.7 million were mothers. These working mothers included 4.4. million women who had children under the age of six years. Licensed day care centers and family day care homes were available for less than a million of these.[4]

The U.S. Office of Education reports on the children between the ages of three and six years who were attending "organized public and non-public education programs" in October 1972.[5] The figures exclude children in programs offering "essentially custodial care." A little more than 76 percent of all five-year-olds are enrolled in educational programs, the majority of them in public kindergartens. The number of four-year-olds in school is much smaller, amounting to 33.5 percent, while a still smaller proportion of three-year-olds (15.5 percent) attend school. The number of children ages three to five attending educational programs has increased slowly but steadily from 1964, when 26 percent of all children in those age groups attended, to 1972, when 40 percent attended.

COMPARING EARLY CHILDHOOD PROGRAMS

What features do the diverse kinds of programs described above have in common? What is the nature of the differences, some of which are immediately apparent, others less so? How do they affect the children, the teachers, and the parents who are involved? Some such analysis of these specific programs and of programs across the country is essential not only to describe the field of early childhood education as it now exists but also to begin to prescribe needed changes in both programs and professional training.

[4] "Day Care Facts," Women's Bureau Pamphlet No. 16, Employment Standards Administration (Washington: U.S. Department of Labor, 1973), pp. 1–2.

[5] Linda A. Barker, *Preprimary Enrollment, October, 1972* (Washington: HEW, Office of Education, National Center for Educational Statistics, 1973).

Characteristics of the Children

The one feature that all programs have in common is that they are directed to children younger than age ten. Whether early childhood programs encompass the primary grades, usually defined as first through third, or are limited to preprimary programs appears to vary with school systems and with authors. One recent study clearly states that "early childhood education is a term commonly used to describe programs of formal schooling for children under six years of age."[6] On the other hand, Lilian G. Katz, director of the Educational Resources Information Center for Early Childhood Education (ERIC-/ECE), reports that the official responsibility for that clearinghouse is for research documents related to the development of children from birth through the primary grades. The *Encyclopedia of Education*[7] defines the age range for early childhood education as from two or three years to eight years.

Until recently, most authorities assumed that the lower limit for early childhood education would be age three, or possibly two, holding to the view that children younger[8] than that should be cared for (and taught) in the home setting. The reality of the need for day care for many infants and toddlers, coupled with research highlighting the nature of infant learning, has led them to reexamine this assumption.

Because there are few schools or centers that encompass the age span from infancy to age seven, it is not unusual for children to make as many as three transitions before they reach second grade. If the mother works, the child may be transported to whatever center has a program for infants or toddlers, then shifted to another more accessible nursery school or child care center program when he is three or four, and finally enrolled in the public school, which may or may not have provisions for after-school care, when he is five.

Although age is the most clearly specified characteristic of the population of children served by a program, a variety of others may also be established. Some schools in communities such as that of the Masters School discourage children whose performance on an individually administered intelligence test is not considerably better than average. Children with physical handicaps may also be excluded, although in recent years increasing effort has been made in many schools to include children with manageable handicaps. In some communities special nursery schools have been developed for service to children

---

[6] William P. McClure and Audra May Pence, *Early Childhood and Basic Elementary and Secondary Education; Needs, Programs, Demands, Costs,* National Educational Finance Project, Special Study No. 1, Bureau of Educational Research, College of Education, University of Illinois at Urbana-Champaign, 1970.

[7] Lee C. Deighton, ed., *Encyclopedia of Education,* vol. 3 (New York: Macmillan, Free Press, 1971), p. 137.

[8] From a practical point of view the question of whether or not a younger child had been toilet trained often served as the basis for admission or refusal.

with specific handicaps such as blindness, deafness, or cerebral palsy. Some programs, with special facilities and teachers with special training, have sometimes focused on a particular defect or disease, unfortunately excluding children with similar needs stemming from diseases less well publicized or funded.

"Emotional disturbance," a term that may cover anything from mild behavior disorders to severe psychosis, serves to exclude children from some programs, and on the other hand may make them eligible for those with more therapeutic orientations.

In some programs it is not so much the characteristics of the children as the socioeconomic status of the parents that determines their eligibility. Thus, until the advent of Head Start and a number of experimental programs intended for the "disadvantaged,"[9] early childhood programs for children younger than five were rarely available to children whose parents could not afford to pay tuition.

Program Goals

Programs clearly differ in the missions they have set for themselves. Day care programs place first priority on the safety and physical well-being of the children. Programs such as the Masters School, Wonder Center, and Hill City Early Childhood Center are not unconcerned with such matters, but give major emphasis to the promotion of intellectual development and academic skills.

Program goals may be explicit, spelled out in a descriptive brochure or a proposal for funding, or they may be implicit, sometimes obvious in the activities that the program encompasses but not set forth in words. Perhaps to no one's surprise, the goals that are stated are not always reflected in what goes on in a program. For example, in a number of public school kindergartens, even before the decade of the sixties with its pervasive concern for the academic, the avowed intent of the program was to promote each child's mental, emotional, social, and physical development. Nevertheless, a visitor, watching the children spend a major part of their morning bent over reading readiness workbooks and given little opportunity to move about or to talk with one another, could only conclude that the mission of the program was to get the children "ready" for the next grade. In other programs, with the same avowed goals, often stated in terms of the development of the "whole child," an observer watching youngsters playing with a minimum of adult intervention, was often convinced that the program actually provided very little for the minds of the children.

---

[9] Throughout the decade of the 1960s euphemisms such as "culturally deprived" and "socially disadvantaged" were used to describe children whose parents were poor. Both terms reflect middle-class ethnocentrism. Throughout this book I shall use these terms only in the context of the 1960s.

In the sixties the global, undifferentiated goals held by traditional early childhood education programs were called into question on many sides. On the one hand, curriculum reforms intended to modernize the teaching of the disciplines, particularly mathematics and science, extended downward into kindergarten. On the other hand, it became apparent that a large number of children in the public schools were not learning the elementary skills of reading and computation, let alone being able to cope effectively with the abstractions of the new curricula. Developmental and educational psychologists turned their interest and research to cognition and learning in the early years. The federal government began support of innovative programs for young children.[10] Even those programs that resisted giving priority to cognitive goals found themselves giving consideration to the ways they were providing for the children's mental development.

In the 1970s a reordering of priorities appears to be under way in many programs. It is not that cognition is no longer fashionable, but rather that its place in the functioning of the young child is beginning to be better understood. As the psychologists turn their attention to motivation and affect, and as a generation of young parents are more concerned with what it means to be human than with what it takes to attain material success, it is not unlikely that more programs will again see their mission as one of facilitating the development of the "whole child." But the accomplishment of that mission will undoubtedly take place in different ways in different centers, depending not only on the characteristics of the children and their parents, but also on the pedagogical theories espoused by those responsible for the center.

Theoretical Bases for Programs

Once a society becomes self-conscious about the nurture of its young, the seed of educational theory is sown. Because men are anxious to control the educative process, they hypothesize as to how the outcomes they envision for their pupils can best be secured. As their observation becomes refined and their thinking more precise, educational practice ceases to be mechanically conventional or blindly empirical. The systematic concern with what to teach and how to teach it stimulates the growth of educational theory both among the professionals who apply it and among the laymen who, in all history, probably have never been completely satisfied with what schools do to and for their children.[11]

---

[10] Doxey A. Wilkerson, "Compensatory Education: Defining the Issues," in Jerome Hellmuth, ed., *The Disadvantaged Child*, vol. 3, *Compensatory Education, A National Debate* (New York: Brunner/Mazel, 1970), pp. 24–35.
[11] Harry S. Broudy and John R. Palmer, *Exemplars of Teaching Method* (Chicago: Rand McNally, 1965), p. 1.

Prior to the 1960s the pedagogical theories espoused by most early childhood educators could be traced back to Comenius, Pestalozzi, and Froebel,[12]
and reflected the influence of Maria Montessori, John Dewey, Arnold Gesell,
and of Sigmund Freud particularly as interpreted by Susan Isaacs and Erik
Erikson. Most early childhood educators before the 1960s would have agreed
with John Anderson's statement in the 1947 yearbook of the National Society
for the Study of Education that in the curriculum for early childhood

> content should be minimized and stress should be placed on adjustment and mode
> of attack on problems. It is not what the child learns in formal terms which is
> important but what he learns in the way of self control, emotional balance, interest
> and enthusiasm for the materials in question.[13]

In the 1960s, however, it began to appear that the content of the curriculum was important. Without attention to what the child learned, how
could he be assured of having the basic skills and concepts needed for meaningful learning in early elementary school? New, or at least different, theories were
brought to bear in the planning of early childhood programs.

With the exception of Montessori, most of the theories had not originally
been developed for pedagogical purposes. A major question for the sixties, and
it continues in the seventies, has to do with the feasibility of adapting psychological theories to the exigencies of the classroom. Great advantage accrues
when the teacher can operate on an understanding of principles, and not
merely intuitively. But some teachers are impatient at the necessity for considering the theory that underlies their work. Others question the relevance to the
classroom of theory that was developed elsewhere.

The theories most often brought to bear on early childhood practice in
the sixties were those of behavior reinforcement and social learning, particularly as derived from Skinner, and the cognitive-developmental theory of
Piaget.[14] In the Hill City Early Childhood Center, for example, the instructional procedures and the sequencing of the tasks presented to the children had
been developed by researchers who identified themselves as behaviorists, al-

---

[12] Samuel J. Braun and Esther P. Edwards, *History and Theory of Early Childhood Education* (Worthington, Ohio: Charles A. Jones Publishing Co., 1972), parts 2 and 3.

[13] John E. Anderson, "The Theory of Early Childhood Education," in Nelson B. Henry, ed., *Early
Childhood Education,* Forty-sixth Yearbook of the National Society for the Study of Education, part II
(Chicago: University of Chicago Press, 1947).

[14] Theories bearing on practice are discussed in Chapter 6. For background, see Alfred L. Baldwin,
Theories of Child Development (New York: John Wiley & Sons, 1969), esp. pp. 171-289, 391-494; Lawrence
Kohlberg, "Early Childhood Education, A Cognitive-Developmental View," *Child Development,* 39:1013-
62, 1968; Jonas Langer, *Theories of Development* (New York: Holt, Rinehart and Winston, 1969); and Paul
H. Mussen, ed., *Carmichael's Manual of Child Psychology* (New York: John Wiley & Sons, 1970), parts III
and IV.

though Piaget's empirical findings very likely provided an initial framework for much of the content of the program. Behavior theory likewise guided much of the program at Wonder Center.

The theory of Piaget has to do with the way the child's comprehension of his world changes, becoming more organized, more objective, and more capable of dealing with relationships among abstractions. It is a developmental, not a pedagogical, theory, although as Piaget has shown in his *Science of Education and the Psychology of the Child,*[15] it carries many implications for education.

Piaget's theory and the experimental work he has done have been interpreted in different ways by different educators. Many have drawn on his theory and findings to determine the order in which various concepts are to be presented to the children. Some have adapted for classroom use the tasks that he has presented to children in order to ascertain the level of their reasoning ability.[16] Others, including proponents of the modern British Infant School, have taken most seriously these aspects of the theory that relate to the child's intrinsic motivation and have developed curricula that provide large blocks of time for children to work at their own pace following their own interests.[17]

Proponents of both Piagetian theory and behavior theory are concerned that an ultimate effect of the educational program should be increased competence and feelings of self-esteem on the part of the child. Accordingly, theories about self-differentiation and enhancement are implicit in the thinking that guides program development. In the 1960s such theories received much less specific attention than did the theories of cognitive development. In the seventies, theories relating to both motivation and affect are more and more called into use.

The Role of the Teacher

Different psychological and pedagogical theories specify different guidance and instructional strategies on the part of the teacher. For example, in centers like Hill City Early Childhood and Wonder where behavior theory predominates, the teacher focuses on shaping the behavior of the children in desirable ways. The adults try to avoid giving attention to the children's "misbehavior" while providing frequent positive reinforcement for correct responses. Teach-

[15] Jean Piaget, *Science of Education and the Psychology of the Child* (New York: Orion Press, 1970).
[16] See, for example, Celia Stendler Lavatelli, *Piaget's Theory Applied to an Early Childhood Curriculum* (Boston: American Science and Engineering, Inc., 1970).
[17] See, for example, Molly Brearley, *The Teaching of Young Children: Some Applications of Piaget's Learning Theory* (New York: Schocken, 1970), and Lillian Weber, *The English Infant School and Informal Education* (Englewood Cliffs, N.J.: Prentice-Hall, 1971).

ers who have had Montessori training, as at the Masters School, function more as observers and seldom intervene in the children's activities except to assist them in the correct use of the materials.

Traditionally, the early childhood teacher has thought of herself more as guide than as instructor, particularly where children younger than five were concerned. She taught the rules for the use of materials and for social living directly; for example, "The sand stays in the sandbox" and "*Ask* John for the shovel. You do not need to grab it"; but she gave little, if any, direct instruction in more academic matters. A child might be asked to do a simple one-to-one correspondence when he matched four napkins to the four children sitting at his table for a snack, but should he prove unable to do it, his teacher was not likely to assemble sets of objects and provide tutorial assistance until he could. In contrast, in Hill City Early Childhood Center, each teacher spends a considerable portion of her time moving from child to child, interrogating each on the task in which he is engaged and helping him to correct his errors.

Probably as a result of the emphasis on instruction in innovative programs in the 1960s, the instructional aspects of the early childhood teacher's role have been highlighted in recent years. British Infant School teachers, for example, although they may not give direct instruction in the ways prescribed by behavior theory, are active facilitators of the child's learning, often using questions designed to facilitate his thinking.

The emphasis on instruction is widespread. For example, many of the receiving mothers in East Side Houses Family Day Care Program have asked for help in teaching the children so that they would be "better equipped for school." The Lakeview Center for Infant Day Care, although placing primary emphasis on the caretaking function, requires its staff to see that each baby has periods of active interaction with an adult in order to facilitate learning.

Since babies and young children are so dependent on adults, the nurturance or guidance function is essential. The instructional function may be interwoven with the caretaking or dealt with separately, at least for purposes of analysis. Nevertheless, even at these early ages, children need in a sense to be taught as well as cared for. Their learning is inextricably interwoven in their exchanges with the caretaker.

Materials and Equipment

Teaching the young child, despite the avidity with which he acquires proficiency in his native language, involves instruction that is more than verbal. Since at least the days of Pestalozzi and especially since Froebel, early education has considered that objects, toys, games, and other equipment are as essential to the program for the young child as books, paper, and pencils are for the older elementary school child. When the decade of the sixties began, the equipment and materials for nursery schools and kindergartens had become remarkably stereotyped. Aside from the facts that some classrooms had many building blocks and others few, that some were chaotically cluttered and others orderly, that some had easily accessible outdoor space and equipment and others lacked it, most classrooms looked very much alike.

As interest focused on cognitive development, and as some programs attempted to teach academic skills to children as young as four, classrooms changed in appearance. Montessori equipment, neglected for many years, was reintroduced in some. The manufacturers, capitalizing on the psychologists' interests, produced an ever-increasing number of "toys and games that teach." Few classrooms could afford the variety of electronic devices of the Wonder Center, but tape recorders equipped with earphones so the children could listen individually to tapes prepared either commercially or by their teacher or themselves, 8 mm projectors, and a variety of simple machines intended to program the children's responses appeared in many centers.

Programs relying heavily on commercial materials and equipment, such as the Masters School, contrast sharply with centers like Barrett Avenue or University Student Center, where the combination of insufficient funds and a concern for ecology have forced the staff to find discarded materials with which they can "make do." In both of these centers, fortunately, the staff has both the ingenuity and the understanding of children necessary to be able to improvise appropriately.

Parent Involvement

Just as programs vary in the extent to which they are dependent on commercial materials and equipment, they also vary in the kinds of relationships they have with parents. There is no evidence of a direct relationship between these two aspects of a program, although it is clear that parents who help to equip a school have different feelings about it than do parents who have no such role. However, parent involvement can take many forms.

In Wonder Center, for example, the elaborateness and unusualness of the equipment, the conduct of the learning counselors and assistants, the diagnostic procedures and reports are all calculated to further the parents' realization that they are entrusting their children to experts. The parents are not involved in the center program (although they can watch through closed-circuit television), but the reports they are given immediately following their child's visit, and the prescriptions provided for their guidance of the child's play at home during the week intervening between visits, are intended to make them feel both more responsible and more competent.

Many programs hold similar goals for parents, although most do not put so much stress on staff expertise. In contrast to those centers that do not encourage—or, in fact, discourage—parent participation, although observation may be permitted, are those that are dependent on parent involvement for their existence. Cooperative nursery schools were established by middle-class parents in the 1920s and have expanded in number through the years. Until after the mid-sixties they provided the best example of parental involvement in early childhood education. Then both poor parents and student parents, sometimes in collaboration, began to develop their own programs. The Barrett Avenue Day Care Center and Community School and the University Student Child Care Center are typical examples.

In both instances, the centers were established through the militancy of the parents. Initially, too, all the work of the centers was allotted to the parents, and any involvement of professional early childhood teachers was strongly resisted. However, as it became apparent that those who have been trained to work with groups of young children had skills and resources not immediately available to parents, the hostility toward the professional abated somewhat. Now, as in many similar centers, some professionals are employed, with their responsibilities to the parent group as policy makers increasingly clearly spelled out.

What has come to light also is the fact that some parents have great but often unrecognized potential for teaching young children. In certain innovative programs, for example the " paraprofessionals," who are often parents from the community, while initially lacking in training, have proved themselves more adaptable as well as more committed to the innovations than some teachers with years of experience.

In the 1970s many parents in all walks of life are looking for some kind of educationally oriented group experience for their young children. The kind of experience they are seeking varies widely as does their wish to be involved in the actual operation of the center where they find it. Nevertheless, nearly all of them want to be informed about what goes on, and a great many of them desire to have a real voice in policy making. Such interest has great promise not only for early childhood education but also for revitalizing public schools that have too long been indifferent to parents.

Evaluation and Research

The notions parents have about the values of early education appear to be derived from two major sources. On the one hand, many parents have seen their own or their neighbors' children apparently benefit from a particular program. On the other hand, the mass media, especially since 1965 and the advent of Head Start, have stressed the importance of the early years and have given considerable publicity not only to innovative programs actually in operation, but also to researchers and others with ideas for facilitating learning and development in those years. Less publicity, it appears, has been given to the evaluation of the programs and their effectiveness in realizing the goals they set themselves.

In perhaps no other aspect of current early childhood programs is there as much diversity as in the provision made for their evaluation. At one end of the spectrum, for example, is the Hill City Center where the goals for individual children are highly specific, and each child's recorded progress through the tasks prescribed for him provides a definite evaluative measure. At the other end of the spectrum the Barrett Avenue Center and School have much more global goals and measure their success in terms of the continued willingness of the parents to fight to maintain the programs. Wonder Center, which is like Hill City Center in the specificity of its stated goals, in one way resembles Barrett Avenue. Since it is designed for profit, it too cannot afford to have parents lose interest.

A growing concern for "accountability," that is, for proof that a program is effectively carrying out the mission set for it, parallels an increasing sophistication on the part of parents and the general public with regard to the possibilities for education. They have begun to recognize that a program with goals so global and socially desirable that no one could question them may easily fail to produce *evidence* of success even in what might be regarded as related subgoals. On the other hand, they are not misled when narrow and specific goals fail to take into consideration the variety of effects the program may have on children. In the case of Head Start, for example, the Westinghouse evaluation found no evidence that the program had affected later school achievement, but many parents bore witness that it had changed their own attitudes toward the possibilities for their children's education and their part in it.[18]

When programs begin to give priority to the development and learning of the child as a person, placing less emphasis on the academic, as appears to be the current trend, new ways of evaluating program effectiveness need to be devised. It seems likely, however, that much as at present, some programs will devote more time and effort to gathering valid evidence of accomplishment than will others.

In the long run, the critical test of any program lies in the reality it

---

[18] Westinghouse Learning Corporation, Ohio University, *The Impact of Head Start: An Evaluation of the Effects of Head Start on Children's Cognition and Affective Development* (Washington: U.S. Office of Economic Opportunity, 1969). For a discussion of the role of parents in Head Start, see *A National Survey of the Impacts of Head Start Centers on Community Institutions* (Albuquerque: Kirschner Associates, 1970), ERIC document no. 046 516.

presents to the children and to the teachers involved in it. Whether or not, from the child's viewpoint, the differences among programs described here are readily discernible is not known. Nor is it clear that differences in all the aspects of the programs are equally important in the eyes of the teacher. In the case of many innovative curricula, observers have noted a tendency for programs using them to become increasingly similar the longer they are in effect. Such a tendency, if verified, may reflect the coercion of the nature of young children on the teaching situation; or it may reflect a tendency for teaching strategies to come to represent, over time, the personality of the teacher more than the prescription of the curriculum.

SUMMARY

In the United States many children under the age of seven are involved in programs intended to provide for their care and education. Many other children, not now participating, could benefit from the expansion of such programs.

Existing programs differ in goals, in the theory on which they are based, in their expectations of the teacher, and in the materials and equipment they require, as well as in the role they assign to parents. Some programs are greatly concerned with obtaining evidence as to their effectiveness. Others are less so.

If programs are to expand, and if they are to meet adequately the needs of both children and parents, they will require increased knowledge of child development and learning and skills in working with both children and adults. To bring such knowledge and skills is the function of the early childhood educator, whose role is described in the next chapter.

Chapter 2

The Early Childhood Educator: An Emerging Role

If . . . early childhood program objectives are to be realized, we need to develop a new professional role. . . . Whatever it is called, this position should be occupied by a new kind of professional who knows how to locate and coordinate the resources needed to foster full human development. [1]

The decade of the sixties demonstrated many kinds of possibilities for the expansion of early childhood education. In the 1970s the need for programs clearly continues, but whether the promise that seemed so obvious in the 1960s can be realized is less certain. The history of education in this country is replete with instances of promising ideas that never reached fruition and of other ideas that were incorporated into educational practice but eventually withered away. Progressive education is a classic instance of the latter, and the expansion of early childhood education programs may prove to be another.

[1] David L. Elliott, "Needed: A New Early Childhood Educator," *Educational Leadership,* 28(8): 837 (May 1971).

Why do such promising ideas fail? The reasons are many. They may not gain sufficiently wide acceptance to attain the necessary financial support. They may be incompatible with the institutional structures that have come to be associated with schooling. Or the practitioners may not understand them well enough to use them effectively. In the case of progressive education, for example, many spoke in the words of Dewey and Kilpatrick, but few comprehended how their ideas were to be implemented. As Cremin notes regarding the situation following World War II:

> The movement had lost its intellectual vitality, but not its reformist thrust; the presence of the one without the other resulted in a short-lived Alexandrian period in which refinements were elaborated one upon the others, but in which insistent realities were studiously ignored. What eventuated was a complex pedagogical mystique, mastered by the initiates but virtually incomprehensible to laymen concerned with the making of educational policy.[2]

Early childhood education, like progressive education, may be doomed to lose its intellectual vitality and, indeed, its effective role in our society. If it is unable to muster a sufficient number of teachers who are specialists in both theory and practice, we may indeed witness the erosion of the fine ideas of the sixties into mere prescriptions for an extended and glorified baby-sitting service.

The need for the new specialist, whom I call "the early childhood educator," can be viewed against traditional and current views of the role of the teacher in the elementary school, in the kindergarten, and in the nursery school.

THE ROLE OF THE TEACHER

Teaching, according to Dreeben, is an occupation, not a profession, nor will it be a profession "until we discover what the tasks of the job are, how to do them and understand why we do them."[3] In recent years many researchers have engaged in systematic observation in classrooms. Their studies should help to specify what teachers do.[4] One group of studies that dealt with the

---

[2] Lawrence A. Cremin, *The Transformation of the School* (New York: Alfred A. Knopf, 1961), pp. 332–333. Copyright © 1961 by Lawrence A. Cremin.

[3] Robert Dreeben, *The Nature of Teaching* (Glenview, Ill.: Scott, Foresman, 1970).

[4] For an analysis of these studies, see Barak Rosenshine and Norma Furst, "The Use of Direct Observation to Study Teaching," in Robert M.W. Travers, ed., *Second Handbook of Research in Teaching* (Chicago: Rand McNally, 1973), pp. 122–183. For studies at the early childhood level, see Ira J. Gordon and R. Emile Jester, "Techniques of Observing Teaching in Early Childhood and Outcomes of Particular Procedures," in Robert M. W. Travers, ed., pp 184–217.

verbal exchanges in the classrooms found that teachers follow the rules of the same game, whether they are teaching first grade, fifth grade, or a high school subject.[5] On the other hand, it seems reasonable that the characteristics of the students should have some effect on the way the teacher functions.

Katz, for example, has identified four functions of the teacher of young children: caretaking, providing emotional support and guidance, instructing, and facilitating.[6] The caretaking function closely resembles that associated with the maternal role, and would be expected to diminish in number of services performed as the children involved become older.

Emotional support and guidance functions also seem to be less obviously required by older youngsters than by younger ones. A considerable amount of the time of the so-called "traditional" nursery school teacher was given over to this function and to the function of facilitating, that is, arranging the environment in such a way as to encourage the child's exploration and discovery. In contrast, the first grade teacher, responsible for the child's initiation into academic work, spent most of her time in instructing. The kindergarten teacher, depending on her orientation, might spend relatively large amounts of time in either instruction or facilitation. As Weber's analysis[7] shows, the role of the kindergarten teacher as originally conceived by Froebel first underwent modification in the direction of less didactic instruction and then, on being more widely accepted into the public school, often became more didactic.

Parallel to or perhaps inherent in all these functions is the model for behavior provided by the teacher. Teachers may not be fully aware of the extent to which what they do becomes a pattern for the children to follow. The kind of modeling they do is most evident in the instructional function in which they consciously demonstrate the behavior they expect from the children. But it is also evident in the facilitating function where the teacher's exploratory and investigative attitude toward materials can be copied by the children. Furthermore, one has only to observe the way children in some classrooms take care of each other and provide comfort in the time of distress to realize that the caretaking and guidance functions of the teacher can also be copied by the children.

The effect of the teacher as a female model has been little investigated. There is evidence that in the early grades, and perhaps also at the preschool

[5] Arno A. Bellack, Herbert M. Kliebard, Ronald T. Hyman, and Frank L. Smith, Jr., *The Language of the Classroom* (New York: Teachers College Press, 1966); Felice W. Gordis, "A Piagetian Analysis of the Teaching of Seriation Concepts in Four First-Grade Classrooms" (unpublished doctoral dissertation, Teachers College, Columbia University, 1970); James T. Fey, *Patterns of Verbal Communication in Mathematics Classes* (New York: Teachers College Press, 1970).

[6] Lilian G. Katz, "Teacher-Child Relationships in Day Care Centers," 1972, ERIC 046 494.

[7] Evelyn Weber, *The Kindergarten: Its Encounter with Educational Thought in America* (New York: Teachers College Press, 1969).

level, male teachers, more than their female counterparts, create an atmosphere that is compatible with the needs of boys.[8]

One would expect the extension of education to younger and younger children to carry with it an inevitable increase in the caretaking and emotional-support functions of the teacher. In fact, however, the emphasis of the innovative programs of the 1960s was on instruction. Currently, under the impetus of interest in the British Primary School and open education, the facilitating role of the teacher is being stressed. Clearly, all four functions are necessary for the fullest development and learning of young children. But the teacher needs to know when each of the functions is most appropriate and, having decided on the proper function, which of a variety of strategies may be most effective. Furthermore, there is good reason to believe that in order to keep functioning at an effective level many, if not most, teachers need considerable support. Occasional teachers, deeply interested in theory, are sustained by their reading. But most teachers also need the help that comes from discussion and colleagueship. Supporting the role of the teacher is seen as one of the important functions of the early childhood educator.

THE ROLE OF THE EARLY CHILDHOOD EDUCATOR

The role of the early childhood educator includes the functions of the teacher but it extends and deepens these and adds others. The need for such a new role can be traced to a number of developments in the last decade.

Factors in the Emerging Need for a New Role

Individuals who have both a wide range of practical skills and a deep understanding of child development and learning are currently in short supply. These are individuals described by Farnham-Diggory as "double specialists," able to translate theory into reality, and reality into theory.[9] The most obvious reason for needing more such people is related to the expansion in services for young children.

Head Start and most of the innovative programs for young children that evolved in the sixties were initially unable to find a sufficient number of staff members who had had training to work with preschool children. In some

[8] Patrick C. Lee, "Male and Female Teachers in Elementary Schools: An Ecological Analysis," *Teachers College Record,* 75(1), September 1973, reviews the available research on the ways the sex of the teacher affects interaction with the children. He includes some studies at the preschool level. His analysis suggests that male teachers can be particularly effective in the early grades but cautions that their effectiveness is constrained by the nature of the school as an institution.

[9] Sylvia Farnham-Diggory, *Cognitive Processes in Education* (New York: Harper & Row, 1972), pp. xxviii, xxix.

instances, where the new program placed a major emphasis on instruction, nursery school teachers were not sought since it was believed they would not be prepared to instruct. In other instances it quickly became apparent that the experience of the nursery school teacher was a great help in organizing the environment and in group caretaking. Head Start, which was designed in part to provide employment for the poor, and also many of the other innovative programs employed many individuals who had had no teaching experience to function as aides or assistants.

One effect of the new programs was to increase the number of individuals with skills in dealing with preschool children in groups. Some who worked as aides and assistants moved into the colleges and universities for more advanced training. At the same time the new programs also increased awareness of the complexities involved in teaching young children. The need for practice to be guided by deeper knowledge became more apparent. Yet it is unlikely that programs can afford to have every teacher a specialist in all aspects of child development and learning. Accordingly, a need emerges for specialists who can closely support the work of the teachers.

The extent of this need becomes even greater when present and projected day care services are taken into account, nor is it necessarily lessened if the present impetus for home-based programs continues. The U.S. Office of Child Development, Department of Health, Education, and Welfare, attested to the continuing need for trained personnel to work with young children when it established its program for "Child Development Associates."[10] These would be individuals with demonstrated competence but minimal training in working with young children.

At the kindergarten-primary levels of the elementary school, teachers also need support of the kind the early childhood educator should be able to give. Both the trends toward increased individualization and open education demand deep understanding of child development and learning. Several of the Follow Through models have demonstrated how an advisor may facilitate the work of the classroom teacher by helping her to find the ways that both work for her and are productive for the children. This effort presents a marked contrast to earlier, and in some instances continuing, efforts to "teacher-proof" materials, that is, to prescribe their use in minute detail.

Recognition of the need for a new role in early childhood education is implicit in recent California plans for the establishment of a credential for the

---

[10] Jennie Klein and C. Ray Williams, "The Development of the Child Development Associates (CDA) Program," *Young Children,* 28(3):139–145, February 1973; and Jennie Klein, "A New Professional for the Child Care Field—The Child Development Associate," *Child Care Quarterly,* 2(1):56–60, Spring 1973. See also [Anon.], "The Federal Government, Child Care and the Child Development Associate: A Dissenting View, *Child Care Quarterly,* 2(2):136–141, 1973.

"Early Childhood Education Specialist."[11] The functions of such a specialist include teaching children and adults, directing and supervising programs, serving as a resource person, evaluating children's progress and program goals, and establishing opportunities and procedures for research. The mere granting of credentials is, of course, no guarantee that the role will be fulfilled as described. Indeed, it seems likely that the role may evolve in different ways in different settings and as enacted by different individuals. Furthermore, it is not clear at this point what mixture of formal education and practical experience may constitute the most appropriate mixture for preparation.

The essential elements in the role of the early childhood educator may best be described by relating them to that of the teacher of young children, which is also central in the role of the early childhood educator.

Comparison of the Teacher and Early Childhood Educator Roles

As described above, the teacher in varying degrees, depending on the ages of the children with whom she[12] is working and the nature of the program in which she is involved, cares for children, provides emotional support, instructs them, and in various ways facilitates their development and learning. Implicitly, of course, the teacher also assesses development and learning and modifies her teaching strategies accordingly. The early childhood educator is also skilled in all these functions.

The early childhood educator, however, may deal with a larger number of children, having less contact with them than the teacher. Thus, she may be a team leader, a head teacher, a director, and advisor, or a supervisor. Although she may be responsible for a small group of children, it is perhaps more likely that she "floats" from one group to another, or works with the children in some special activity, for example, music or science. Knowing the children reasonably well, she is in a good position to demonstrate different teaching strategies with them. At the same time, since she has a deep knowledge of development and learning to draw on, she is particularly adept at assessing individual children's needs and the appropriateness of particular instruction or experiences for them.

---

[11] *Manual for Developing, Evaluating and Approving Professional Program Preparation Plans for the Early Childhood Specialist Credential* (Sacramento: Commission for Teacher Preparation and Licensing, State of California, 1973).

[12] Like other authors who write about early childhood education, I have been bedeviled by the problem of whether to use the feminine or masculine gender for the teacher and the early childhood educator. Generally these roles are filled by women, but men are increasingly involved. Initially I was inclined to use the masculine pronoun in its generic sense since I find "he or she" too cumbersome and welcome male participation in early childhood care and education. As the writing progressed, however, custom seemed to prevail and I found myself using "she" to the exclusion of "he."

The teacher, particularly with the younger children, has long had the responsibility for setting the stage for learning. She makes materials and equipment available to the children, deciding when and how they are to be introduced and when replaced with new or different things. This is an area in which the early childhood educator has special expertise. She is alert to resources for a variety of materials. She not only knows what is available commercially but also the criteria on which they may be judged. Her expertise also extends to the variety of community agencies that may be called on to facilitate needed health, psychological, recreation, or welfare services for children or their families.

Traditionally, the teacher of preschool children shared her classroom with an assistant teacher or aide. Kindergarten and first grade teachers were likely to have self-contained classrooms, and especially in the case of the first grade teacher, no assistants. In the last decade or so this picture has changed somewhat, and early childhood teachers at all levels often have paid or volunteer assistants and work as team members. For those individuals who prefer working with children to working with adults, this change has necessitated considerable adjustment.

Teachers must also learn to collaborate with parents. As the effectiveness of the public schools has been called into increasing question, as parents are called on to take more active part in their child's schooling, and as minority groups have become more articulate about their concerns, many teachers have found themselves ill-prepared for this aspect of their work. The number of schools and centers where parents and teachers regard each other with completely mutual respect and trust is very likely matched by the number in which the relationship can only be characterized by suspicion and fear. For the great number between these extremes much can be done to establish more equitable and harmonious working relationships.

Until recently the evaluation of the teacher's effectiveness tended to be quite informal. Often it was a matter of the opinion of the parents, and of the principal or the center director, based on diverse kinds of evidence. To some extent also the teacher was a self-evaluator. She monitored her own performance, and changed or did not change it, depending on how she perceived its effectiveness. The current call for accountability has made the matter of teacher evaluation a more public and formal matter, sometimes a source of anxiety and resentment to the teacher.

The early childhood educator understands the necessity for evaluation of both teaching and programs. Her knowledge of the processes of development and learning, and the nature of evidence regarding them, enhances her appraisal of the available methods for teacher evaluation. She has, in addition, an interest in experimentation, in demonstrating empirically how particular procedures and curricula affect children and teachers. In this sense she is a researcher.

In summary, the role of the early childhood educator is an extension of the role of the teacher. Such extension brings to the role deeper understanding of the processes of development and learning, more skill and understanding in working with adults, more awareness of the resources to support teaching, and some expertise in research.

PERSONAL CHARACTERISTICS OF THE EARLY CHILDHOOD EDUCATOR

An old question asks whether good teachers are "born" or "made" by training and experience. To the extent that the role of the early childhood educator encompasses that of the teacher, the question is equally applicable to it. Essentially the question has to do with whether certain kinds of people, those with particular personality characteristics, are more likely to be effective than those with different characteristics.

The available research regarding teachers provides no sure answer to this question. Ryans's (1960) extensive study of teacher characteristics did not include nursery school teachers.[13] Furthermore, as Gordon and Jester point out, "The long history of classroom studies of teacher personality in relation to pupil achievement has borne little fruit.[14] Accordingly, recent studies have focused on directly observable teacher behavior, rather than attempting to infer personality characteristics either from the behavior or from a questionnaire or interview. But the question of personality is still viable. Gordon and Jester acknowledge this when they comment, "However, when we turn to the young child, the studies . . . although far from conclusive and but a mere beginning, indicate that this personality dimension may be more important than it seemed to be for older children."[15] Beller, commenting on a series of studies that included teacher personality variables, notes that they "give continuous support to the notion that an evaluation of teacher functioning must include not only the techniques the teacher employs but also her personality and the teaching situation in which she functions.[16]

Assuming that a range of occupations, each with similar financial rewards, is available, it seems that those individuals who, as the cliché goes, "just

---

[13] David G. Ryans, *Characteristics of Teachers* (Washington: American Council on Education, 1960).

[14] Ira J. Gordon and R. Emile Jester, "Techniques of Observing Teaching in Early Childhood" in Robert M. W. Travers, ed., *Second Handbook of Research on Teaching* (Chicago: Rand McNally, 1973), p. 212.

[15] Gordon and Jester, p. 212.

[16] E. Kuno Beller, "Research on Organized Programs of Early Education" in Robert M. W. Travers, ed., *Second Handbook of Research on Teaching,* p. 586.

love little children" will be most likely to choose early childhood education. Not all who avow their devotion to the young find actual satisfaction in the nose-wiping, shoe-tying, mess-cleaning, comforting, and protecting that are an inevitable component of working with them, but those who are successful in dealing with them are likely to have sizable components of warmth and nurturance in their personalities.

Common sense also suggests that patience is an essential attribute of the successful teacher of young children. In early childhood the child "learns to learn" and is not yet attuned to the ways of thinking of the older child and adult. The lack of fully developed motor skills also contributes to his ineptness in many situations. His teacher must match her pace and her expectations to his level of performance and bear with him as he moves ahead. Patience is also a virtue for the teacher of older children and adults, but it may be less essential for them than for the younger children.

Another essential for the teacher of young children is energy. Farnham-Diggory, in describing the teacher characteristics essential for a "free learning environment," says:

> For whatever reason, the common denominator of our good teachers is available, well-directed energy. Energy to notice and attend promptly to the individual needs of children; energy to generate a special, personal task for a child; energy to be pleasant and cooperative despite numerous demands from the children; energy to direct aides and volunteers cheerfully and sufficiently; energy to plan, plan and replan ways of keeping the children busy and independent; energy to keep track of the effectiveness of lessons and other kinds of activities, to keep notes and written guides; energy to explain details of the program to parents and administrators; and above all, energy to respond warmly and sensitively to children.[17]

Farnham-Diggory's good teacher is well into the role of the early childhood educator, as I have described it, but the early childhood educator has some characteristics in addition to the warmth, nurturance, patience, and energy already described.

Three are noteworthy. One has been suggested in the preceding analysis of the two roles, as well as in Farnham-Diggory's description of the good teacher. This is an interest in, and desire to work with, adults that is parallel to the interest in and desire to work with children.

Another characteristic may be described as an attitude of mind. Such an attitude encompasses openness to new ideas, some tolerance for ambiguity, an

[17] Farnham-Diggory, p. 590.

interest in unraveling cause-and-effect relationships, together with an ability to think and organize data in multidimensional categories. Something of what I have in mind here has been described by Harvey, Hunt, and Schroder as an "abstract" conceptual system, as contrasted with one that is "concrete."[18] In Piaget's terms, it seems to imply the ability to move easily back and forth from the concrete thought of the child to the formal level where possibilities can be dealt with as systematically as actualities.

Some teachers of young children demonstrate this ability. According to a study by Harvey and others,[19] those with an abstract attitude are, among other things, warmer, more perceptive and more flexible in meeting children's needs, more encouraging of individual responsibility, and more ingenious in improving teaching and play materials, than their colleagues who think more concretely.

For the early childhood educator, who must deal with complexities that go beyond the classroom, the ability to depart from the concrete seems imperative. To what extent it is an ability that can be nurtured and trained is at present unknown, although there are some teacher education programs in which the question is being investigated.[20]

A third characteristic is perhaps best described as "maturity." To be able to handle the closeness, competition, and crises that are inevitable when adults —teachers and other staff members, parents, administrators, funding agents— collaborate, and at the same time to deal with the impulsivity and high energy level of young children takes a person who is truly "grown up."

As with the teacher, there is no reason to believe that the role of early childhood educator cannot be filled as well by a man as by a woman. The critical question is not sex but the kinds of characteristics that the person possesses.

In summary, the early childhood educator role may be seen as that of "double specialist" in a variety of ways: In teaching young children and in assessing their development and learning; in working with children and in working with adults; in thinking concretely (maintaining insight into the child's thought) and thinking formally, in practice as well as in theory.

[18] O. J. Harvey, David E. Hunt, and Harold M. Schroder, *Conceptual Systems and Personality Organization* (New York: John Wiley & Sons, 1961).

[19] O. J. Harvey et al., "Teacher Belief Systems and Preschool Atmospheres," *Journal of Educational Psychology,* 57:373–381, 1966.

[20] David E. Hunt, "Matching Models for Teacher Training," in Bruce Joyce and Marsha Weil, eds., *Perspectives for Reform in Teacher Education* (Englewood Cliffs, N.J.: Prentice-Hall, 1972); and Lawrence F. Lowery and John David Miller, "Research in Teacher Education," School of Education, University of California, Berkeley, in progress.

EARLY CHILDHOOD EDUCATOR:
AN ANOMALOUS ROLE?

The new role of early childhood educator is easily described. Individuals whose functions fit the role can be identified. But whether it becomes widely accepted as necessary to the effective education of young children will depend on how it is seen by the public and by the profession.

Having shown how the functions of the role both resemble and differ from the usual functions of the teacher, it may be well to examine it in the context of teaching as an occupation.

Teaching, particularly at the elementary school level, has been identified, along with nursing and social work, as a "semi-profession."[21] This statement, which may startle teachers whose professors have urged them to take professional attitudes, is not intended to derogate the work of the teacher. It reflects, rather, on the way schooling has developed in this country. Teaching fails, according to sociological analysis, to meet the criteria for a true profession, such as the law, medicine, or the ministry. These criteria have to do with professional knowledge[22] and with the service performed.

As far as its knowledge is concerned, teaching derives much more from such a discipline as psychology than it generates itself. Furthermore, many teachers rely more on their own experience than on pedagogical theory. Like the public, they tend to believe that the teacher's personality is more important than her knowledge. This position impelled one observer to comment that teaching is a profession in search of its own expertise. Lortie notes:

> The subjects teachers themselves believe useful in teaching (e.g. child psychology) are primarily the property of others. Lacking the clear autonomy which leads to the assurance that professional knowledge will provide the basis of action, teachers have not developed codified and systematic bodies of knowledge; lacking that knowledge, their stance vis-à-vis laymen is, in turn, weakened.[23]

The professional renders a service directly to a client whose needs he appraises and treats accordingly. This professional-client relationship is highly regarded and protected by standards that have evolved within the profession. In contrast, the relationship of teacher to client is decidedly ambiguous. She is caught between her obligations to the children and their parents and to her

---

[21] William J. Goode, "The Theoretical Limits of Professionalization," in Amitai Etzioni, ed., *The Semi-Professions and Their Organization* (New York: The Free Press, 1969), © 1969.

[22] Geraldine Joncich Clifford, "A History of the Impact of Research in Teaching," in Travers, ed., *Second Handbook of Research on Teaching*, pp. 1–46.

[23] Dan C. Lortie, "The Balance of Control and Autonomy in Elementary School Teaching," in Etzioni, *The Semi-Professions and Their Organization*, p. 24.

employers—the school system and the taxpayers. She has, in a sense, "a big client" and accordingly less autonomy than the professional who is not part of a bureaucracy. Nevertheless, traditionally, the rather loose formulation of school goals and the protection of the self-contained classroom together with the comparative remoteness of superintendent and principal have afforded teachers more freedom than might be anticipated in such a bureaucratic structure.

Against this background the introduction of the early-childhood-educator role may be viewed as an attempt to upgrade a segment of the teaching profession. If it is seen as such, it clearly runs counter to many of the traditions inherent in elementary school teaching—including an intuitive approach and the freedom of the teacher to make her own decisions about the specific group of children she has. Furthermore, "teachers have consistently opposed attempts to introduce differentiation in money, prestige and power within their ranks."[24] They have preferred to emphasize the intrinsic, rather than the extrinsic, rewards in teaching. "Differentiation, they argue, will lead to envy and hostility among teachers, preventing the cooperation which is necessary to effective education."[25]

The reality of these traditions cannot be denied. They may well account for much of the unhappiness experienced by a large number of teachers during the past decade. Prescribed curricula and evaluative techniques, the introduction of aides, volunteers, program advisors, and consultants have considerably changed the conditions of teaching, but not, in the opinion of many, necessarily for the better.

On such grounds, the person who fills the role of early childhood educator may be expected to encounter resistance from those whose work she plans to support and extend. On the other hand, to the extent that the work of the early childhood educator enhances the satisfaction the teacher derives from her work, the tradition of intrinsic rewards may serve to diminish resistance.

It should be noted that the view of teaching as an occupation sketched above may not correspond to the view of teaching held by those who have not been affiliated with public education. Nursery education, for example, as it originated in this country, based its knowledge in child development research.[26] Those who taught in nursery schools initially held graduate degrees

[24] Lortie, p. 40.
[25] Lortie, p. 41.
[26] G. M. Whipple, ed., *Preschool and Parental Education*, Twenty-eighth Yearbook of the National Society for the Study of Education, part I, Chapters 2, 8 (Bloomington, Ill: Public School Publishing Co., 1929). See also Samuel J. Braun and Esther P. Edwards, *History and Theory of Early Childhood Education* (Worthington, Ohio: Charles A. Jones Publishing Co., 1972), pp. 149–151, 156–159.

at a time when the elementary school teacher less often had a baccalaureate.[27] This situation changed as nursery education expanded under WPA in the 1930s, and as cooperatives and commercial schools grew in number. Nevertheless, my impression is that nursery school teachers more than elementary teachers accepted the notion that teaching is to be informed by research, and not solely by intuition.

The nursery school teacher's relationships to her clients also differed somewhat from those of the elementary school teacher. The involvement of the parents, either directly or through observation, and in the instance of the cooperative, through participation, was a strong tradition in the nursery school movement.[28] Furthermore, only in rare instances, at least until the decade of the sixties, was the nursery school teacher put in the position of having a "big client." Rather, in both the cooperatives and to a considerable extent in the commercial schools, the responsibility of the teacher to the parents and children appears to have been fairly direct. If what she did with the children was not satisfactory to the parents they could in effect withdraw their financial support.

This is not to say that the nursery school teacher was, in general, more professionalized than the elementary school teacher. It would be more appropriate to say that the variation among nursery school teachers was greater than among elementary teachers. As indicated in Chapter 4, nursery school teachers worked in a wide variety of settings. Since the nursery school teacher was usually not required to hold a teaching certificate,[29] the preparation for nursery school teaching could range from experience in baby-sitting, or with one's own children, to a master's degree. Remuneration was, in general, not comparable to that received by kindergarten and primary teachers.

There is some evidence that the nursery school teacher has resisted professionalization rather than demanded it. Although there have been occasional local efforts to establish qualification for membership in organizations devoted primarily to the education of young children, these have met with little success on the national level. Membership in the National Association for Nursery Education, which later became the National Association for the Education of Young Children, has always remained open to all who shared an interest in

---

[27] Ilse Forest, *Preschool Education* (New York: Macmillan Co., 1927), pp. 293–309.

[28] Whipple, ed., op. cit.

[29] Thirty-three states (including the District of Columbia and Puerto Rico) do not require the certification of nursery school teachers, presumably because nursery schools are not publicly funded. (Only 8 states report state or local government support for nursery schools. Kindergartens are publicly funded in 37 states.) Forty-seven states require kindergarten teachers to be certified if the kindergarten is publicly funded. Nineteen states require teachers in both nursery schools and kindergartens that are publicly supported to hold certificates. T. M. Stinnet with Geraldine E. Pershing, *A Manual on Certification Requirements for School Personnel in the United States* (Washington: National Education Association, 1970), p. 27.

its purposes. Currently, this purpose is "to serve and to act on behalf of young children with primary focus on the provision of educational services and resources." Membership is urged on "persons engaged in work with young children."[30]

The lack of impetus for professionalization may be regarded either as a liability or an asset for the work of the early childhood educator. In the context of current concern for enhancing and supporting parental authority and parental involvement, it may serve more as an asset than a liability. Morgan, noting the "inability of professionals to communicate across their specializations," adds:

> While professionals are holding discussions about how to create more and better programs that are staffed in their own image, they seem unable to hear the concerns of hard-to-read bicultural groups; young families with changing concepts of family life and life style; and the poor.[31]

To suggest that successful fulfillment of the role of the early childhood educator should depend more on her commitment to children and their parents than on her status in the bureaucratic structure is idealistic. But it represents an idealism that is strongly supported by many of the current generation of young people.

The early childhood educator can, if she chooses, acquire the kinds of knowledge and develop the kind of expertise that characterizes the "true" professional. She can also work with her clients, parents, children, and sometimes teachers, in ways that are similar to those of the "true" professions. On the other hand, in so doing she may run counter to the bureaucratic traditions in public schooling, and in other public agencies. The way will not be easy. However, as I see it, a genuine professionalism is essential for the development and maintenance of effective programs for early education and care.

RECRUITMENT AND TRAINING OF EARLY CHILDHOOD EDUCATORS

Although early childhood education programs, including day care, are no longer expanding at the rate envisioned in the late sixties, there appears to be considerable demand for individuals who can fill the role of the early childhood educator. Recruitment goes on for those now qualified and for those who might receive training to qualify.

---

[30] Cover statement, *Young Children,* vol. 38, no. 4, April 1973.
[31] Gwen C. Morgan, *Regulation of Early Childhood Programs* (Washington: Day Care and Child Development Council, January 1973), pp. 123–124.

Where are such individuals to be found? The obvious place to look is in the ranks of those who are currently working with young children. Those who have demonstrated success with them and with their parents, who are looking beyond the confines of their own group or their own classroom, who are asking questions about what they do and why—these are potential candidates for further training and for employment.

Such individuals need not have come through the usual academic ranks. In Head Start and Follow Through programs, and in day care centers across the country, women and men, often with little formal education and from varying socioeconomic and ethnic backgrounds have demonstrated the qualities that are essential to good teaching. (The Child Development Associate Program was devised to recognize and extend their competence.) Some of them have also shown the kinds of interests and skills that suggest potentiality for filling an expanded role. Given sufficient time for reflective study and inquiry, particularly in the areas of child development and learning, they would have much to offer. Unfortunately, time to pursue the knowledge they need, and the financial support to make such pursuit feasible, are often lacking.

A younger group with fine potential for the early childhood educator role is also coming along. This includes college and university students who have had an intense interest in day care. They have volunteered or been work-study students in a variety of centers throughout their college years. Many of them have studied psychology or anthropology or sociology and have a working knowledge of the methods of those disciplines. There is no reason to believe that they should not fulfill the role of teacher on the way to the larger role, but it is conceivable that they may pass through the usual stages of development of the teacher[32] more rapidly than others because of what may be regarded as an early apprenticeship.

With the current decline in the population of elementary and secondary schools leading to possible teacher unemployment at those levels, some movement of teachers downward may be anticipated. As were some elementary and secondary teachers who moved into WPA nursery schools in the 1930s, they may be effective at earlier levels. In all probability they will need training and support. Some of the teachers who are currently working in preschools and kindergartens may find themselves moving into the early childhood educator role to supply them.

The training that will be needed is suggested by the variety of functions that the role of early childhoood educator may encompass. The knowledge needed in this training, it should be noted, is interdisciplinary. It draws not

---

[32] Lilian G. Katz, "Developmental Stages of Preschool Teachers," *Elementary School Journal,* 73:50–54, 1972.

only on psychology but also on pediatrics, nutrition, sociology, and anthropology.

POSITIONS TO BE HELD BY EARLY CHILDHOOD EDUCATORS

Those who prepare to fill the early childhood educator role will find that it carries a number of different titles. Within the public schools they are likely to be directors of early childhood centers, early childhood specialists, coordinators of early childhood education, supervisors of early childhood education, or early childhood program advisors. In the community they may be in charge of infant or children's centers or schools for young children, or serve as educational directors of these. They may be instructors or professors in colleges and universities. In health and welfare services their title may well be that of early childhood consultant or specialist. They may also be involved in the productions of television programs for young children, or in commercial or industrial services for young children and their parents.

Not all these positions encompass all the functions that have been described as part of the role of the early childhood educator. Each of the possible functions is considered in greater detail, beginning with Chapter 6. First, however, we return to a consideration of the field in which the early childhood educator will work and some of the issues to be encountered there.

Chapter 3

Persistent Issues in Early Childhood Education

There can be no gain, least of all for children, when educational theory is conceived as a perpetual conflict. For the middle ground is not a neutral territory where reasonable men come together to fashion a treaty of peace; it is a no-man's-land where virtually nothing of rational educational theory survives at all.[1]

The history of early childhood education is replete with instances where opinion has become so polarized that, if one were to believe the rhetoric, the very existence of the children was threatened by some method or theory. Whether a visitor from outer space, or even an intelligent but educationally uninformed earthling come to observe in the classrooms would have shared the opinion of the opposing factions is questionable. Why, then, should a text written in the 1970s pose again the issues that might long since have been resolved? And particularly, why pose them at a time when the technological revolution has

---

[1] Harold Entwhistle, *Child-Centred Education* (London: Methuen & Co., 1970), pp. 211–212. Distributed in the United States by Barnes & Noble.

created a new world in which so many of the ideas of the past appear increasingly obsolescent?

These recurrent issues are not all of a kind. Some reflect different philosophies about the nature of man and the human condition. Some stem from the evolving but not highly developed science of pedagogy and to a considerable extent represent competing theories related to human development and learning. Others have to do with the art rather than the science of teaching. Accordingly, they vary greatly in the kinds of evidence that can be brought to bear on them. But whether the side one takes is supported by data or by conviction there is little question that the beliefs one holds shape and color the classroom realities one perceives. The early childhood educator needs to be aware of the differing views that may be held by parents and by teachers.

To analyze these issues in depth is not within the scope of this text.[2] Rather, its intent is to make the reader alert to his own biases and predilections and wary of simplistic views that fail to take into account the complexities of both the children and the settings provided for their education, together with those inherent in the larger society.

THE YOUNG CHILD IN A PLURALISTIC SOCIETY

Someone has said that every generation uses its children to its own purposes. More recently Bronfenbrenner, contrasting the status of children in the United States and the Soviet Union, has proposed that the worth of a nation is to be read in its concerns for the young.[3] But it is not easy in the United States to appraise what those concerns are. Some of the statistics cited in Chapter 1 suggest that children are not highly valued by our society. To what extent this situation may be changing is uncertain. Similarly unclear is the nature of the future for which we should be preparing them. The 1970s have not lacked predictions for the future, but there is little consensus among them.

One observer points to the "blinding succession of new temporary cultures" to which children growing up will be expected to adapt.[4] In contrast, other observers see the emergence of a new consciousness,[5] and more humane "mutually complementary alternative subcultures."[6] Still others, concerned

---

[2] For such an analysis, see Ellis D. Evans, *Contemporary Influences in Early Childhood Education* (New York: Holt, Rinehart and Winston, 1971), and Evelyn Weber, *The Kindergarten: Its Encounter with Educational Thought in America* (New York: Teachers College Press, 1969).

[3] Urie Bronfenbrenner, *The Two Worlds of Childhood: U.S. and U.S.S.R.* (New York: Simon & Schuster, 1972).

[4] Alvin Toffler, *Future Shock* (New York: Bantam Books [Random House], 1970), p. 37.

[5] Charles Reich, *The Greening of America* (New York: Bantam Books, 1971), p. 241.

[6] Jean-Francois Revel, "Without Marx or Jesus the New American Revolution Has Begun," *Saturday Review,* July 24, 1971, pp. 14–31.

with the tightening economic situation and current population trends take less sanguine views, predicting that economic survival will become increasingly difficult,[7] and the world increasingly dull, unable to maintain cultures that are "interestingly different."[8]

As indicated in Chapter 1, less than a fourth of the young children of working mothers are cared for in licensed centers or homes. Many are adequately cared for in their own homes by relatives and sitters. But "own home" care may also be care by a slightly older child, or by a father who works a night shift and sleeps days. An unlicensed home may also provide adequate care, but a recent study of working mothers reports that less than half of those with preschoolers were satisfied with such care.[9] Statistics cited in this report indicate that 15 percent of the children accompany their mothers to work. At least 18,000 children are "latchkey children" who are responsible for their own care. Probably the best, if not the only, way to deal with today's children becoming tomorrow's citizens is to confront the present-day realities impinging on them and their parents. The long-term significance of these realities may, at least partially, be inferred from what is now known about human development and learning.

The Status of Childhood in Present-Day Society

An astute observer from outer space would not need many hours in the United States to be able to infer that differences in the size and sex of human beings are in some way related to the way they are treated.[10] In general, the smaller individuals are more often associated with one of the sexes than the other. Those who are the smallest tend to remain in close proximity to a particular larger individual, for almost the entire time. But there are other small individuals who at certain periods of the day leave their particular larger individual, and together with those of a size approximating their own shift to an association with a small number of different larger individuals. In many places small individuals are never seen; in others they do appear, usually, however, accompanying larger individuals.

Were the astute observer to stay longer, he would also note that the activities of the small individuals differ in many respects from those of the larger, and that they seem to occupy themselves with different objects from

[7] Peter F. Drucker, "The Surprising Seventies," *Harper's Magazine,* July, 1971, pp. 35–39.

[8] Kenneth Boulding, *Berkeley Gazette,* July 28, 1971, p. 4.

[9] Mary Keyserling, *Windows on Day Care* (New York: National Council of Jewish Women, 1972).

[10] I am indebted to Seymour Sarason, *The Culture of the School and the Problem of Change* (Boston: Allyn & Bacon, 1971), for a number of insights derived from the objective observations of an "outer-spacer" who, although he does not comprehend language, can see and hear everything and can discern the regularities.

those used by the larger individuals. Eventually he would also discern certain regularities about the activities and the objects apparently depending somewhat on the places where the individuals eat and sleep. He would be close to the discovery that in the United States young children do have special status, but its significance varies depending on such factors as socioeconomic status of the child's family, and whether he lives in an urban, a suburban, or a rural area.

The recognition that the child is not merely a miniature adult and the notion that childhood is a special phase of life are, according to Ariès,[11] relatively modern ideas, rooted in the moralization of society that began in the sixteenth and seventeenth centuries, and are reflected in the gradual development of new family attitudes oriented around the child and his education. These attitudes, "raising a wall of private life between the family and society," constitute an important deterrent to current efforts to supplement the family as the primary institution involved in early care and education.

THE INSTITUTIONALIZATION OF EARLY CARE AND EDUCATION

The astute observer from outer space, who discerns the regularity with which children at the age of five or six, not only in crowded innercity areas, but in the wider spaces of suburbia and the more remote country, disappear into school buildings, must surely be puzzled at the diversity of what happens to those who are younger. Some of them, rarely younger than three, do go to school. Others are taken to buildings not usually limited to the young as are the schools—for instance, churches, stores, factories, homes—where they are left with others of similar age. Meanwhile the mother may return to the home, but very often she too disappears for a considerable period of time into another building. Sometimes the child, or there may be several, remains in its home and another adult seems to carry on while the mother disappears. Occasionally, and most often but not exclusively in the innercity, very young children and even infants are left alone, sometimes in hazardous situations, for long periods of time.

If the observer who does not understand the language were suddenly to acquire it, he might still have difficulty arriving at any rational explanation for the apparent chaos. Clearly children under the age of five or six need care. Clearly also many of their mothers have responsibilities that make it impossible for them to supply that care twenty-four hours a day. The varied kinds of

[11] Philippe Ariès, *Centuries of Childhood, A Social History of Family Life* (New York: Random House, 1962).

arrangements they make for the children when they cannot be available might represent personal choice.

The fact is that most parents have very few options. The mother's choice too often is not between a play group and a nursery school, or between a good day care center and a competent baby-sitter, but between leaving the child with an indifferent neighbor or relative and remaining on welfare, or subsisting on alimony when she has skills and competencies to contribute in the world of work. Even the mother in an intact home who seeks only a few hours of respite from the daily demands of child rearing confronts a limited range of possibilities, particularly if she demands that these be educative for the child.

Why, despite the evident need, does day care remain relatively unavailable? Why is early education, given so much publicity in the last decade, still largely limited to children who have reached the age of five? Why have some early childhood programs aroused antagonism among the parents of the children for whom they were intended? The answers to these questions are not simple and are embedded in political realities beyond the scope of this book. However, the polarization of opinion around three issues deserves the consideration of the early childhood educator.

One of these issues has to do with the role of the family and the state in the upbringing of children. Another has to do with the belief that care and education can be dealt with separately. A third relates to the question of whether schools and centers operated at public expense are to have homogeneous programs based on middle-class values or to reflect the diversity that characterizes the culture of the United States.

The Family and the State

The traditions of the United States were built around the notion of a strong family within which the child received care and protection but also learned right from wrong and the skills necessary to work. Over the years the functions once held primarily by the family have been taken over by other institutions. Families, particularly in the middle class, have grown smaller and more isolated, their functions largely reduced to child care and the giving of affection. While social scientists question the survival of this nuclear family and young adults experiment with various kinds of communal living in attempts to restore some of the vestiges of the extended family, it appears that most Americans cling to the ideas of the sanctity of the family.

Along with strong feelings about the family go equally strong feelings about the role of government, again stemming from American traditions. Thus, while it is clear that in many respects today's citizen is powerless to protect himself except through reliance on government, many people deplore its expansion into more and more areas of living.

It was, perhaps, an attempt to steer between the Scylla of removal of one more function from the already threatened family and the Charybdis of increasing bureaucracy that prompted President Nixon to veto the Child Development Act of 1971. In so doing he reflected a concern that many people have.

The issue of family versus state with regard to child care is, however, more complicated than may be evident immediately. The critical question has to do with the numbers of children who are currently in need of care and the adequacy of the care they are receiving. When is it deleterious to the child's safety, health, and development? Although we may cling to the notion that the best place for the young child to be is at home with his mother, the hard facts are that many mothers of young children are employed, and that the arrangements they are able to make for their children are often makeshift at best.

The changing role of women is obviously an important factor in the increasing demand for day care services. Although the need for such services has long existed among families at the poverty level where women's work has been an important, if not a major, source of income, it is likely that the middle-class woman's demand for equal rights has brought the need for day care to wide public attention. Not willing to accept the fact that equal opportunity for employment added up to holding two jobs, one in business or profession and the other at home, the middle-class woman has highlighted the plight of all women.

Many middle-class women have also articulated a concern, shared by some of their less-privileged sisters, that the care received by the children be educative as well as protective.

Care and Education

The idea that no particular provision need be made for a child's learning before he reaches the age of five or six and begins to read and write has a long history. Despite an ever-increasing body of evidence testifying to the nature of the young child's mental, emotional, and social development, it is only recently that concern for the factors contributing to these areas of development has become widespread. While few people would deny that every child has the right to adequate food and protection from health and safety hazards, many still appear to believe that what he learns before the age of six has little consequence. Thus, for example, one finds the Department of Social Services in one state seeking to find a kind of child care that is "not child-centered," a euphemism that may be taken to mean "custodial" and "cheap."

What is too often overlooked in the quest for care that is minimally expensive is that care inevitably has educational consequences. If it is care in which the caretakers have respect for and understanding of the learning abilities of the children, if the interactions of the children with the caretakers and with other children are such as to make them increasingly aware of themselves and of the rights and needs of others, if the environment is one that increasingly satisfies and challenges their growing intellectual powers, then its consequences should be favorable to the child's further development and learning.

The consequences of any kind of care are, of course, intimately tied to the kinds of care and education the child receives within his home. When the quality of the relationships the child has with his mother (and his father) is strong and positive, he is better equipped to withstand supplemental care that is less than adequate. Such parents can, of course, distinguish good care from other kinds, but they do not always have the options for securing it.

Other parents are less well prepared for parenthood. Evidence on the incidence of extreme inadequacy at all socioeconomic levels may be derived from current evidence regarding child abuse.[12] Here the need for high-quality supplemental care and education seems obvious.

Uniformity and Cultural Diversity

Any attempt to extend education downward raises the question of whether the new ventures are to perpetuate the traditions of American education. One such tradition, or myth, is that of the "melting pot," in which succeeding generations of immigrants have become Americanized. The public schools have been seen as a major source of fuel for the pot—teaching a common language, describing political and economic institutions as though they were monolithic, and inculcating "American" moral standards. But what has seemed, at least on the surface, to work for many second-generation Americans is clearly unsatisfactory for other minorities[13] —Afro-, Spanish-, and Asian-Americans —and Indians. The tradition of middle-class uniformity is equally unsatisfactory to a growing number of young parents, graduates of the public schools and of colleges and universities, who, although they have been brought up in middle-class homes, now question many middle-class values.

In the 1960s, preschool programs for the disadvantaged were generally directed toward readying children for the traditional elementary school program. Although there was considerable diversity among the preschool programs, and although the need for modification of primary grade programs (as in Follow Through) was widely recognized, their goals, at least initially, were established by psychologists and educators, not by the clients.

Katz,[14] in *Class, Bureaucracy and the Schools,* hypothesizes that the

---

[12] *Crisis in Child Mental Health: Challenge for the 1970's,* Report of the Joint Commission on Mental Health of Children (New York: Harper & Row, 1969), pp. 344–345.

[13] Marjorie S. Friedman, "Public School: Melting Pot or What?" *Teacher's College Record,* 70: 347-351, January 1969.

[14] Michael B. Katz, *Class, Bureaucracy and the Schools: The Illusion of Educational Change in America* (New York: Praeger Publishers, 1971), pp. 121–122.

extension of education downward, not only in recent years but also a century ago when kindergartens began to spread, is a conservative, not a radical, measure. He writes:

> Early childhood education has a long history, dating from the infant school movement in late-eighteenth century England. At that time philanthropists, concerned with the problem of juvenile crime, urged the establishment of schools for very young children, aged two or three. Although the infant school movement failed to spread widely in America, its emphasis on early childhood education became a permanent feature of educational thought. Later schoolmen, including those of the mid-nineteenth century, developed that emphasis. They, too, stressed the importance of counteracting the unfavorable influence of the home and argued that the primary purpose of early education was formation of attitudes rather than the development of skills. It was this emphasis on the relationship of early childhood education to social order that fed the kindergarten movement, in the same way, quite obviously, that widespread concern with crime and welfare expenses has given impetus to movements for preschool education today.

Today's preschool programs, however, tend to involve parents to a considerably greater extent than was the case when they were initiated. In the meantime, community control of local schools has been established in some large cities and ethnic minorities have become better organized and more vocal. Accordingly, the question of whether early childhood programs can and should reflect cultural diversity continues to be a very live issue.

Ultimately, given the complexities of our changing society, the diversity of kinds of care and education available for the young child is likely to increase. But if it is to meet the needs of families and children effectively, it will be a diversity based on a range of choices, all of which guarantee the child protection in a physical and social environment adapted to his level of development. Progress toward such options for all children demands careful analysis of the processes involved in socialization.

SOCIALIZATION OF THE YOUNG CHILD

How does the newborn infant become the school-age child? How does the helpless neonate become the independent, beginning-to-talk two-year-old, and the strong-willed two-year-old the competent, adaptable five-year-old? In the past fifty years, and more rapidly in the last ten, hundreds of psychological studies have dealt with these and similar questions. Consequently, a wealth of material is available for those who plan care and early education. But there are hazards in its use. Kessen suggests the nature of these when he says:

> The history of child study is a history of rediscovery. With remarkable regularity the same themes appear, are elaborated for a while, then fade. . . .
>
> The very intransigence of the problems posed by children has also contributed to the iteration of themes; unresolved issues pop up in new form with each generation of searchers for certainty among the confusion of babies.[15]

With regard to the empirical studies of children that have been conducted over the last hundred years, Kessen says that

> scientists, at least, remain committed to the eighteenth century postulate of remediable ignorance and the stability of this commitment has led, slowly but steadily, to the accumulation of a body of reliable facts about children. It is our greater knowledge of the child as well as our changed attitude toward him that marks the passage of many years of study. The history of child study is a history of rediscovery; it is also a history of modest advances toward truth.[16]

The problem for the educator lies in the fact that the "small advances toward truth" are not always clearly marked, while the latest research, espousing a particular theory, receives much publicity. Often a theorist's position becomes distorted by would-be followers who, not fully grasping its complexities, present simplified versions. These are not adequate to the practical applications to which they may be put. Consequently, the theory is rejected and some other becomes the slogan of the day. The educator who is sophisticated regarding the nature of psychological theory and research may be less likely to fall into the trap of oversimplification than his less well-informed colleague but he is not without risk.

Some issues recur so often in consideration of the ways the child becomes socialized that they seem to demand special attention from the early childhood educator. In some instances these are really "dead" issues or pseudo issues no longer regarded as viable when posed in such simplistic fashion. In other cases they represent alternate ways of looking at the child, or alternate approaches to his socialization. Three issues are closely related. They are heredity and environment, maturation and training, self-regulation and extrinsic control.

---

[15] William Kessen, *The Child* (New York: John Wiley & Sons, 1965), p. 1.
[16] Kessen, p. 6.

Heredity and Environment

The issue of heredity and environment, simply put, has to do with the extent to which the child becomes what he has to be in accord with his genetic inheritance and the extent to which he is shaped by his environment. But to put it so fails to do justice to the complexity of the interactions among genetic and environmental factors. McClearn notes:

> It is most important to appreciate that the influence of the genes is not manifested only at conception or at birth or at any other single time in the individual's life history. Developmental processes are subject to continuing genetic influence, and different genes are effective at different times.[17]

Scheinfeld, in 1950, wrote that the mechanism of heredity "now stands fully revealed."[18] Since then, tremendous strides have been made in understanding the intricacies of genetic processes. Nonetheless, it is probably still true that "not much of this understanding has seeped through to the general public, and even among many professional people the knowledge of modern genetics remains hazy."[19]

People, including professionals, continue to take strong positions regarding the relative importance of heredity and environment, particularly with regard to their influence on intellectual development. The nature-nurture controversy of the 1930s, well-represented in the thirty-ninth yearbook of the National Society for the Study of Education,[20] appears to have subsided during the forties and fifties, when the notion of fixed intelligence had rather wide acceptance. J. McV. Hunt called this notion into question in 1961.[21] His extensive review of the literature related to intellectual development led him to the often quoted conclusion that "it might be feasible to discover ways to govern the encounters that children have with their environments, especially during the early years of their development, to achieve a faster rate of intellectual development and a substantially higher adult level of intellectual capacity." That he did not rule out the contribution of genetic factors is made clear by a later, but seldom quoted, sentence: "Furthermore, these procedures, insomuch as they tended to maximize each child's potential for intellectual development, would not decrease individual differences in intellectual capacity as assessed by tests but would increase them."[22]

---

[17] Gerald E. McClearn, "Genetic Influences on Behavior," in P. Mussen, ed., *Carmichael's Manual of Child Psychology* (New York: John Wiley & Sons, 1970), p. 61.

[18] Amram Scheinfeld, *The New You and Heredity* (Philadelphia: J. P. Lippincott, 1950), p. 2.

[19] Scheinfeld, p. 2.

[20] G. M. Whipple, ed., *Intelligence, Its Nature and Nurture.* Part I: *Comparative and Critical Exposition;* Part II: *Original Studies and Experiments,* Thirty-ninth Yearbook of the National Society for the Study of Education (Bloomington, Ill.: Public School Publishing Co., 1940).

[21] J. McV. Hunt, *Intelligence and Experience* (New York: The Ronald Press, 1961). Copyright © 1961.

[22] Hunt, p. 363.

The question of how much of the individual variation observed in a population with regard to some specified trait may be attributed to genetic factors has been addressed in a number of studies of *heritability*. Some of these have precipitated controversy among scientists and educators that is even more heated than that of the forties.[23] Not all those involved in the controversy, and certainly not all those who have commented on it, have grasped the point made by McClearn:

> The key concept of heritability explicitly and necessarily involves the simultaneous consideration of both genetic and environmental determinants. With this formulation, an attempt to describe a trait as being "genetic" or "environmental" in origin is seen to be meaningless. It is also important to know that the heritability estimate obtained from a particular set of operations, . . . is not an external, fixed value of the trait. Depending simultaneously upon environmental and genetic variance sources, the heritability will change as a given population is subjected to different environmental circumstances, or as its genetic composition changes. Thus a heritability value refers to a given trait at a given time in a given environment.[24]

For the educator to assume a predominantly hereditarian position would be to deny to children their right to the best possible environment both in and out of school. On the other hand, to overlook the contribution that genetic factors make to development also denies the child the right to an environment that takes into consideration his unique qualities.[25]

Maturation and Training

The maturation and training issue may be taken as a particular instance of the larger heredity-environment question. Stated as a set of alternatives it is so obviously an oversimplification that it no longer receives consideration in most child development textbooks. The related educational question of "readiness" is also currently given little prominence even in books dealing specifically with early childhood education. This may well be because so much of psychological and educational research of the 1960s showed that young children could succeed in learning tasks once thought too difficult for them, if the task was

[23] Arthur R. Jensen et al., *Environment, Heredity and Intelligence,* Reprint Series No. 2, *Harvard Educational Review,* 1969. This contains Jensen's "How Much Can We Boost IQ and Scholastic Achievement?" and replies to it.

[24] McClearn, "Genetic Influences on Behavior," p. 49.

[25] For further discussion of this issue see two articles by Sandra Scarr-Salapatek: "Unknowns in the IQ Equation" (a review), *Science,* 174:1223–1228, December 17, 1971; and "Race, Social Class and IQ" (report of her research), *Science,* 174:1285–1295, December 24, 1971. The articles are also the subject of further discussion in letters to *Science,* 178:229–240, October 20, 1972.

carefully analyzed, broken into its component parts, and taught step by step in situations providing optimum encouragement.[26]

One of those who contributed to the view that young children are capable of learning and thinking at a level considerably above that traditionally expected of them was Jerome Bruner. In reflecting on the sixties, he comments on the many times in different curriculum projects that good teachers found it difficult "to get to the limit of the child's competence." It was, he notes, easy to conclude that "any subject could be taught in some honest form to any child at any stage in his development."[27]

Unfortunately not all who read this conclusion understood that a subject could not be taught in its final form but had to be translated into a form that was within the child's intellectual grasp. Some attempted to teach complex mathematical and scientific concepts to first graders without translating them to the child's level of thinking. Others expected three-year-olds just introduced to a school environment to cope with tasks that were more suitable for six-year-olds.

In the 1960s studies of early experience and its effects on both animals and human beings, studies of infant behavior, learning and perception, and studies of early language development were also rather well publicized, probably contributing to a popular notion that given the proper environment or the proper training procedures, the young child's potential for learning was practically limitless. But the sobering realization that many children exposed to the cognitive curricular innovations of the sixties were not enthusiastic about learning, at least in school, and that the programs for young disadvantaged children have not been as successful as had been anticipated, leads to many questions. One of these has to do with the appropriateness of the training provided in relation to the maturity of the children. Despite the tremendous increase in knowledge of the ways children develop and learn, it is unlikely that the early childhood educator can escape

the question of the timeliness of what we wish to teach in the light of the child's ability to take it. Does the child possess the requisite capacity and background of experience? Is it economical to devote time and energy to a certain undertaking now or should it be postponed until the child is more mature?[28]

[26] Benjamin S. Bloom et al., *Handbook on Formative and Summative Evaluation of Student Learning* (New York: McGraw-Hill, 1971), especially pp. 43–57, "Learning for Mastery." See also Robert M. Gagné, "Contributions of Learning to Human Development," *Psychological Review,* 75:177–191, May 1968, and Lauren Resnick, "Hierarchies in Children's Learning, a Symposium," *Instructional Science,* 2:311–362, 1973.

[27] Jerome S. Bruner, "The Process of Education Revisited," *Phi Delta Kappan,* 53:18–21, September 1971.

[28] Arthur T. Jersild et al., *Child Development and the Curriculum* (New York: Teachers College Press, 1946), p. 31.

Postponement, of course, need not mean that the child is to be protected from any instruction in skills that appear to be precursors of later accomplishment, if those skills are clearly within the range of his abilities. On the other hand, it is not at all clear that experience specifically programmed to relate to particular concepts pays off better at the next level of development than does a generally varied, rich experience.[29]

Self-regulation and Extrinsic Control

When the early childhood educator opts for a curriculum that permits the child many choices in preference to one in which most of the activities are prescribed, she reveals a conviction that the child is the best arbiter of his own learning. She rejects the notion that her job is to shape the behavior of the child through the reinforcement of certain responses and not others. In so doing she espouses those theories of development (especially that of Piaget) that place the primary source of the interaction between the organism (the genetic factors) and the environment with the organism in clear contrast to those that place primary emphasis on the environment.[30] However, she must bear in mind the nature of the available developmental theories. As Baldwin commented in the mid-sixties, they represent a patchwork quilt in which

> there are few issues on which any two theories actually confront each other and produce different predictions in the same situation. The theories generally talk past each other; each is concentrated on some particular area of child behavior and development to the exclusion of many of the questions which other theorists regard as fundamental. At certain points the theories deal with the same subject matter in different terminologies, but these points of contact are less common than the place where they are non-overlapping.[31]

Given this state of affairs and the fact that the early childhood educator must be concerned with many aspects of the child's development and learning, she needs to consider carefully which theories are applicable to which situations. This involves looking at development and learning from different stances, but it also implies the necessity for a consistent approach. For exam-

---

[29] See, for example Lawrence Kohlberg, "Early Childhood Education: A Cognitive-Developmental View," *Child Development,* 39:1013–1062, 1968; Joachim Wohlwill, "The Place of Structured Experience in Early Cognitive Development," *Interchange,* 1(2):13–27, 1970; and Sheldon White, "Possibilities and Plausibilities in Early Education," *Pediatrics,* 44:901–904, December 1969.

[30] Theories of development are discussed at some length in Chapter 6.

[31] Alfred L. Baldwin, *Theories of Child Development* (New York: John Wiley & Sons, 1967), p. 583. Since Baldwin's comment, the literature of developmental psychology has expanded tremendously. In some studies of cognitive learning, behavioral and Piagetian theories have both been brought to bear on prediction. In general, however, Baldwin's statement still seems appropriate.

ple, a teaching procedure selected for its short-term efficacy ought not to carry undesirable consequences when long-term development is concerned.

Immediate and Long-term Goals

Both teachers and parents of young children frequently confront situations in which short-and-long-term goals seem in conflict. For example, immediate punishment will stop behavior that is deemed undesirable, but its cumulative effect in terms of the child's relationship to himself and to the adult may be negative. Again, the kindergarten and first grade teacher may program the tasks the child undertakes so that he never makes a mistake, but so doing may have consequences in his ability to make realistic judgments.

Although the consideration of long-term effects seems imperative, the juxtaposition of particular short-and-long-term goals against one another without regard to related goals and to the probable nature of the child's progress toward them seems fruitless. Punishment may be necessary when the child is too young to reason about consequences. If it is not pervasive and if it frees him for safe exploration of his environment, then its long-term consequences are likely not detrimental. Similarly, when the kindergarten or first grade teacher considers programming various learning tasks (something that most teachers of young children were doing long before the term came into popular use), she needs to consider not only the long-term effects of such programming, but also how extensive it is to be. Certain aspects of the child's living in the classroom may need to be routinized, certain skills and information taught directly to free him for other kinds of learning and thinking. What these aspects are, and the nature of the skills and information provided will depend on the stage of development of the children involved.

Continuity and Stages of Development

Certain psychologists have questioned both the reality and the utility of the concept "developmental stages," preferring to focus on quantitative rather than qualitative changes over time. In contrast, such theorists as Freud, Erikson, and Piaget have segmented the child's development into periods with characteristic concerns and ways of thinking. Stages, by themselves, are only descriptive and explain nothing. To the extent that such concerns and ways of thinking are pervasive in any age span, however, they do provide the teacher with some notion of what to expect from children of those ages. Knowledge of the succession of stages can also provide the teacher with insight into some of the observed changes. For example, the argumentative behavior that disrupts a group of children who have previously been quite agreeable toward one another may be seen not as deterioration but as evidence of progress toward thought that is less self-centered and more adapted toward the view of others.

Beyond this it would be helpful to know the factors involved in the transition from one stage of development to the next, so that the social and physical environment could be of a nature to facilitate that transition. According to the theory of Jean Piaget, these factors include maturation, the child's action on his physical environment, social transmission, including both the tuition of adults and collaboration with other children, and the processes of self-regulation or equilibration.[32] But Piaget's theory provides few specifications for either the proper mix or the timing of these factors. As Sinclair has commented,

> Educational applications of Piaget's experimental procedures and theoretical principles will have to be very indirect—and he himself has given hardly any indication of how one could go about it. His experiments cannot be modified into specific teaching methods for specific problems, and his principles should not be used simply to set the general tone of an instructional program.[33]

The evidence for Piaget's principles, it might be added, is derived from individual interviews with groups of children. These provide normative data. In only a few studies have the children been followed over an extended period of time. There have also been relatively few studies in which the same child has participated in interviews designed to probe his understanding of a variety of concepts.[34]

The Norm and the Individual

Norms refer to average or typical performances for specified samples of children. In the case of a standardized test such as the Stanford-Binet, the sample is supposed to approximate that of the total United States. In practice, intelligence and other standardized tests are often based on norms from groups that are unrepresentative of the groups with which they are used. Obviously the normative figures provide only a backdrop against which the performance of a particular individual can be viewed. The circumstance of the interview or test situation, the competence of the interviewer, whether the child was relaxed and attentive, the background of experience (including being interviewed or tested)

---

[32] Jean Piaget, Foreword to Millie Almy et al., *Young Children's Thinking* (New York: Teachers College Press, 1966), pp. v, vi.

[33] Hermine Sinclair, "Piaget's Theory of Development: The Main Stages," in Myron F. Rosskopf, Leslie P. Steffe and Stanley Taback, *Piagetian Cognitive-Development Research and Mathematical Education* (Washington: National Council of Teachers of Mathematics, 1971), p. 2.

[34] Our studies, *Young Children's Thinking* (New York: Teachers College Press, 1966), and *Logical Thinking in Second Grade* (New York: Teachers College Press, 1970), both present longitudinal data. The latter study also provides data on the relationships among several cognitive tasks of the sort posed by Piaget.

that the child brings to the situation—these are all factors that are relevant.

Clearly norms can be and frequently are misused. The norm is a statistic, not a model for the individual to match. It is much more important to know that a particular child's performance shows continuing progress than it is to be able to peg him as being above or below others of his age.

For reasons that will be discussed in greater detail in a later chapter on assessment, two contradictory trends are currently apparent in early childhood education. On the one hand, tests of all kinds have proliferated. On the other hand, in a number of centers and schools all kinds of tests and any attempts to relate individual performance to normative data have been called into question. Well-constructed tests, carefully conducted interviews, and the normative data derived from these all have their place in the early childhood education program as long, of course, as they are used *for* the child and not *against* him.

The Whole Child or a Specified Aspect?

The concept of the "whole child," intended to emphasize both the uniqueness of each child and the fact that physical, mental, emotional, and social development cannot really be divorced one from the other, has a history in early childhood education going back at least to the 1930 White House Conference on Children.[35] To the extent that it implies the necessity for considering the effects of whatever experience one provides for the child on all of the aspects of his development, it is a powerful concept. But it can, and too often does, become a mere cliché. For in planning, teaching, and evaluating, some analysis must be made of the child's body movements. of his apparent reasoning, of the pleasure or fear or animosity he reveals, and of the ways he relates to other people. Furthermore, within any one of these domains, the teacher, if she is to be effective, must be able to observe many fine and subtle behaviors, She never teaches anything but a whole child, but she needs to understand all the aspects that contribute to that wholeness. Similarly, research, if it is to throw light on the intricate processes of development and learning, cannot always limit itself to consideration of the whole child, but must also investigate specific, and at times exceedingly limited, aspects.

Cognitive and Affective Aspects of Development

Research, particularly in education, appears to reflect the larger concerns of the nation. In the 1960s, the years following Sputnik when there was concern

---

[35] White House Conference on Child Health and Protection, §I. Medical Service; §II. Public Health Service and Administration; §III. Education and Training (Washington: 1930; published 1931–1932).

not only for the production of scientists and engineers, but also for scientific literacy on the part of the general public, interest turned to the ways scientific knowledge develops. The work of Jean Piaget served as a stimulus for much of the research that ensued. At about the same time, the realization that the schools at all levels were failing to meet the needs of children living in innercity and other impoverished areas also precipitated an increased interest in cognitive development.

The theory of Piaget which increasingly dominated the research of the sixties does provide for the affective aspects of development. Indeed such aspects are inseparable from and complementary to the cognitive. The affective aspects have to do with the "energetics," or economics of behavior.[36] Affectivity, according to Piaget, proceeds from a lack of differentiation between the self and the physical and human environment toward the construction of a group of exchanges or emotional investments which attach the differentiated self to other persons (through interpersonal feelings) or things (through interests at various levels).

Although the thinking child is also the feeling child, it seemed to many observers that the researchers, and many of those who constructed educational programs in the 1960s, had forgotten that fact. By the beginning of the 1970s, however, the pendulum of interest was clearly swinging in the other direction, and the affective and expressive aspects of development were beginning to receive more attention.

As Piaget has indicated, his views on the cognitive and affective development of the child can be integrated with the ideas inherent in the psychoanalytically oriented developmental studies of such theorists as Spitz, Wolf, and DeCarie,[37] as well as Bowlby and Erikson.[38] Work has also been done relating his theories to the moral and social development[39] of children. All this gives promise of the emergence of a more comprehensive theory of development to be eventually validated through empirical research.

CURRICULA FOR YOUNG CHILDREN

What goes on in any early childhood program—the activities the children engage in and the materials and equipment available for their use—reflects

---

[36] Jean Piaget and Bärbel Inhelder, *The Psychology of the Child* (New York: Basic Books, 1969).

[37] Piaget and Inhelder, pp. 21–27.

[38] Jean Piaget, "The General Problems of the Psychobiological Development of the Child," in J. M. Tanner and Bärbel Inhelder, eds., *Discussions on Child Development*, vol. 4 (New York: International Universities Press, 1955), pp. 3–27, 77–83.

[39] Lawrence Kohlberg, "Stage and Sequence: The Cognitive-Developmental Approach to Socialization," in David A. Goslin, ed., *Handbook of Socialization Theory and Research* (Chicago: Rand McNally, 1969), pp. 347–380.

adult notions of the way children should be socialized and adult theories about child development and learning. It also reflects pedagogical notions about the content of the children's experience and the ways they should be taught.

In the 1960s, the "rediscovery of early childhood" brought with it much controversy about many of these notions. Sufficient consensus about curriculum matters among early childhood educators had led to what the innovators called a "traditional" curriculum, even though at the nursery school level it was barely thirty years old. The issues that were raised, however, were not new and can be paralleled in the struggles between the Froebelians and the followers of Dewey with regard to the kindergarten in the 1890s, in the contrasting points of view of psychoanalysis and behaviorism represented in nursery schools in the 1930s and 1940s, and in the controversies surrounding the progressive elementary school in the 1940s. In all these periods the role of the teacher was open to question.

Instruction or Guidance?

The younger the child the more he requires care and nurturance. Is his instruction to come through the medium of his care, or is it to be separated? Shall it then be didactic, or is the teacher to provide guidance but not direction? According to what became the tradition, at least for the nursery school, "The teaching function is conceived in terms of setting the stage in such a way that she [the teacher] is a part of the situation without seeming to be; she is only rarely in the foreground but is always significantly in the background."[40]

At the kindergarten and certainly at the early elementary level where the numbers of children in relation to each adult are usually greater, and where the business of acquiring academic skills looms larger, few have questioned that the teacher's role includes instruction, sometimes of a very direct sort. There is need, however, for analyses of what teachers, with different groups of children at different ages, and using different curricula, do with children, and with what effects. Such analyses are now being made.

The Planned and Emerging Curriculum

Teachers of young children often note that the children's interests are unpredictable. They can, as Anderson suggested, set the stage, but they are never sure what will emerge. While the element of unpredictability is certainly a reality, it is also true that it may become a rationalization for doing very little

---

[40] John Anderson, "The Theory of Early Childhood Education," in Nelson B. Henry, ed., *Early Childhood Education,* Forty-sixth Yearbook of the National Society for the Study of Education, Part 2 (Chicago: University of Chicago Press, 1947), p. 95.

planning. There are aspects of the curriculum for which step-by-step planning (and teaching) is appropriate, and other aspects where the teacher need only see that the necessary props are available. Even in the latter case, some planning is required if the teacher is to provide props that are appropriate to the children at a particular time in their development.

The Academic versus the Intellectual

If the major focus of a program is academic, that is, geared toward teaching the skills and concepts that underlie the elementary school reading and mathematics program, it will entail much detailed planning, and much direct instruction. If, on the other hand, its concern is with the development of the child's thinking, it will probably not demand any less planning and perhaps no less instruction. But it will be instruction (or stage-setting) of a very different order. The teacher's question in relation to the activities in which the children engage will less often be "What did they learn?" and more often "How did they think?"

The program that focuses on intellectual development need not ignore specific concepts and specific skills. It is rather that these concepts and specific skills are seen in the context of the child's total development. The aim is not to fit the four- or five-year-old into a program that has been simplified from the first or second grade, but rather to capitalize on his four- and five-year-old powers in ways that are appropriate to his present level of development.

Specifically Programmed Skills and Concepts versus General Experience

It is a moot question whether the carefully ordered, highly prescribed activities imposed on young children in some curricula serve to enhance their total development. As Wohlwill has noted:

> While narrowly defined, stepwise organized learning sequences may result in limited success with respect to the specific content area at which the learning material is directed, the young child is not apt to make the generalizations to other related concepts or concepts of his own. However, he is apt to achieve concepts perhaps more slowly, but on a broader front, if presented with a more loosely structured, at the same time more wide-ranging, experiential context, such as would allow the imagination freer rein.[41]

[41] Joachim F. Wohlwill, "The Place of Structured Experience in Early Cognitive Development," *Interchange,* 1(2): 25, 1970.

The curriculum question, Wohlwill further notes, is one of the optimal balance between externally imposed and programmed tasks and unstructured activity initiated and directed by the child himself.

Play versus Work

Perhaps the same question is being raised when one considers the role of play in the early childhood curriculum. Traditionally, programs, particularly for children younger than six, have capitalized on the child's propensity for play, even maintaining that play is young children's work. Theoretical analyses of play[42] raise doubts about some of the assumptions that early childhood educators have made regarding children's play. Whether children who are playing are always cognitively employed, and whether for the sake of their all-around development they should be so employed, is a matter of current debate. Clearly, however, play is the prerogative of the child, and whether he can be made to play, even in an environment of toys and games, is dubious.

SUMMARY

The import of this chapter is *not* that the more things change, the more they stay the same. It is rather that promising new possibilities carry with them varied consequences, all of which need examination.

Society changes, new problems are confronted, new "solutions" arise. Young children are regarded in different ways. Programs and their emphases change.

Those responsible for the care and education of young children cannot expect to find direction from the past. But knowledge of concerns that have persisted over the years may throw some light on those that are now in the foreground. Such knowledge provides the early childhood educator a base and perhaps some hypotheses for analyzing current early childhood programs in whatever setting they are found.

---

[42] Brian Sutton-Smith, "The Playful Modes of Knowing," in *Play: The Child Strives toward Self-Realization* (Washington: National Association for the Education of Young Children, 1971). See also Jerome L. Singer, *The Child's World of Make Believe* (New York: Academic Press, 1973).

Analysis of Early Childhood Programs

There is only one subject-matter for education, and that is life in all its manifestations.

Alfred North Whitehead

After several years devoted to the development of innovative curricula for young children, extending downward to infancy and focused particularly on children from low-income families, attention in the 1970s began to turn to the child as a person and to the totality of his experiences.[1]

The term "curriculum," originally referring to a course of academic study and in the 1960s used broadly to mean the experiences of the classroom, or more narrowly, a set of activities prescribed for some clearly specified purpose, now seems to be used less frequently. It is often replaced by the term "program." Programs are conceived as planned experiences that may occur in the

---

[1] See, for example, the September 1971 issue of *The National Elementary Principal* which is devoted to early childhood education.

classroom but often expand beyond the classroom into the home and the community. Planning, furthermore, is no longer the prerogative of the educator but is to involve the parents as well.

The necessity for such widening of concern for the education and well-being of young children can be supported in many ways. But the undertaking is tremendous and not without hazards. All too often in the history of American education, lip service has been given to broadening the scope of the curriculum without materially changing the realities of the classroom. Or, at the other extreme, breadth has been achieved but at the expense of the acquisition of certain essential skills. The trick, in the present instance, is to capitalize on extensive knowledge of the development and individuality of the young child without losing sight of the educative possibilities in some of the more narrowly conceived curricula designed to meet specific needs. The problem in essence differs little from that described by Ruth Updegraff nearly twenty-five years ago as the need for integrating research findings and the curriculum of early childhood education.[2]

Unfortunately, the research dealing with the long-term effects of particular kinds of curricula is neither as extensive nor as definitive as the early 1970s emphasis on the importance of the early years might lead one to believe. Some evidence indicates that curricula based on rather different theoretical conceptions, given careful supervision and implemented by highly trained teachers, are equally effective in producing gains in cognitive performance and academic achievement. Evidence also indicates that programs designed to produce gains in *specific* cognitive areas show greater gains in those areas than programs not so oriented.[3] To what extent these gains can be sustained is an open question. Also, most of the curricula dealt with in recent research have focused on cognitive and academic goals. Changes in self-concept, motivation, persistence, curiosity, and initiative, although sometimes predicted, have been demonstrated in only limited ways. Furthermore, changes in other aspects of the child's development, whether socioemotional, perceptual-motor, moral, or esthetic, have frequently been filtered through the more pervasive concern with cognition and academic achievement.

Some educators and many young adults, parents, and parents-to-be are now insisting on a reordering of goals for themselves and for their young children. They relegate cognition to a place parallel to socioemotional develop-

[2] Ruth Updegraff, "Research and the Curriculum," in Nelson B. Henry, ed., *Early Childhood Education,* Forty-sixth Yearbook of the National Society for the Study of Education, part II (Chicago: University of Chicago Press, 1947), pp. 172–179.

[3] Joan S. Bissell, "The Cognitive Effects of Preschool Programs for Disadvantaged Children," in Joe E. Frost, *Revisiting Early Childhood Education: Readings* (New York: Holt, Rinehart and Winston, 1973), pp. 223–240.

ment and include ways of knowing that are not merely verbal. They value self-expression and the uniqueness of each individual over conformity to the traditional and normative. For these young people the major goal of early education, which is best when it is least institutionalized, is to create an environment in which the child can be "free to grow."[4]

In contrast, many, perhaps most, educators and many parents are skeptical or afraid of education largely based on a notion of freedom. Nonetheless, a great number are concerned with the depersonalization, fragmentation, impermanence, and insecurity that characterize so much of modern life. They acknowledge that the times demand renewed attention to human values. They support the notion that education, and most especially education that is directed toward the young child, should concern itself with the totality of his experience.

When parents are more deeply involved in the planning of early education programs, and when the parental role, whether or not it includes participation in a particular program, is seen as coextensive with the teacher role, the present diversity in programs seems likely to increase. Some programs, for example, may emphasize "freedom," others "structure," some a broad range of activities, and others a more limited number.

From the standpoint of the child, and from a concern with his development as an individual, there needs to be a way of analyzing curricula as they are enacted to see how they do impinge on him. Whatever goes on within the confines of a particular program can then be related to the experiences the child has outside of it. Obviously no one program will be equally appropriate for all children.

This chapter sketches some guidelines for such an analysis. It assumes that the effectiveness of any program depends on the way the child experiences it. This holds whether the curriculum is enacted in an environment in which all the interactions (teacher-child, material-child, and in some instances child-child) are tightly prescribed or whether it occurs in one where few prescriptions are apparent.

The analysis begins with a statement about the nature of the young child. The idea that schooling must be adapted to the capabilities of the child can be traced through at least two centuries of educational literature. But it was not until the 1930s that the study of child development became a generally accepted approach to the development of curriculum. Jersild describes the point of view:

---

[4] Rachel Elder, "Three Educologies," Far West Laboratories, San Francisco, 1971, p. 3. (Mimeographed).

The child development approach to the curriculum means an effort to apply to the education of children the lessons learned from the study of children themselves. Research in child development has provided many findings which have implications for education. . . . But the child development approach does not represent merely a collection of facts. It represents also a point of view.

Basic to this point of view is a spirit of inquiry—a desire to learn about the ways of children. This means an effort to obtain knowledge, to test this knowledge by repeated study, to state the findings in clear terms so that others can understand and, if they so desire, repeat the study.[5]

In the quarter of a century that has elapsed since Jersild wrote these words the literature of child development, as noted in Chapter 3, has proliferated almost astronomically. The concern in this chapter is not so much with children as a particular developmental theory conceives them but rather with the developmental realities that must be taken into consideration when programs are planned for children younger than the usual elementary school age.

THE NATURE OF THE YOUNG CHILD

Whatever the goals of a particular program for infants or preschoolers, it confronts what have been described as "universal functional problems of socializing the impulse life of children" and "other functional universals in insuring infant survival and giving children positive competence and role training for future social participation."[6]

Those who plan the program and more especially those responsible for its execution participate to a greater or lesser extent, depending on the age of the children enrolled and the portion of each day they spend in the program, in various aspects of child training.

According to Whiting et al.:

. . . Child training the world over is in certain important respects identical. . . . Parents everywhere have similar problems to solve in bringing up their children. In all societies the helpless infant, getting his food by nursing at his mother's breast and having digested it, freely evacuating the waste products, exploring his genitals, biting and kicking at will, must be changed into a responsible adult obeying the rules of his society. . . . Child training everywhere seems to be in considerable part concerned with problems which arise from universal characteristics of adult culture which are incompatible with the continuation of infantile behavior.[7]

[5] Arthur T. Jersild, *Child Development and the Curriculum* (New York: Teachers College Press, 1946), p. 1.

[6] Robert A. Levine, "Cross-Cultural Study in Child Psychology," in Paul H. Mussen, ed., *Carmichael's Manual of Child Psychology* (New York: John Wiley & Sons, 1970), p. 589.

[7] J. W. M. Whiting, I. L. Child, and W. W. Lambert, *Child Training and Personality* (New Haven: Yale

It is not without significance that throughout the world, instruction in academic subjects has generally not been initiated before the age of five, and usually later. Although this fact may be related to the usual progress in cognitive development,[8] it is also likely that only rarely were those in charge of schooling willing to take on responsibility for socialization of the young child. A probable attitude is summed up in the facetious comment of an American superintendent of schools: "The most important evidence to be gained from any test administered to determine whether a child is ready for kindergarten comes not from his performance, but rather from his ability to sit through it without needing to go to the toilet."

Reports of the learning abilities of infants and young children, particularly as reported in the popular press, sometimes give the impression that the child functions as a miniature adult. They fail to make clear the kind and extent of environmental support that goes into the demonstration of these abilities. In the experimental laboratory, the child is observed under optimal conditions. Any stimuli that might be regarded as distracting are ruled out. He is brought at the time of day when he is most likely to be responsive. The tasks confronting him are paced to his interests. In this situation the child may perform at levels above those usually expected for his age. The psychologist, in describing the results, may emphasize the adaptability of the youngsters, but it is equally clear that he has adapted his procedures to what he knows to be their nature. In a sense, at a given point in development, by taking account of the essentials of the child's *being,* he is able to demonstrate something of the process of his *becoming.*

Being and Becoming in Infancy and Early Childhood

The educator, like the psychologist, is confronted with two aspects of the child's development. There is, on the one hand, his being—his present ways of living in, acting on, and relating to his world. On the other hand, there is his future, the child and the adult he is becoming.

When the infant held closely in the adult's lap pushes himself to a more erect posture, laughing and gurgling as his feet make incipient stepping motions, the immediacy of his pleasure is clear. When he matches his vocalizations to the words he hears from the adult, it is to the immediate satisfaction of both of them. These are major events, not only in themselves but as landmarks indicating that he is *becoming* a walker, *becoming* a talker. Similarly, when the older child manifests an interest in printed words, his curiosity and his present pleasure also signify that he is *becoming* a reader.

University Press, 1953), pp. 63–64.

[8] Sheldon H. White, "Plausibilities and Possibilities in Early Education," *Pediatrics,* 44:901–904, December 1969.

A balance between these ways of looking at the child seems essential for those responsible for early childhood programs. Without a sense of the direction of development, programs will lack direction and sufficient challenge. Or, as Vygotsky notes, "The only good kind of instruction is that which marches ahead of development and leads it; it must be aimed not so much at the ripe as at the ripening functions."[9] But without an equally clear sense of where the child *is,* of the state of his *being,* so to speak, the program will allow insufficient opportunity for the child to assimilate the instructional experiences it provides.

Just as the child's being and becoming can only be separated for purposes of analysis, so too the active role which he plays in shaping his own destiny cannot be isolated from the role that is played by other human beings.

The Activity of the Young Child

The infant's inability to provide for his own care and nurture is not to be taken as a mark of passivity. Almost from birth his active manifestations of distress can elicit the care he needs. Increasingly thereafter the waking state finds him active—babbling, wriggling, sucking, grasping, looking at his own hands and other objects within his reach. This active manipulation and the eventual effects it produces (the "feedback" he gets from it) constitute his knowledge of his world.

That world expands and his knowledge with it as he begins to get around under his own powers of locomotion. His increasing language ability is also expansive, but it is still through action and not merely through talking that he develops his understanding, demonstrates his knowledge, verifies his hunches. Actions that seem on the surface to be random and unrelated gradually evolve into systematic, purposeful routines for investigation. Take, for example, the actions involved in water play. The infant splashes in his bath; the two-year-old appears to test the properties of a variety of containers, including sieves; the older youngster "washes" clothes and dishes and sails boats, and eventually returning to the possibilities of containers may work out the concept of unit measure.

Environments differ in the kinds of actions they permit, encourage, or prohibit. In some cultures the young child is relatively free to explore, using the repertory of actions he is developing, in almost any way he chooses. In other cultures his active tendencies are channeled into real responsibilities at earlier ages. In any event, from earliest infancy on, the young child is an active being, and any program designed to meet his needs must provide ample opportunity for him to engage in action.

[9] L. S. Vygotsky, *Thought and Language* (Cambridge, Mass.: MIT Press, 1962), p. 104.

The Young Child and Other People

The infant's actions are intertwined with his relationships to his caretakers. Initially, certain of his behaviors elicit nurturing responses from the adult. As time goes on, he begins to differentiate the central caretaking figures, especially the mother, from other individuals. He acts to maintain contact with them, and many of his increasingly complex action patterns are elaborated in interaction with them. Attachment to the mother, which may be intense through the toddler stage, may be described as a pivotal relation. Using her as a source of security, the child makes increasingly extended excursions into the larger environment, but always with an eye to where she is or to her return. Other children manifest less intense attachment to the mother but display similar behaviors in relation to other caretakers.

The attachments of the infant and toddler appear to provide an important base not only for the child's relations with other adults and his peers, but also for his cognitive development. Although he is to a considerable extent self-propelling in his exploration of his world, his expectancies regarding the effects he may have on it depend in large part on the stability of his relations to significant others. Accordingly, an important question for any program designed for children under the age of three has to do with the extent to which it builds on or disrupts these attachments.

From the toddler period the child shows increasing interest in and ability to relate to other people, both those who are near his age and those who are older. Individuals vary greatly in this regard. For example, some three- to five-year-olds, confronted with a situation with several teachers, seem to accept care and direction as readily from one as from another. Others, perhaps most, express clear preferences for a particular one.

Considerable variation is also apparent in the ways children relate to their peers. As early as toddlerhood some children play relatively peacefully with those with whom they have had close associations. Encounters among children who do not know one another, and who have had little experience with others, may be stormy, not so much from animosity as from lack of understanding. In any event, although three- and four-year-olds often associate with one another pleasantly, the ability to sustain a cooperative endeavor may need time and encouragement for full development. Sharing in both actions and ideas of other children is, however, essential to the child's growing understanding not only of his world but also of himself.

The Developing Self

The child's awareness of himself and the feelings he has about himself are the product of his encounters with his physical and social environment. The process of self-development is complex. The impact of a particular encounter and the cumulative effect of many encounters depends as much on the unique characteristics of the child as it does on the nature of his environment. In the early months of life a kind of mutual regulation occurs between the infant and his mother. She learns his style and tempo and he adapts to her ways of caring for him. Being fed, and taking an increasingly active part in the process; being held, being carried about, and later propelling himself about; playing peeka-boo; babbling and hearing the mother respond—all these are interchanges contributing to the core or body self. Whether such mutual regulation takes place as readily when several caretakers are involved is an open question.

Beyond the infancy period, as the child begins to walk and to talk, an awareness of himself as a person with both needs and capabilities may be reflected in an assertive "Me do!" and an uncompliant "No." He begins to imitate some of the behaviors that he observes, particularly those of individuals who are significant to him. As he grows he engages himself in an ever-widening range of activities, and the effects he gains from these, whether through his own pleasure or the approval of others, are incorporated in his developing picture of who he is.

To enhance the child's self-image seems to be both a reasonable and a desirable goal for any program designed for young children. But it is a goal whose implementation demands extensive knowledge of the child and whose realization is difficult to assess.

The adult can make some inferences about the child's developing self from the way he behaves and from his expressions of feeling. When the general direction of the child's development is toward increasing competence and the child's emotions appear appropriate to the situations in which they are expressed, taking into account the probable nature of his cognitions, the adult has some assurance that all goes well. Note, however, that a valid inference requires an adult who is open to the child's feelings and to his ways of thinking.

Thinking and Feeling in Young Children

Adults, noting the spontaneity of the child's emotional expression and his whole body involvement in it, tend to think of the child's emotional life as very different from their own. On the other hand, once the child begins to use language, they often assume that what he says reflects thinking not dissimilar to theirs. They overlook the evidence, so cogently assembled by Piaget, that adult logic and adult reflectiveness are in fact the products of a long period of development, and qualitatively very different from the thinking of the young child. Accordingly, from a subjective view, the affectionate, angry, or fearful feelings of the infant or preschooler may not differ greatly from those experienced by his parent or teacher. But what cues off those feelings may be very different.

The infant, in the sensorimotor period of development, knows the world through the patterns of action he applies to it. Thought, in the sense of reflection on one's actions or on events, is largely lacking. Feelings of pleasure derive both from the exercise of patterns of action and from the comfort of being cared for. When the care is well adapted to the infant's individuality, as expressed in his tempo and rhythm and the way he responds to different kinds of stimulation, he comes, in Erikson's terms, to be trusting both toward people and toward things. When, on the other hand, the care is less appropriate for him, and most especially when his emotional attachments are disrupted, he runs the risk of acquiring a basic mistrust that may imperil not only his interpersonal relationships but also his learning and competence.

By the age of eighteen months or two years the child constructs a stable reality in which objects are permanent and independent entities, related to one another in space and time. By then he gives evidence that he mentally represents his experience to himself. Such representation can be seen in instances in which he imitates something that is no longer directly observable. It is also evident in his play, in which an object can stand for some other object, or an action can symbolize some object or event.

Mental representation and the beginning of preoperational thinking brings with it an awareness of the self. The toddler, into everything, now confronts the need to control himself. Still basically dependent on adults, he begins to savor his own independence and insists on demonstrating his competence. The central conflict revolves around his autonomy and self-esteem and whether his life can be so ordered that these, rather than shame and self-doubt, will be its resolution.

Preoperational thinking was initially described by Piaget more in terms of its lacks than its positive attributes. It is clear, however, that as the child continues his active investigation of his world, he stores up a tremendous amount of information about it. He derives social knowledge from his own observations and from adults' responses to his "What's that?" and "Why?" From his experimentation with objects he develops knowledge of their physical properties.

Piaget's more recent studies highlight the fact that the preoperational child understands such functional dependencies as that it takes a push from someone or something to make a block move. The preoperational child, though he may lack an understanding of quantitative identity, does grasp the nature of qualitative identity—changing the shape of a piece of wire does not alter its essential properties.

The child's thinking in the preoperational period tends to be egocentric, in the sense of lacking awareness of viewpoints that may differ from his own. His logic is not systematic, but better described as a "semilogic." He sorts objects and events according to some guiding criterion, but he lacks an understanding of hierarchical classifications. He knows which of a group of objects is the longest, and which the smallest, but he has no systematic method for putting them into serial order.

The preoperational child cannot yet readily reverse his thinking to recapture the thought of a moment before. He gets caught up in the way things look, and in a typical conservation experiment asserts that the equality of two sets of objects no longer holds when one set is transformed by some rearrangement of its members. He also has difficulty with reciprocal relationships—the idea that just as he has a brother, his brother has a brother eludes him.

Erikson sees a third nuclear conflict arising within the period of preoperational thinking. This is the conflict between the initiative that the child displays in testing his powers and comparing himself with others, both his peers and adults, and the feelings of guilt that are engendered in his transgressions.

Toward the end of the early childhood period, around the age of seven, a gradual transformation in the child's thinking occurs. It becomes more logical and systematic, more like the thinking of an adult. The child is accordingly more amenable to instruction. He has reached the level of concrete operations. The term "operation," as Piaget uses it, refers to the transformations implied in such symbols as $+$, $-$, $\times$, $>$, $<$, and to the mental activity of carrying out the transformations. The term "concrete" refers to the fact that the child can perform mentally actions he previously carried on in actuality.

From the viewpoint of Erikson's analysis, the change in the child's thinking is paralleled by a change in the child's attitudes. He is no longer so concerned with testing himself and his limitations, but rather with the accomplishment of real tasks. In some societies he would begin to share important responsibilities. In a society dependent on technology, he must find satisfaction in schoolwork. The danger is that he may come to feel inferior and inadequate.

From the standpoint of both the child's emotional well-being and his intellectual development, the program for the young child needs to be adapted to his ways of thinking. The way routines are planned, the provisions for his physical safety, the number of adults available, as well as the kinds of activities provided are all matters demanding knowledge of the child's cognitive and emotional development.

Special Vulnerabilities of the Young Child

It might be said that the young child is vulnerable in an environment that is ill-adapted to his nature—that fails to provide for his activity, both physical and mental; that exposes him to too many adults or to those who treat him in perfunctory, routine, or punitive fashion; or that offers him insufficient opportunity for interaction with other children or expects him to cope with them in too great numbers. To say this does not deny the fact that children do survive such environments, and some of them go on to reasonably meaningful and productive adulthood. It is not clear what strengths in their particular genetic endowments or what supports in their later experience distinguish them from the less fortunate whose existence seems to hold little that is good either for themselves or for others. Certainly, however, programs that are deliberately planned for children can only opt for what is, on the basis of present knowledge, best adapted to them.

Furthermore, those who plan programs need to bear in mind that the infant and young child are not only psychologically vulnerable, but equally important, physically vulnerable. Birch and Gussow remind the educator of this when they write:

> It is inevitable and quite fitting that when the educator, the psychologist, and the sociologist attempt to alter educational achievement they should concentrate on features of curriculum, familial environment, motivation, cultural aspects of language organization, and the patterning of preschool experiences. But the fact is that the child who is both the subject and the object of all this concern is a biological organism—a statement the obviousness of which is exceeded only by the extent to which it can be, and has been forgotten in the face of our fragmented administrative concern with health and with education. As an organism, the child is not only a mind and a personality capable of being unmotivated, unprepared, hostile, frustrated, understimulated, inattentive, distracted, or bored; he is also a body which can be tired, hungry, sick, feverish, parasitized, brain-damaged, or otherwise organically impaired.
>
> . . . The child who is apathetic because of malnutrition, whose sequence of prior experiences may have been modified by acute or chronic illness, whose selectivity as a perceiver and whose organizing ability as a learner may have been affected by previous exposure to risks of damage to the central nervous system, cannot be expected to respond to opportunities for learning in the same way as does a child who has not been exposed to such condition; for the effective environment of any organism is never merely the objective situation in which he finds himself, but is rather the product of an interaction between his unique organismic characteristics and whatever opportunities for experience his objective surroundings may provide.[10]

The fact that the damage done the child by malnutrition, chronic fatigue,

---

[10] Herbert G. Birch and Joan Dye Gussow, *Disadvantaged Children: Health, Nutrition and School Failure* (New York: Harcourt, Brace and World, Inc., 1970), p. 7.

and inadequate medical care may not easily be remedied does not exonerate those responsible for his care and education from concern for it. Furthermore, whatever program is designed for him, or for the more fortunate youngster whose physical being has not been at risk, needs to ensure good physical care. This includes adequate nutrition, the balance of rest, activity, and stimulation that prevents undue fatigue, equipment and materials physically safe for an individual still largely lacking in judgment, and adequate protection against the diseases that are hazardous to him.

Planning and programming that take proper account of the nature of the young child are inevitably concerned with him as a total being. Whatever is designated "the early childhood (or infant) curriculum" is part of the total fabric of his life. It may occur during a few hours each day outside his home, or it may be woven into a larger and more extensive child care program outside the home, or it may become part of what goes on within his home.

ANALYZING CURRICULA FOR EARLY CHILDHOOD

In the 1960s a great number of curricula for early childhood were devised, followed by curricula for infants and toddlers. The available curricula vary considerably in the psychological theories underlying them, in the instruction and guidance strategies they require, and in the kinds of equipment and materials they use. Most of them were designed to correct what were perceived to be the deficits of children coming from poverty homes. They gave primary focus to language and cognitive development. A number of curricula have been extended from prekindergarten or earlier upward to include kindergarten, first grade, and beyond.

Interest in the relative effectiveness of these programs has led to a number of attempts to compare them. For example, Maccoby and Zellner[11] examined materials describing ten different primary education programs of an experimental nature. Many of these were programs originally designed for prekindergarten. All were part of Project Follow Through, a federally funded "intervention" program for elementary school children coming from poverty areas. After analyzing program descriptions, talking with the sponsors of the programs, and visiting some of them, Maccoby and Zellner noted the points of similarity and difference among the programs.

The programs compared agreed on the necessity for assessment of the child at the beginning of the program. They agreed that the child's prior learning and development must be taken into account, and that the program

---

[11] Eleanor E. Maccoby and Miriam Zellner, *Experiments in Primary Education, Aspects of Project Follow Through* (New York: Harcourt, Brace, Jovanovich, 1970).

must be sufficiently individualized to allow for a range of differences. They agreed that when the program and the methods of teaching are so adapted to the child, the child will learn. Proper adaptation includes finding ways of capturing the child's attention and understanding his motivation. Furthermore, the child should find success and enjoyment in the program. They also agreed that programs must specify their objectives in detail.

The programs Maccoby and Zellner compared differed in their views about the nature of learning, placing different kinds of emphasis, for example, on learning through discovery or through carefully sequenced tasks and on the role of language in learning. They also differed in the emphasis they gave to extrinsic as contrasted with intrinsic motivation. Some stressed competition, others cooperation.

More extensive comparisons deal with the details of instructional and guidance procedures, the materials and equipment used, staff requirements, and evaluation procedures. Guidelines for such comparison, for example, were developed for the Association of Supervision and Curriculum Development by a team of early childhood educators.[12]

Interest in comparison also extends to the programs in operation. As Maccoby and Zellner's report implies, programs differing in avowed philosophy may not differ very much in what is taught, nor even in some cases in how it is taught. Accordingly, some attempts have been made at systematic observation of classrooms with differing curricula. (See, for example, studies by Soar and Soar[13] and the Stanford Research Institute.[14])

Perhaps the most important question that can be raised when programs are compared has to do with which aspects impinge meaningfully on the children and the teachers participating in them.

Structure in Early Childhood Programs

When many of the innovative preschool programs came into being in the early 1960s, teachers affiliated with the "traditional" nursery school often labeled the newcomers "more structured," or "too structured." Currently, teachers in the primary grades also refer to themselves as preferring "more structure," or sometimes "less structure." Or they may say, "I like the open classroom, but of course it has structure." Obviously, then, the term has meaning for teachers, but it may mean different things to each of them.

Some researchers (for example, Karnes[15] and Weikart)[16] have made com-

[12] *Educational Leadership,* 28(8):788–843, May 1971.
[13] Robert S. Soar and Ruth M. Soar, "An Empirical Analysis of Selected Follow Through Programs," in Ira J. Gordon, ed., *Early Childhood Education,* Seventy-first Yearbook of the National Society for the Study of Education, Part II (Chicago: University of Chicago Press, 1972).
[14] Stanford Research Institute, "Longitudinal Evaluation of Selected Features of the National Follow Through Program," ERIC document no 067266 and 057267, 1971.
[15] Merle B. Karnes, *Research and Development Program on Preschool Disadvantaged Child,* Final Report

parative studies of preschool programs based on relative differences in structure. However, as Mayer has pointed out, "structure" is a term that applies not to a single dimension, but rather to the "interrelation of parts or the principle of organization in a complex entity."[17] Noting that the basic components of a preschool classroom are teachers, children, and materials, she shows how their interrelationships can be described in terms of the frequency of interactions—between teacher and child, child and material, and child and child. Programs can then be ranked relative to each other on the basis of the frequency of each type of interaction. In Mayer's scheme, frequency is measured by the amount of the child's time spent in learning mediated either by the teacher, by materials, or by other children.

Clearly these interactions can occur in different modes. For example, learning mediated by the teacher can be directed toward the right answer or toward the child's discovery. Similarly, materials may be programmed so that the child's use of them leads him to the expected learning, as is the case with much of the Montessori apparatus, or may invite the child's exploration and lead to a variety of learnings, as is more typical of traditional nursery school equipment. Even the learning that is mediated through other children may vary depending on whether the children are left more or less to their own devices as in spontaneous play, or participate in a game or in a child-child tutoring session.

A concern with the modes in which classroom interactions occur seems inherent in an analysis made by Bussis and Chittenden.[18] Their attempt to describe the Education Development Center program, a Follow Through patterned to some extent on the British Infant School model, suggested that it was *both* child-centered *and* adult-centered. They propose a double classification scheme for describing classrooms based on the extent to which (1) the teacher or (2) the child is an active contributor to decisions on the content and process of learning. In the EDC model, for example, the contribution of both child and teacher is high, while in traditional nursery schools the teacher's contribution is often relatively low and the child's is relatively high.

Bussis and Chittenden note that this scheme can be applied to many different programs and that it can serve as a device for evaluating the extent to which a curriculum in operation conforms to the expectations of those who devised it.

vol. 1, University of Illinois, Contract No. OE 6-10-235, U.S. Office of Education, 1969.

[16] David P. Weikart, "Preschool Programs; Preliminary Findings," *Journal of Special Education,* 1:163–182, 1967.

[17] Rochelle S. Mayer, "A Comparative Analysis of Preschool Curriculum Models," in Robert H. Anderson and Harold G. Shane, eds., *As the Twig Is Bent: Readings in Early Childhood education* (Boston: Houghton Mifflin, 1971).

[18] Anne M. Bussis and Edward A. Chittenden, *Analysis of an Approach to Open Education,* Interim Report (Princeton: Educational Testing Service, August 1970).

Any scheme setting forth the dimensions of curricula tends to mask the dynamics it is intended to reveal. Figure 1 depicts such a scheme. It is derived in part from the analysis by Mayer, cited above, and in part from an analysis by Lay and Dopyera. [19]

Child encounters	Teacher and other adults	Other children	Materials and equipment	Self

Density
Variety
Complexity

Mode:
    Didactic
    Sequenced
    Paced
    Open

In space
Through time

Fig. 1 Child's-Eye View of the Curriculum (Adapted from Margaret Lay and John Dopyera, *Analysis of Early Childhood Programs,* Urbana, Ill., ERIC Clearinghouse on Early Childhood Education, May, 1971).

Since curricula are designed for children, it seems reasonable to think how they perceive them. Unfortunately, with the youngest children it is difficult, if not impossible, to get systematic evidence on this, although their willingness to participate gives some indication of their perceptions.

With children who can communicate verbally, more direct evidence can be obtained. Cazden, [20] for example, had Polaroid snapshots made of children at work and play in "open" classrooms. Then she discussed the pictures with them individually, finding out how they saw the activity in which they were engaged, and what else they thought were "good things to do." Other investigators (for example, Almy, [21] Biber and Lewis, [22] and Koslin [23]) have used sketches of standard classroom situations to check children's perceptions and expectations.

[19] Margaret Lay and John Dopyera, *Analysis of Early Childhood Programs,* Urbana, Ill. ERIC Clearinghouse on Early Childhood Education, May 1971.

[20] Courtney B. Cazden, "Transplanting English Infant School Ideas to American Classrooms and Some Effects on Language Use," ERIC document no. 040 756, 1970.

[21] Millie Almy, "Exploratory Study of Team Teaching in First Grade" (unpublished paper), 1962.

[22] Barbara Biber and Claudia Lewis, "An Experimental Study of What Young Children Expect from Their Teachers," *Genetic Psychology Monographs,* 40:3–97, 1949.

[23] Sandra Koslin et al., "Effect of Race on Peer Evaluation and Preference in Primary Grade Children," *Journal of Negro Education,* 39:346–350, Fall 1970.

The scheme presented in Figure 1 does not imply any assumption that the child takes conscious note of all the dimensions included, or that he could report on them. It does imply an assumption that he is aware of some of them, and that they all, to greater or lesser degree, affect him and contribute to his learning and his self-esteem or lack thereof. Whatever effects there are depend, of course, on the kind of child he is, and on his age and maturity.

Looking across the top row of Figure 1, the reader will note that the scheme takes account of the child's encounters with teachers and other adults, with other children, and with materials and equipment. It also includes a column headed "Self" as a reminder that each of the encounters is experienced by the child in a personal way that depends on his unique characteristics and history. Cumulatively, the child's encounters, in combination with those he has outside the program, are incorporated into and shape his concept of himself.

The first column at the left lists some of the ways in which the child's encounters may vary depending on the particular curriculum. The last two rows in this column refer to the space and the time within which the encounters occur. Some of the kinds of relationships among the dimensions listed in the rows and the columns are discussed below. The reader may wish to consider other possibilities.

Density In Lay and Dopyera's scheme "density" refers to "the total amount of sensory stimulation within a given time span." Note, however, that it may be applied to each of the kinds of child encounters. In a Montessori program, for example, the child probably has more frequent encounters with materials than with either children or adults. But these material encounters may be less dense in a traditional Montessori school where materials are displayed so as to be accessible to children, but must be returned to their places when used, than is the case in a traditional nursery school where a great variety of materials seem to be in use all at the same time. The consequences of such density are not known, but some children do appear able to function selectively while others seem to be pulled at by each thing their eyes encounter.

Much the same can be said with regard to the density of encounters with people. Although the necessity for limiting these is fairly clear where infants and toddlers are concerned, there may also be optimal numbers for children of older ages. The kinds of comments teachers make when there are "too many adults," "too many children," and sometimes "not enough children" or "not enough adults," tend to support this. On the other hand, careful examination will probably reveal that sheer numbers of people are not as important as *who* those people are and what kinds of demands their presence makes on the child.

Variety   In how many programs is the variety of people the child will encounter strictly predictable? What is the effect on his learning of encounters with males as well as females, with members of ethnic groups other than his own, with old people as well as young, with children of other ages as well as his own age? Perhaps variety is more often sought in materials than in people, but even with materials the possibilities in variety are not always exploited fully. For example, Lay and Dopyera note that one program reported teaching size discriminations through the use of seriated rings, different length straws, stacking blocks, Cuisinaire rods, building blocks and toys, coins of different denominations, and the children's reflections in mirrors. This may be contrasted with another program that reported children learned such terms as large, small, big, little, thick, thin, short, and tall, and distinguished between size proportions but referred to no materials other than pictures of animals.

Complexity   Lay and Dopyera use the term "complexity" to refer to the extent to which children encounter stimuli or situations in their natural complex state as compared with encountering prepared simplified versions. In the example given above, comparisons of pictures of animals would be less complex than comparisons of live animals or even the mirrored reflections of the children themselves. For the older child and the adult, learning may be facilitated by presenting a concept stripped of elements that may be distracting. The situation may be different where young children are concerned. Sigel,[24] for example, found that kindergarten children from poverty areas were unable to classify the pictures of objects as adequately as they could classify the objects themselves. Greenfield,[25] following a series of experimental studies designed to teach the mathematical concepts "square" or "round" to two- and three-year-olds, noted that the simultaneous representation of the concept in three modes—enactive (events encoded in terms of action), ikonic (in terms of images), and symbolic (in terms of arbitrary systems such as language)—during training was effective, whereas presentation in a single mode was not. Greenfield also notes that variety may improve learning through enhancing attentional processes. She cautions, however, that some preschool education approaches have emphasized direct experience but have not specified the importance of the communicative context in which the learning occurs.

Mattick,[26] in a discussion of language development, points to the ways

[24] Irving E. Sigel and Bonnie McBane, "Cognitive Competence and Level of Symbolization among Five-Year-Old Children," in Jerome Hellmuth, ed., *Disadvantaged Child*, vol. 1 (New York: Brunner/Mazel, 1967), pp. 433–453.

[25] Patricia M. Greenfield, "Teaching Mathematical Concepts to Two- and Three-Year-Olds: Some Experimental Studies," ERIC document no. 037 234, 1968.

[26] Ilse Mattick, "The Teacher's Role in Helping Young Children Develop Language Competence," *Young Children,* 27(3):133–142, February 1972.

in which the complex and varied nursery school situation *may* facilitate learning provided the adult is sensitive to the focus of the child's attention. Her illustration of a teacher who attempts to teach a math lesson by pouring the children different amounts of milk at snacktime suggests that the children's encounters with adults, like those with materials, vary in complexity. The children are concentrating on getting their cookies and are reacting to the fact that the teacher has given some children less milk than others. The teacher, however, does not respond to the children's reaction but simply reiterates the lesson, "Billy's glass is three-fourths full, Jimmy's glass is one-half full," and so on.

In this instance, the teacher apparently intends to teach through the complexity of the "real world." When she does not get the children's attention, her attempt fails. She has not really understood the complexity of the children's involvement with the real world.

In contrast to such a single-minded adult are those individuals who come to the classroom with a wealth of knowledge and information that may potentially be shared with the children. Those who understand the way the children think and feel start where the children are, or perhaps come to where they are as an encounter proceeds, and do not overwhelm them with complexity. Others, less sensitive to young minds, may leave them confused and disinterested.

Another aspect of adult complexity that may be revealed in different ways in different programs is emotional expression. The Montessori program, for example, calls for a teacher who is an observer and "indirectress."[27] One cannot conceive of a teacher who maintains this tradition giving vent within the classroom to feelings of irritation or anger, or even of strong affection. In contrast, many of today's "free schools" place a high premium on the authentic expression of feeling by all involved, including the teachers. The line between the situation where the adults are themselves genuine but also insightful about the thinking and feeling of the children and the situation where the adults are unwittingly exploiting the children is not always easily drawn.

Children have their own complexities. Undoubtedly programs present more or less complexity to the child, depending on whether the other children included are similar in age and background or more mixed. Traditionally, many nursery schools were organized by age, sometimes limiting groups to as little as six-months' range, on the assumption that children of near age were likely to have similar capabilities and interests. Mixed age groups, some teachers thought, perpetuated the kinds of rivalries the children might experience

---

[27] Thomas J. Banta, "Montessori, Myth or Reality?" in Ronald K. Parker, ed., *The Preschool in Action: Exploring Early Childhood Programs* (Boston: Allyn and Bacon, 1972).

with siblings. More recently, as Piaget's work has revealed the sequence of the development of children's thinking, the narrow age groupings are often questioned. However, evidence on the child's perception of either the mixed or the more homogeneous group is largely lacking.

Mode   Many ways of teaching (to be discussed in greater detail in Chapter 6) are available, but some are more effective for certain kinds of learning than for others. Thus the variety of modes of presentation of ideas and materials *may* be a measure of the success of a program, particularly when that variety takes into account both the material to be learned and the nature of the child for whom the learning is intended. Some of the variations in mode are considered here.

Didactic instruction   "Didactic," originally meaning "intended to instruct," has come to refer to instruction which relies predominantly on associative, or rote, learning. In its simplest form, the child hears and is led to repeat a "correct" answer. The patterned drill of the Bereiter and Engelmann program[28] is one example of this mode. So is the learning of nursery rhymes, and learning to count and to say the alphabet. Obviously much that children learn in the preschool years, regardless of whether they are deliberately instructed or not, is learned in this fashion. In recent years, educators and psychologists have debated at length regarding the extent to which early childhood programs, particularly those designed for children from poverty areas, should rely on the young child's propensities for rote learning, or should try to promote more conceptually based learning.[29] Clearly, however, both sorts of learning have their appropriate places.

Sequenced instruction   Sequencing has also been much emphasized in recent years. The emphasis has derived from programmed instruction, where considerable effort has gone into empirical demonstration of the most efficient sequences for learning particular tasks (for example, Gagné[30] and Resnick[31]) and from the sequence of development of logical thinking described in Piaget's work.[32]

As Lay and Dopyera[33] point out, the notion that learning should occur

---

[28] Carl Bereiter and Siegfried Engelmann, *Teaching Disadvantaged Children in the Preschool* (Englewood Cliffs, N.J.: Prentice-Hall, 1966).
[29] Arthur R. Jensen, "How Much Can We Boost IQ and Scholastic Achievement?" in *Environment, Heredity and Intelligence,* Harvard Educational Review Reprint Series no. 2, 1969.
[30] Robert M. Gagné, "Learning and Instructional Sequence," in Fred N. Kerlinger, ed., *Review of Research in Education* (Itasca, Ill.: F. E. Peacock Publishers, 1973), pp. 3–33.
[31] Lauren B. Resnick, "Hierarchies in Children's Learning," *Instructional Science,* 2: 311-362, 1973.
[32] See, for example, Jean Piaget and Bärbel Inhelder, *The Psychology of the Child* (New York: Basic Books, 1969), and Jean Piaget, *Science of Education and the Psychology of the Child* (New York: Orion Press, 1970), especially pp. 65–80, 151–180.
[33] Lay and Dopyera, op. cit.

in a predetermined order may apply either to the specific tasks posed the children and the materials or equipment they used, or it may apply to the teacher's ideas about the kinds of learning that should emerge as the child moves through the year in a program featuring relatively free interaction between the children and the materials.

Paced instruction In certain respects the notion of pacing parallels that of sequence. Pacing, however, carries with it greater concern for appropriate individualization and for matching instruction to the level of thinking the child seems to have reached in such a way as to provide appropriate challenge.

Indirect instruction or "guidance" In this mode, "the stage is set for learning through the varieties of materials the teacher provides and the range of experiences she makes possible for the children. She extends and enriches these by her guidance. She makes comments or asks questions, and above all she listens."[34] The theory underlying this mode was stated by Anderson some years ago:

> *Learning is self education.* If a child is given a problem which can be solved, and if he is motivated to respond, correct responses will appear in time, regardless of whether or not a teacher is present or instruction given. All that is essential is that right and wrong responses have different outcomes. If guidance and demonstration of good procedures are added, the child will make greater progress. [The teacher] guides a process inherent in the child which could go on even if she were not present but which should go on more effectively if she is present.[35]

It seems likely that most programs provide some mixture of the modes of instruction described here, and perhaps other modes also. Traditionally, the nursery school adhered most closely to the mode of indirect instruction or guidance. Beginning in kindergarten, more direct instruction came into the picture, and in first grade still more. Reports from some of the British Infant Schools that have been taken as models for experimentation in kindergarten-primary education in America suggest that although British teachers stress self-education, they also provide very direct instruction as it appears to be needed by particular children.

With regard to the effects that the mode of instruction may have on the child's developing self, there seems little question that *all* work (direct instruction) with no opportunity for exploration and play makes Jack a very dull boy. However, the effects of whatever modes of instruction are used also depend on

---

[34] Katherine H. Read, *The Nursery School: A Human Relationships Laboratory* (Philadelphia: W. B. Saunders, 1971), p. 28.

[35] John Anderson, "The Theory of Early Childhood Education," in Nelson B. Henry, ed., *Early Childhood Education,* Forty-sixth Yearbook of the National Society for the Study of Education, Part II (Chicago: University of Chicago Press, 1947), p. 92.

the density, variety, and complexity of the child's encounters and on the spatial and temporal contexts in which they occur.

Space Environmental designers know very well that space and its organization have profound effects on the behavior of human beings, but relatively few studies have specified the nature of these effects so far as young children are concerned. Two recent exceptions are to be found in the work of Kritchevsky[36] and Shapiro.[37] Kritchevsky, in summarizing data from fifty day care centers, notes:

> . . . Our data have shown that space strongly influences behavior in day care centers but also that space itself is subject to influence by other factors, and that by and large the staff has little or no awareness of either influence. . . . Clues to the need for spatial improvement can be found primarily in teachers' and children's behavior. Tired or irritable teachers, apathetic, hyperactive or uninterested children, high noise level, high restriction and direction, and a large amount of teacher-directed activity all have a high likelihood of being spatially induced.

Kritchevsky adds that instruction of a didactic nature may come to be preferred simply because teachers have had unsatisfactory experiences with other modes in poorly organized space.

Well-organized space appears to clarify for the child the expectations the program has for him. Books are not destroyed by crayon marks when the library corner is clearly a place separated from other activities, for example. Space can also be organized to encourage the child either to try all the possibilities or to be more selective. It can propel him into constant friction with his peers, or it can invite cooperation among small groups. It can offer him no respite from the group, or it can provide nooks where he may be an onlooker or, should he prefer, enjoy privacy.

The kind and amount of space a child needs in a particular program, and the effects it has on him, appear to be related to the length of time he spends in it and to the space available to him at other times. As Margaret MacMillan[38] noted half a century ago, children who live in cramped and crowded quarters find space for running exhilarating. Small quarters, with little space for vigorous exercise or for privacy, on the other hand, are of less importance for the child who has ample opportunity for these at home and spends only a few hours in the program.

[36] Sybil Kritchevsky, "Physical Settings in Day Care Centers: Teachers, Programs and Space," in Elizabeth Prescott and Elizabeth Jones, *Day Care as a Child-Rearing Environment* (Washington: National Association for the Education of Young Children, 1972), p. 40.

[37] Sylvia Shapiro, "Preschool Ecology: Selected Environmental Variables and Classroom Behavior" (unpublished doctoral dissertation, Teachers College, Columbia University, New York, 1971).

[38] Margaret MacMillan, *The Nursery School* (New York: E. P. Dutton, 1919).

Time   Time, like space, provides a backdrop against which the child's encounters occur and probably has much to do with their ultimate meaning to him. The slow-moving, cautious child in a program in which a great deal happens all the time has a very different experience from that of his more volatile, adventuresome peer. Yet both may need periods for reflection, for living through in play or in creative expression what they have learned or at least have been exposed to in other aspects of the program or in other aspects of their lives. Some children have time for this kind of being in their home life. Others do not.

In some programs time almost seems to govern the program. There is a time to arrive, a time for toileting, for snack, for music and stories, and a time to go home. How much adherence to a clock schedule, how much regularity in the day-to-day order of things is necessary to give small children a sense of security and how much is just a matter of the teacher's (or the school system's) convenience? How often do teachers and parents in a program come together to discuss the meaning time has for them, what it means to the children in whose education they are involved, and how the program can operate reasonably efficiently without making time the master of all concerned? Lay and Dopyera[39] express a similar concern for the meaning of time in programs when they note that *regularity* (the extent to which patterns of encounters recur on a daily or weekly basis) is a dimension on which programs may be compared. Under certain circumstances, they suggest, regularity may become stultifying.

In contrast, a dimension of programs which Lay and Dopyera describe as *emergence* provides evidence of vitality. It has to do with the extent to which new materials (or new patterns of encounters among children and adults, presumably) are introduced as the program progresses. In the Montessori program, for example, new materials are introduced continuously. In some traditional nursery schools the materials may not change, but expectations for their use do.

Time also relates to the objectives of the program. Is the program intended to bring all the children to a certain state of readiness for the kindergarten or first grade program that is imminent? Do the children meet for only a few hours a day? Does that make teachers more prone to use direct teaching, less apt to take cues from the children? Or, in contrast, is the program intended primarily for day care, so that the children are present for long hours? Are they, then, less involved in learning? Again, if the program is designed for older children, must the program objectives be realized within a single year, or does the program encompass, as in the British Infant School model and some ungraded schools, a period of several years?

[39] Lay and Dopyera, op. cit.

Although it is unlikely that the children themselves will give consideration to questions such as these, each will, it seems, register in some way the
time pressures, or lack of them, that the adults feel or impose on them.

SUMMARY

An essential facet of the work of the early childhood educator is the analysis
of programs from the viewpoint of the child.

The child's-eye view presented here assumes that there are many elements
in a program that influence not only the way the child responds in a program
and the learning he demonstrates, but also the way he feels about it, and the
motivation for further learning and thinking it engenders. This view also
assumes that the influence the program has is determined not by the elements
the program presents but by the nature of the child's interactions with them.
Thus the kind of child he is, the experiences he has during the time when he
is not involved in the program are all factors contributing to the effect it has
on him.

Settings and Sponsors for Early Childhood Care and Education

The child grows up in a world of things, surrounded by people who serve as models for skills and values. He finds peers who challenge him to argue, to cooperate, and to understand; and if the child is lucky, he is exposed to confrontation or criticism by an experienced elder who really cares. Things, models, peers, and elders are four resources each of which requires a different type of arrangement to ensure that everybody has ample access to it. [1]

Illich writes out of the conviction that present arrangements for schooling the young are no longer adequate to the needs of society. He calls for new "networks" designed to bring would-be learners whatever resources they need. His emphasis on "deschooling" society contrasts sharply with the view that public schools should expand downward to include the very young. Illich's critique accords with the view of those who prefer to have the needs of young children for care and education met somewhere other than in the public schools. Like

---

[1] Ivan Illich, *Deschooling Society* (New York: Harrow Books, Harper & Row, 1972), p. 109.

Illich, these people also seek new arrangements. They turn to the home and, in some instances, to other existing community agencies, but not to the school. Current concerns for changing arrangements for the care of young children can be understood in the dual context of traditional arrangements and new arrangements designed for the children of poverty.

TRADITIONAL SETTINGS FOR EARLY CHILDHOOD CARE AND EDUCATION

Lazerson,[2] discussing the historical antecedents of early childhood education, notes that three themes have dominated its development in the United States. These three themes (discussed briefly in Chapter 3)—the ethic of social reform, the uniqueness and importance of childhood, and the reform of the educational practices of the public schools—were evident in the decade of the 1960s. They also appear in current concern as to where early childhood education should occur, and how it is to be sponsored and funded.

The Home

The law protects the right of the family to provide whatever early education it deems necessary. Education generally does not become compulsory until the age of seven.[3] Practically, however, parents are urged to send their children to kindergarten in those states where kindergartens are available, and about 80 percent of all children do begin school when they are five.[4]

The responsibility of the family for the early care and education of its children is also supported by law, Under provisions of the Social Security Act, federal funds have provided aid to certain needy families with dependent children since the 1930s. Such funds were intended initially for the protection of children in families where the father was absent, incapacitated, or dead. The mother, in effect, was paid to stay home to care for her children, rather than leaving them in the care of someone else while she worked. In practice, both the minimal levels of support, and the pervasive American ethic have led to considerable question about the operation of Aid to the Families of Dependent Children (AFDC) and other welfare programs.

According to recent studies, a majority of women receiving AFDC believe

[2] Marvin Lazerson, "The Historical Antecedents of Early Childhood Education" in Ira J. Gordon, ed., *Early Childhood Education,* Seventy-first Yearbook of the National Society for the Study of Education (Chicago: University of Chicago Press, 1972), p. 33.

[3] U.S. Office of Education, National Center for Educational Statistics, *Digest of Educational Statistics* (U.S. Government Printing Office, 1973), p. 29.

[4] This figure includes children enrolled in public and private kindergartens but excludes those in nursery schools (from U.S. Office of Education, *Digest,* p. 8).

that there are great advantages in employment as contrasted to welfare support.[5] Employment means independence and pride as well as a better standard of living. Many, however, lack the skills required for well-paying jobs and can earn only minimal amounts. Like most mothers not receiving public support, they have a strong commitment to their children, particularly those of preschool age, and believe that they should be at home to take care of them. They worry about the difficulty of securing adequate child care should they find employment.

The belief that the home is the proper place for the care of young children is reflected in the fact that day care for the preschooler and infant is more often provided in homes than in centers. Most working mothers have little choice for care other than that of finding a caretaker to come to the child's own home, or more likely, one who cares for the child in her home. Until recently most social work agencies regarded day care homes as more suitable for young children than day care centers.

The Public Schools

Prior to the decade of the 1960s, only twenty-two states had state-supported kindergarten programs.[6] Programs for children under the age of five were rare.

The kindergartens had come into the public school system for the first time in 1873.[7] First established as private institutions for the children of relatively affluent parents and later for the children of the poor, their acceptance as part of the public schools represents all the themes described by Lazerson. Having become part of the bureaucratic structure, they became somewhat isolated. They were no longer so concerned with improving the lot of the poor. Nor did they influence the values of elementary teachers in the way their original proponents had hoped. They held, in general, to a child-development view, but the child development they espoused was often that of an earlier era. Weber sums up the situation by suggesting that a kindergarten teacher from the twenties would have felt comfortably at home in many kindergarten classrooms in the sixties.[8]

The nursery school, with very different origins from the kindergarten, came only briefly into the public elementary school picture prior to the 1960s. That was during the depression era of the 1930s when, in order to provide jobs

---

[5] Joyce B. Lazar, "Sources of Family Income and Attitudes toward These Sources," in Barbara J. Sowder and Joyce B. Lazar, *Research Problems and Issues in the Area of Socialization* (Washington: The Social Research Group, George Washington University, September 1972), p. 243.

[6] "Population Trends and School Enrollments," *National Education Association Research Bulletin,* 47(1): 26, March 1969.

[7] Evelyn Weber, *The Kindergarten* (New York: Teachers College Press, 1969), p. 28.

[8] Weber, p. 206.

to unemployed teachers, and nutrition to children whose parents were out of work, federal emergency legislation created the Work Projects Administration nursery schools. Many of these operated in the public schools.

In the high schools, where there were home economics programs, nursery schools were sometimes established to provide experience in child care to the students.[9] Nursery schools also became part of some programs of adult education where they served as laboratories for parent education. California, for example, has had an extensive program of this sort for many years.

World War II, following on the depression, marked the public schools' first extensive experience with child care. In some instances WPA nursery schools were converted to child care purposes. In others, new centers were created. Most received federal funding under the Lanham Act. The end of the war brought the end of the funding; however, in a few schools, programs were continued under other auspices. In California, they were continued and later included with other programs under the state education department.

Universities and Colleges

Although the nature and extent of the influence of the universities and colleges on some aspects of education is problematic, it was clearly direct in the case of the nursery schools. Most of the early nursery schools established in the 1920s were located in the universities, specifically to contribute to the knowledge of normal child development.[10] Although the total number of nursery schools now far outnumbers those located in the universities and colleges, Moore and Kilmer are probably correct when they note that the colleges and universities continue to influence programs for young children through their demonstration, research, and training facilities.[11] By the 1960s some of them had also begun to sponsor or to collaborate in nursery school and child care programs that were located off campus and served a wider range of clients than was usually the case in the campus school.

Other Community Agencies

Kindergartens, nursery schools, and child care centers, before the 1960s and now, are found in a variety of places and are sponsored by a variety of agencies.

In many communities, churches use their Sunday School classrooms for weekday kindergartens or nursery schools. In some instances the church rents

[9] Samuel J. Braun and Esther P. Edwards, *History and Theory of Early Childhood Education* (Worthington, Ohio: Charles A. Jones Publishing Co., 1972), pp. 164–167.

[10] Braun and Edwards, pp. 156–159.

[11] Shirley G. Moore and Sally Kilmer, *Contemporary Preschool Education: A Program for Young Children* (New York: John Wiley & Sons, 1973), p. 16.

or donates space to private groups; in others the program is operated more directly, often as part of the religious education program. Sometimes preference is given to the children of church members, and the program may have some religious aspects. Frequently, however, the program is operated in the same way as a secular program.

Both kindergartens and nursery schools may be operated as nonprofit educational institutions, in combination with private elementary schools, or separately.[12] The cooperative nursery school, owned and sometimes operated by the parents of the children, has enjoyed wide popularity, especially in certain areas of the country.

Settlement houses, where many kindergartens originated in the 1800s, community centers, and park and recreation departments often operate nursery school programs and sometimes child care centers. A number of women's organizations such as the Young Women's Christian Association, the National Council of Jewish Women, and the National Council of Negro Women have long been interested in day care. Many agencies that initially sponsored nursery schools to meet what they saw as community needs for parent education shifted to child care as more mothers sought employment outside the home.

Some agencies with a primary focus on a handicapping condition such as blindness, cerebral palsy, mental retardation, or emotional disturbance began operating nursery school programs well before the decade of the sixties.

In large cities a number of philanthropic agencies were originally established, at the end of the previous century or the beginning of this one, to provide day care that can only be described as custodial. Most of them were gradually influenced by the child development and nursery school movement so that by the 1950s programs for nursery school and for day care have been described as "indistinguishable."[13]

Proprietary Agencies

Those who romanticize childhood are repelled by the notion that there is money in the provision of care and education for young children. Those who are more realistic note how the stocks for the toy industry soar and are not surprised that nursery schools and child care centers can be made to pay.

Such private commercial ventures may be regarded as a legacy from

---

[12] Private or commercially operated nursery schools and kindergartens in middle-class neighborhoods have often employed housewives who are willing to work for small salaries because they find the location and the hours convenient. In many such settings professionalism has not been encouraged or rewarded.

[13] Greta G. Fein and Alison Clarke-Stewart, *Day Care in Context* (New York: John Wiley & Sons, 1973), p. 22. This excellent analysis of the complex issues involved in day care makes the important point that the children attending nursery school differed in many respects from those in day nurseries. It questions whether all the tenets of nursery education were appropriate to the children in day care.

World War II when the need for care was so great that "make-shift day care of all kinds mushroomed."[14] In states and cities where regulatory codes regarding safety and sanitary provisions were applicable, there was often insufficient staff to see to their enforcement. Accordingly, it was relatively easy to establish and maintain a center. By the 1960s, when early childhood education received much publicity and the needs for day care grew steadily, the already established schools and centers expanded their facilities and others desired to imitate them.

As might be expected, commercial schools and centers vary greatly in quality. "A rare few are successful in achieving a type of environment in which young children can grow and develop in all areas—physical, social, emotional and intellectual—without sacrificing one for the other."[15]

As far as business success goes, in a state where regulatory codes limit the number of children that can be cared for by a given number of staff, the profits are not great. "The owner of a successful nursery makes an adequate living, somewhat more on the average than his bureaucratic counterpart, the head teacher in a public center, but his responsibility is considerably more inclusive and sweeping.[16]

The Effects of Setting and Sponsorship

The preceding description depicts the situation in the United States in the early 1960s as the "rediscovery" of early education and the injection of federal funds that speeded its expansion began.

The reader may well ask, "Does this diversity matter? Do settings and sponsorship influence program quality?" An American predilection for analyzing things in terms of their costs might suggest that what matters most is not the setting, nor who sponsors the program, but the adequacy of the funding.

Surprisingly little research has gone into questions such as these, but the little that is available suggests that the assumption about cost is in error. Prescott and Jones, in 1964, studied fifty California child care centers including those that were proprietary, nonprofit, and public. They found that the size of the centers was related to program quality. In large centers there was more emphasis on rules and routine guidance than in smaller centers. Smaller centers provided the children more opportunities for "pleasure, wonder and delight." Sponsorship did not directly influence program or teacher performance.

---

[14] Elizabeth Prescott and Elizabeth Jones, The "Politics" of Day Care (Washington: National Association for the Education of Young Children, 1972), p. 8.
[15] Prescott and Jones, p. 8.
[16] Prescott and Jones, p. 45.

Excellence, the investigators found, as well as its absence, occurred under all types of sponsorship.[17] However, sponsorship had considerable to do with the characteristics of the adults in the center and also with the range of experience offered the children. Proprietary centers, which tended to be small in size, were more likely than the others to keep children ungraded by age, to have directors that participated in the teaching, and to have men present to assume a father role with the children.

As far as money is concerned, programs with similar hourly costs ranged in quality from very poor to outstandingly good. What really counts, Prescott and Jones decided, is committed leadership, and that can't be bought.[18]

EARLY CHILDHOOD EDUCATION FOR THE CHILDREN OF THE POOR

Most of the facilities described above—with the exception of the public kinder-gartens, child care centers, and the philanthropic centers—served children from middle-class homes. Occasionally working mothers from poverty areas were able to use strategically located low-cost proprietary centers, but in general poor children had access to few early childhood programs below the kindergarten level. That picture began to change in the mid-1960s.

Experimental University-based Programs

The programs designed for poor preschool children appear to have originated in the universities and colleges. Some school systems and social agencies initiated programs, but the major impetus for their development prior to 1965 when federal funding became widely available came from the universities. They were aided by funds from private foundations. Among the professors whose ideas provided inspiration for the new programs were J. McV. Hunt, Jerome Bruner, Benjamin Bloom, and William Fowler.[19]

As the 1950s drew to a close, the inequities between school performance and school provision for the poor had become of increasing concern. Poor children appeared to enter school at an initial disadvantage and continued to fall behind their more affluent peers. Some investigators began to turn their attention to the design of preschool programs to correct the disadvantages and the presumed cultural deprivation. Their strategy was to compare the func-

---

[17] Prescott and Jones, p. 76.
[18] Prescott and Jones, p. 78.
[19] See J. McV. Hunt, *Intelligence and Experience* (New York: Ronald Press, 1961); Jerome Bruner, *The Process of Education* (Cambridge, Mass.: Harvard University Press, 1960); Benjamin Bloom, *Stability and Change in Human Characteristics* (New York: Wiley, 1964); and William Fowler, "Cognitive Learning in Infancy and Early Childhood," *Psychological Bulletin*, 59:116–152, 1962.

tioning of poor children with the functioning of middle-class children of the same age. They then planned to correct the differences, or deficits, by early educational intervention.

In retrospect, the error of some of the assumptions underlying this strategy has become clear. As Nimnicht, developer of one of the early programs, wrote in 1973:

> "Cultural deprivation" is a misperception of the real problem of minority-group children in this country. "Cultural deprivation" is the explanation that has been given for the outcomes of the minority-group child's encounter with a mono-cultural system that is hostile to him. The real problem for children outside the mainstream is not lack of, or inadequate, stimulation in early childhood, but rather, trying to cope with an institution which is based on somewhat different values, uses a somewhat different language, and has a negative opinion of their life style, their parents, their community and themselves. The real problem for teachers lies not in providing watered down work or in coping with children who seem hard to control, but rather in the difficult task of learning different communication and motivation systems—learning to respond to unfamiliar perspectives and experiences rather than repressing them. The real problem for educational planners and decision makers is not to devise remedial "help-them-to-be-like-us" programs but rather to broaden the institution so that it can adequately accommodate and respond to students from a variety of cultural backgrounds and life-styles.[20]

The suggestion that the real problem is not what the designers of the first intervention programs thought does not necessarily mean that those programs and the others that followed were of no value. Rather, the experience in the intervention programs came eventually to throw the real problems into clearer focus. Furthermore, there are those who now see the real problem and its solution resting not alone in the schools, but rather in the social and economic inequities of the larger society.[21]

To return to the university-based programs, among those getting early starts were the Institute of Developmental Studies (IDS) program under the direction of Martin Deutsch, originally affiliated with the Department of Psychiatry of New York Medical School, later with New York University School of Education, and the Early Training Project, later Demonstration and Research Center for Early Education (DARCEE), under the direction of

---

[20] Glen Nimnicht and James A. Johnson, Jr., *Beyond "Compensatory Education"* (San Francisco: Far West Laboratory for Educational Research and Development, 1972), pp. 25–26.
[21] Christopher Jencks et al., *Inequality: A Reassessment of Family and Schooling in America* (New York: Basic Books, 1972). See also Philip Jackson et al., "Perspectives on Inequality; A Reassessment of the Effect of Family and Schooling in America," *Harvard Educational Review*, 43(1): 37–164, February 1973.

Rupert A. Klaus and Susan Gray at George Peabody College for Teachers.

The IDS, initiated in 1958, developed its program, beginning with four-year-olds, in the New York City Public Schools. The teachers, at least in the beginning, were individuals who were well-trained in traditional nursery school methods. The environment they provided for the children closely resembled that of the traditional nursery school, although all the equipment and materials were selected or constructed with a view to the concepts they might convey to the children. The teachers, much more than in the typical nursery school, intervened directly in the children's play and other activities, in order to elicit cognitive and language responses from them.[22]

The Early Training Project began a pilot study in 1959. In 1962 a study that was to extend for seven years was initiated. It employed experienced primary teachers in a summer program for four-year-olds. Although the program used some materials and equipment that were customary in the nursery school, the teaching procedures involving small groups were more directive and more like those used in the traditional first grade than those used in the nursery school. Positive reinforcement of the children's responses was emphasized.[23]

In addition to the summer program, the children in the Early Training Project were visited in their homes once a week throughout the school year. The home visitor involved the parent as an active participant in the project. She demonstrated activities that the parent could carry on with the child, both in the home and outside. She also informed the parents of opportunities such as adult education, improved housing, and better employment that might be available to them.

The Early Training Project also included a research component. Besides the experimental groups who participated in the summer programs and were visited in their homes, there were local and distal control groups.[24] One experimental group had three summers of special intervention, the other two. The control groups received all tests but had no special programs. Over the years the experimental children remained significantly superior to the control children on intelligence tests. By the end of fourth grade, however, differences on language and achievement tests were not significant. These findings are comparable to the results in most of the intervention projects

[22] For a description of the program, see Fred Powledge, *To Change a Child* (Chicago: Quadrangle Books, 1967).

[23] Susan W. Gray et al., *Before First Grade* (New York: Teachers College Press, 1966), describes the curriculum.

[24] Rupert A. Klaus and Susan W. Gray, "The Early Training Project for Disadvantaged Children: A Report after Five Years," *Monographs of the Society for Research in Child Development*, (120)33(4), 1968. See also Susan W. Gray and Rupert A. Klaus, "The Early Training Project: A Seventh Year Report," *Child Development*, 41(4):909-924, December 1970.

involving preschool programs. The Project also studied the effects that the family's participation in the Project had on the younger brothers and sisters of the children enrolled in the preschool program. The fact that the influence on the younger children seemed to come from the mother had an effect on the later development of programs focused on the teaching of the mother.

In certain other ways these early projects that began a bit in advance of the general concern for providing preschool programs to poor children seem to have set some trends. With the exception of the Bereiter-Engelmann program which relied almost entirely on direct verbal instruction, most programs proceeded from either a modified nursery school or a modified first grade approach.

The North Point Family Project,[25] associated with the Boston University School of Medicine and starting in 1955, is noteworthy not only as an early project but also because of certain other characteristics. It dealt with a group of children from "so-called hard-to-reach, hardcore, multi-problem families." Few of the families were from racial minorities. The program included both nursery school and intensive social work support for the parents. The group of children was small, and the analysis of the dynamic relations of the cognitive and affective factors involved in the children's learning was much more complete than in the more typical program for disadvantaged children. Like other projects of its time it operated from a clearly middle-class orientation; one cannot generalize from this group of children to poor children generally. Nevertheless, the project report shows how deeply the child's ability to cope with the school program is enmeshed in his basic feelings of trust or mistrust, autonomy or self-doubt. The teacher cannot easily help the child toward greater initiative, competence, and mastery until these personality components are strengthened.

As the 1960s progressed, the number of experimental programs for poor preschoolers sponsored by the universities and elsewhere increased. Some of these were eventually incorporated into Project Head Start (launched in 1965) and Follow Through (1967).

In 1967, the National Laboratory on Early Childhood Education, funded under the Elementary and Secondary Education Act of 1965,[26] brought into a loosely knit confederation early childhood education programs from Cornell University, the universities of Arizona, Chicago, and Syracuse, together with

---

[25] Eleanor Pavenstedt, ed., *The Drifters Children of Disorganized Lower-Class Families* (Boston: Little, Brown, 1967).

[26] Funds provided under the Elementary and Secondary Education Act of 1965 served to expand many programs for disadvantaged children including those for preschoolers. For example, in California, Compensatory Preschool Programs were established. In New York State somewhat similar programs were developed as prekindergartens.

DARCEE and later the universities of Kansas and Oregon. A coordination center was established. The mission of the Laboratory was to "provide the knowledge by which all young children may develop the competencies to master their environments and live effectively in a rapidly changing society."[27] The component programs were engaged in programmatic research on early development, applied experimentation, the development of curriculum materials, and evaluation. As time went on, the pressure to produce, test, and disseminate program materials came into conflict with the need to build a broader knowledge base through research. The Laboratory became the National Program on Early Childhood Education anf focused its efforts on the testing and dissemination of already available materials.

Head Start

Project Head Start, a program for poor preschool children and their families, came into being as part of the War on Poverty. Funded through the Economic Opportunity Act of 1964, it began in the summer of 1965, serving 561,000 children in 2,400 communities.[28] Priority for sponsorship went to community action agencies, but school systems and other voluntary organizations could also be involved. It brought early childhood education into many settings, both schools and community agencies, that had never before known a program for such young children.

From its beginning Head Start captured the imagination of many people. Initially, according to one who was involved in the early planning, the goal for the program was rather modest and realistic: " . . . children might be helped to enter school with more pleasure, confidence and courage if they had a preliminary experience in which teachers would help them to feel more positively toward themselves and school."[29] The scope of the program grew, however, to include an educational program, health services to provide medical diagnosis and treatment, social services, psychological services, nutrition, and a parent participation program. As White notes,[30] this was an expensive intervention program, trying to reach all the possible sources of educational deficit. Like the program, expectations regarding its effects grew steadily until the study of its national impact was made by the Westinghouse Corporation in 1969. That study, although imperfect in many respects, produced evidence that, insofar as cognitive development and achievement were concerned, the

---

[27] National Laboratory on Early Childhood Education, *Annual Report,* 1969.

[28] Sheldon H. White, "The National Impact Study of Head Start," in Jerome Hellmuth, ed., *The Disadvantaged Child,* vol. 3 (New York: Brunner/Mazel, 1970), p. 166.

[29] Evelyn Omwake, "Head Start—Measurable and Immeasurable," in Hellmuth, ed., *The Disadvantaged Child,* vol. 2 (New York, 1968), p. 539.

[30] White, p. 166.

summer programs were not producing the anticipated effects, and full-year programs were only marginally effective.[31]

Whether it was reasonable to expect effectiveness from staffs, many of whom were inexperienced in both education at the preschool level and in work with poor children, can be, and was, debated.[32] This is not to say that the staff members were not trainable; many of them have since demonstrated their fine abilities and moved on to increasingly responsible jobs. Nevertheless, the provisions for training in many Head Start programs have too often been minimal.

Perhaps the greatest effect of Head Start has been on the involved parents. Many found employment in Head Start. In addition, they and others became more confident and sure of their goals for their children. The Kirshner report[33] provides evidence that some Head Start parents have been able to secure needed community services adapted to meet their needs more effectively.

In 1969, in order to gather data on the effectiveness of different kinds of curricula, and perhaps also to improve training, Head Start initiated a Planned Variation Study.[34] Essentially this involved the analysis of some of the curricula that had been developed earlier in the universities and elsewhere. Certain Head Start programs implemented certain curricula, and their differential effects were studied. This project operated in conjunction with Follow Through, to be described presently.

Head Start has also initiated several innovative programs, including a limited number of Parent-Child Centers for children younger than three. In 1972, Head Start made a move toward a drastic change in the settings for federally funded early childhood programs when it launched Home Start, to be described later. In 1973, plans were also made for the inclusion of handicapped children in Head Start programs.

Follow Through

One of the major concerns arising from the Westinghouse National Impact Study and inherent in any cognitively oriented preschool program has to do with the nature of the child's later school experience. Is it designed to capitalize

---

[31] Westinghouse Learning Corporation, *The Impact of Head Start* (Washington: Office of Economic Opportunity, 1969).

[32] James O. Miller, "An Educational Imperative and Its Fallout Implications," in Hellmuth, ed., *The Disadvantaged Child,* p. 45.

[33] *A National Survey of the Impacts of Head Start Centers on Community Institutions* (Albuquerque: Kirshner Associates, 1970), ERIC document no. 046 516.

[34] Joan S. Bissell, "Implementation of Planned Variation in Head Start. Review and Summary of the Stanford Research Institute Interim Report," Office of Child Development, April 1971. ERIC document no. 052 845.

on the knowledge and strategies for learning the child has acquired in pre-school? Or may its effect be stultifying because, as one researcher suggested, "the desire to learn goes unfed"?

Follow Through was initiated under the Office of Economic Opportunity in 1967.[35] Administered by the Office of Education, it was directed toward continued special attention for the graduates of Head Start and similar preschool programs. Money from Follow Through could be used for noncurricular matters, including health, welfare, and remedial services. It brought resource specialists, aides, and nonteaching professionals to the assistance of the classroom teacher in the primary grades. Eventually, capitalizing on the innovative programs that had been developed in the universities and elsewhere, Follow Through developed a plan for "educational alternatives." These are, in the main, different curriculum models with theoretical orientations running from behavior theory to Piaget.[36] In some instances the curriculum is highly prescribed; in others the role of the teacher as decision maker is supported. In general, the sponsor of the model, usually its innovator or his representative, provides consultation and training as well as materials to the school systems selecting it. Active parent involvement is required. Research is under way comparing results with the different models in different settings.[37]

Infant Programs

Just as Follow Through programs are needed to support whatever gains children make in Head Start or other preschool programs, some researchers believe that preschool programs should be preceded by infancy programs. This approach to the education of the children of poverty seems likely to move early childhood education back to the home setting, although some programs have been carried on in centers.

Interest in infancy programs has stemmed in part from recent expansion in research related to infancy and in part from the apparent failure of preschool programs to produce lasting changes in cognitive functioning. Assuming that the failure of poor children to achieve in school is due to deficits in their experience, the earlier those deficits are corrected the better.

[35] Robert L. Egbert, "Follow Through Fulfilling the Promise of Head Start," in Hellmuth, ed., *The Disadvantaged Child,* pp. 571-580.

[36] Descriptions of some of the models are included in *A Source Book of Elementary Curricula Programs and Projects* (Far West Laboratory for Educational Research and Development, 1972); E. Maccoby and Miriam Zellner, *Experiments in Primary Education Aspects of Project Follow Through* (New York: Harcourt, Brace, 1970); and Stanley H. L. Chow and Patricia Elmore (Far West Laboratory for Educational Research and Development), *Early Childhood Information Unit: Resource Manual and Program Descriptions* (New York: Educational Products Information Exchange, 1973).

[37] Robert M. Soar and Ruth M. Soar report on one of the studies in "An Empirical Analysis of Selected Follow Through Programs: An Example of a Process Approach to Evaluation," in Ira J. Gordon, ed., *Early Childhood Education,* Seventy-first Yearbook of the National Society for the Study of Education (Chicago: University of Chicago Press, 1972), pp. 229-259.

According to Meier and his colleagues,[38] this view, or one approximating it, prompted Head Start officials to launch the experimental parent-child centers involving children under the age of three years.

Several programs have demonstrated the possibilities for infant intervention in the child's home.[39] Other studies have shown that infants can thrive when the intervention is carried on away from the child's home. Caldwell and her associates[40] found no evidence of the dilution of mother-infant attachment patterns when two-and-a-half-year-old home-reared infants were compared with infants who had spent at least one year in an infant care program. Keister[41] also found that middle- and lower-class infants who experienced enriched day care thrived as well as comparable infants raised at home.

The evidence is not all in, however,[42] and there is some reason to doubt the appropriateness of such early intervention on the basis of present knowledge of infant functioning and cognitive perceptual development. Most studies of the intellectual functioning of children, including most of those with Piagetian orientations, have not found social class differences prior to the age of eighteen months.[43] Several recent studies, reviewed by Gollin and Moody,[44] have found that a variety of enrichment procedures designed to enhance cognitive-perceptual development produced little or no acceleration, and in some instances retarded development.

One factor that seems to need greater consideration and specification in the discussion of infant programs is the matter of the age of the child. Several articles proposing infant programs do not differentiate between infants under eighteen months and those between eighteen months and three years who might perhaps be more appropriately designated as toddlers. Considerably more experience is available for planning programs for toddlers than is the case for infants. It seems likely that whatever success programs for children under eighteen months have can be attributed as much to the interest engendered in the mother or caretaker as to their direct effect on the infants.

[38] John H. Meier et al., "An Education System for High Risk Infants: A Preventive Approach to Developmental and Learning Disabilities," in Hellmuth, ed., *The Disadvantaged Child,* vol. 3, pp. 405-444.

[39] For example, DARCEE, The Intervention Study with Mothers and Infants; Ira Gordon, Instructional Strategies in Infant Stimulation, ERIC document no. 056 751, 1970; Genevieve Painter, Infant Education, ERIC document no. 033 760, 1968; Merle B. Karnes et al., "Educational Intervention at Home by Mothers of Disadvantaged Infants," *Child Development,* 41:925–935;, 1970.

[40] Bettye M. Caldwell et al, "Infant Day Care and Attachment," *American Journal of Orthopsychiatry,* 40:397–412, 1970.

[41] Mary Elizabeth Keister, *"The Good Life" For Infants and Toddlers: Group Care of Infants* (Washington: National Association for the Education of Young Children, 1970).

[42] For a discussion of theoretical and practical problems, see Alice S. Honig, *Infant Development: Problems in Intervention* (Washington: Day Care and Child Development Council of America, 1972).

[43] Beverly Birns and Mark Golden, "The Implications of Piaget's Theories for Contemporary Infancy Research and Education," in Milton Schwebel and Jane Raph, eds., *Piaget in the Classroom* (New York: Basic Books, 1973), pp. 114–131.

[44] Eugene S. Gollin and Mark Moody, "Developmental Psychology," in Paul H. Mussen and Mark R. Rosenzweig, eds., *Annual Review of Psychology,* 24:6–7 (Palo Alto: Annual Reviews, Inc., 1973).

EARLY CHILDHOOD EDUCATION MOVES BACK TO THE HOME

The fact that those early intervention programs that were most successful, whether for infants or preschoolers, so often included a home-visiting component has led to an increasing emphasis on home-based programs. Such programs need not be limited to poor children, but might also involve middle-class children as well. Several different models are available.

Backyard Play Groups

Middle-class mothers have long engaged in cooperative planning for the play of their children. When backyard or other space is available they work out arrangements for one or two mothers to take charge of several children while the others are freed for other activities. Such arrangements have sometimes led to the development of cooperative nursery schools. Gordon[45] used such an arrangement for his home learning center approach to early stimulation. In this instance the centers were homes where at least five children were brought once a week for home learning activities. The center director was a person drawn from the poverty area who had been previously involved in a parent education program. She was assisted by the mother in whose home or backyard the center was located.

Mobile Classrooms

In some programs a classroom on wheels moves into the neighborhoods where the children live. In one rural county in a southern state where kindergartens had just opened, an old school bus was fitted out as an early childhood classroom. The staff served about 24 children a day, working with them in groups of 4 or 5. Although most of the children were the four-year-olds who would soon be moving into the kindergartens, the staff also found some youngsters as old as nine who had never been to school. In other areas of the country campers and vans have been equipped for similar purposes.[46]

Television Programs

Someone has observed that Head Start in 1968 spent $125 million on 465,000 youngsters. Children's Television Workshop in producing "Sesame Street" spent one-sixteenth as much and reached twenty-five times as many children. Many would regard this as a powerful argument for early childhood home-

[45] Ira J. Gordon, "A Home Learning Center Approach to Early Stimulation," in Joe L. Frost, ed., *Revisiting Early Childhood Education* (New York: Holt, Rinehart and Winston, 1973), pp. 98–118.
[46] Rosella Lipson, "A Mobile Preschool," *Young Children,* 34(3):154–156, January 1969.

based programs via television. Two questions are raised. What effects does the program have on the children who watch it? Are the effects similar to or different from those that might result from center-based programs or from a different approach to a home-based program?

The producers of "Sesame Street" had some very specific goals for the children's learning, such as recognizing letters, naming forms, and classifying by size or function. Studies[47] were made of three-, four-, and five-year-olds during both the first and the second year of the program to check on the extent to which the children who viewed the program achieved the intended goals. The children received pre- and posttests. The results indicated, not surprisingly, that those who viewed most gained most. Unfortunately, as a group, poor children for whom the program was intended viewed less than their advantaged peers. Nonetheless, when they viewed they learned, and in both groups, those who watched most tended to have mothers who often watched the show and also talked to them about it.

Despite these findings and the general popularity of "Sesame Street" (now being shown in 48 nations and territories),[48] the program has been criticized by a number of educators who think that the program is a poor substitute for a program such as Head Start. The major complaint lies in the passive learning they believe Sesame Street encourages. Sprigle,[49] for example, found that the adults on "Sesame Street" talk 90 percent of the time and give the children very little opportunity to talk or to exchange ideas with one another.

Whether one likes the "Sesame Street" format or not, it has established a precedent for reaching the young child in his home.[50] It is, of course, not the only model for television programming.[51] Television is currently being used in the Appalachia Project and the Rural Family Development Program in Madison, Wisconsin to reach children and their families in remote areas. A program like "Sesame Street," having both adult and child appeal, but offering a wider range of activity for the children, seems a potentially powerful means of early childhood and parent education.

---

[47] Samuel Ball and Gerry Ann Bogatz, "The First Year of Sesame Street, An Evaluation," a report presented to the Educational Testing Service, Princeton, N.J., October, 1970; and "The Second Year of Sesame Street, An Evaluation," November, 1971. See also Edward L. Palmer, "Television Instruction and the Preschool Child," *International Journal of Early Childhood,* 4(1):11–17, 1972.

[48] Michael Dann, "The Street That Runs Around the World," *New York Times,* August 6, 1972; William Wilson Lambert, "Is Sesame Street Exportable?" *International Journal of Early Childhood,* 4(1):18–20, 1972.

[49] Herbert A. Sprigle, "Who Wants to Live on Sesame Street?" *Young Children,* December 1972, pp. 91–109.

[50] Richard M. Polsky, *Getting to Sesame St: Origins of the Children's Television Workshop* (New York: Praeger Publishers, 1974), reviews and analyzes the decisions that led to the Sesame Street format.

[51] Rose Mukerji, *Television Guidelines for Early Childhood Education* (Bloomington, Ind.: National Instructional Television, 1969).

Toy Library

A project developed by Nimnicht,[52] sponsor of one of the Follow Through models (The Responsive Environment) provides another approach to home-based early childhood education. In this project a number of toys for three- to nine-year-olds were designed to teach certain concepts and skills and to promote verbal fluency and problem-solving techniques. The toys are loaned to parents who enroll in an eight-week course. With other parents they attend a weekly session in which a new toy is demonstrated. The parents then borrow a toy for their child's use during the ensuing week. Their reports of the ways their children play with the toys and their participation with them serve as a base for discussion at the weekly session.

The important difference between toy library sessions and the more usual parent discussion would seem to be that the toys provide focus and objectivity. In addition, the toys provide interest to the child both as toys and as a means of interaction with the parent.

The toy library has had special interest for parents who are not poor enough to be eligible for Head Start and not affluent enough to send their children to nursery school. This is a group that has been neglected in the recent expansion of early childhood education.

Home Start

Head Start initiated Home Start,[53] a demonstration program for disadvantaged preschool children and their families, in 1972. It epitomizes the current trend toward moving early childhood education into the home. In recent years some 200 similar programs have come into operation in various parts of the country.

The objectives of Home Start include involving parents directly in the education of their children and helping to strengthen the parents' capacity for facilitating their children's development. In addition, it aims to demonstrate the delivery of comprehensive child development services to parents for whom a center-based program is not feasible. It also proposes to compare the relative costs and benefits of home-based and center-based programs. Directed to children ages three to five years, the demonstration Home Start programs serve as adjuncts to Head Start programs. They rely principally on home visitors, paraprofessional workers who come from the same community as the families they serve. The role of the home visitor may be augmented in various ways,

---

[52] Glen P. Nimnicht and Edna Brown, "The Toy Library; Parents and Children Learning with Toys," *Young Children*: 110–116, December 1972.
[53] Home Start Fact Sheet, Office of Child Development, Washington, May 1972; Sherry Kapfer, Report of First National Home Start Conference, April 3-7, 1972. ERIC document no. 067 155.

including meetings for parents in groups, television, and mobile classrooms.

Home Start is directed to older children than those in most of the experimental home-based programs. Nevertheless, it bears some resemblance to what Schaefer calls "Ur-education, basic, primitive, early."[54] This education, which has its beginning in the early, positive, and reciprocal relationship between child and parent, engages parent and child together in exploring material. Schaefer sees it as the basis of all later education.

Schaefer believes children should be enrolled in "school" at birth. This would be a matter of providing training for the parents through such means as workshops, home visits, and mass media. Teachers would be prepared as leaders of an educational team having the support of the parental role as its main objective. Teachers would be family educational consultants, teachers without classrooms, who would visit families regularly. Schools for older children would also provide child development materials and toys to them so that they could in turn teach younger children.

The Ur-education model has considerable appeal. Particularly, if it were associated with comprehensive health and nutrition services beginning prenatally, it could assure every child a chance for a good beginning. Whether such a model would be acceptable to the general public and whether it could appropriately replace current center-based programs can be debated.

The proponents of the model appear to make some assumptions that may not be warranted. One is that parents will welcome the visits of the educational counselor from the child's birth. At a time when the invasion of personal privacy seems both continuous and overwhelming, this is a questionable assumption. They also assume that all parents, with the help of the counselor, will be equally desirous and capable of providing effectively for their children. The experience of the North Point Project, cited above, and of others indicates that some parents require psychological support that goes considerably beyond that likely to be provided by the usual educational counselor. In addition, for many of these parents, including those who resort to child abuse, some respite from child care is essential.

Those who see home-based programs not as alternatives but as substitutes for center-based programs seem to overlook the fact that many homes, particularly but not only those of poor families, have inadequate provisions for the active, investigative, experimental play of the young child. It is not unlikely that the parents, whether poor or middle-class, given an effective parent education program, will decide that what their children really need is a place where they can play together.

To the extent that returning early childhood education to the home is a

---

[54] Earl S. Schaefer, "Learning from Each Other," *Childhood Education*: 3–7, October 1971.

matter of recognition of the crucial role of the parents in the development of the child, it deserves the fullest support. However, it seems reasonable to regard the home-based program as an option, but not the only option, for the parents of young children.

DAY CARE: SOME SPECIAL PROBLEMS

According to Child Welfare League Standards,[55] any care that the child receives outside his home for some part of the twenty-four-hour day is day care, whether it be three or four hours in nursery school, prekindergarten or kindergarten, or eight hours or more in a child care center. Since all children, as children, have the same developmental needs, it is reasonable to assume that all programs should have the same essential components; that the children in these programs should benefit from the knowledge and professional skills in child development, early education, medicine, and social work; that the experiences provided should be good for the children; that the arrangements should support and enhance the parental role; and that the program should be fitted to the particular needs of child and parent.

These recommended standards are intended to protect children from less than adequate provisions for care that may be justified on the basis that "the children are only here for three hours," or "this is an educational program, not day care," or "this is not a service that parents use regularly, it is just 'drop-in.' "

In practice, however, when the care of the young child away from his home extends beyond a morning or an afternoon, with or without lunch, the longer day creates problems for him and for those who care for him that are of a different order from those encountered in shorter programs. For the child, fatigue, and in group programs the lack of an opportunity for withdrawal from interpersonal stimulation, are hazards. The longer day also means that a major part of his socialization is being promoted by adults who may or may not share the values of his parents.

For the caretaker, both her own and the child's fatigue are problems. So is the provision of activities that engage the child but do not overtax him. To respond constructively to the demands of perhaps ten or more four-year-olds at the end of eight hours with them places heavy demands on the caretaker in the group setting. Caretakers are, or should be, also concerned about the compatibility of their practices with parental procedures.

The need for day care, outlined earlier, continues to accelerate. It is attributed to a combination of factors, chief of these being the socioeconomic

---

[55] Child Welfare League of America, *Standards for Day Care Service* (New York, 1969), p. 1.

needs that compel mothers to enter the work force. According to a *Wall Street Journal* observer:

> . . . Women workers are more important than ever before in maintaining their families' standard of living, in serving as the sole breadwinner for many families, and in contributing to economic production and growth.[56]

Changes in family and community patterns parallel socioeconomic factors. With increasing mobility and the virtual disappearance of the extended family in middle-class groups, mothers are less often able to call on relatives, older children, or friends for assistance in child rearing. Hired help is also less available and too expensive for many families. Increasing divorce and separation rates are reflected in larger numbers of single-parent families and add to the need for assistance with child care.

For many women, self-fulfillment can no longer be found in work related solely to home and child rearing. The women's liberation organizations pinpoint their demand for a wider variety of child care options at reasonable cost. For those who as single parents carry the full burden of support for their children, the need for day care is imperative.

The situation among parents living in or near poverty is similar in some respects, different in others. Where families are extended, provisions for day care are, in a sense, built in. But families in poverty like their middle-class counterparts are often isolated and are more often beset by illness and other problems that make extrafamilial day care a prerequisite for holding a job.

If the parent in need of day care is fortunate, three options are available —someone to provide care to the child in his own home, day care in the home of another family,[57] or care in a center. Center care receives the most publicity but is the least available. When care in the child's own home means that someone outside the family must be hired, it becomes something that few but middle-class parents can afford. Most parents make arrangements with someone in their neighborhood, if possible, to keep the child while they work. This is family day care.

Child Care Centers

A study of day care facilities carried on by volunteer interviewers found that parents who used center care were better satisfied with it than were those who

---

[56] Mae E. Rosenberg, *Early Childhood Education: Perspectives on the Federal and Office of Education Roles,* Stanford Research Institute, Project 6747, July 1972. ERIC document no. 066 621.

[57] Some families provide what is known as a group day care home. This is for the after-school care of school-age children and may involve as many as twelve children.

used family day care.[58] The quoted comments of the parents suggest that an important factor in their satisfaction is the educational program provided in the center. But a more recent and well-controlled study[59] involving only parents who used centers suggests that convenience is the main reason for choosing a particular center. The investigator believes that what she calls the "warehousing" of children is the predominant motive of parents using centers. Most parents, she finds, view the center's primary responsibility to be one of meeting their own needs rather than providing a service to children. However, a minority of parents, not satisfied with the center they are using, place more emphasis on the well-being of the child than on their own convenience.

Convenience, presumably, is a matter of finding a center open for the appropriate hours and located near enough home or work to make for efficient transportation. This latter factor might seem to argue in favor of locating centers at the place of work.

Work-related Centers   Except during World War II when some exceptional day care centers were operated in conjunction with wartime industry,[60] good care for the child at the parent's place of work has rarely been available. An industry-based center (KLH) was opened in Cambridge, Massachusetts in 1967. It has since closed. Curran and Jordan,[61] who conducted a two-year study of the center, analyze the factors that justify industry-sponsored day care. These include the particular industry's need to secure or maintain a skilled working force of women when recruitment of such workers has been difficult. They note that industry-related care is expensive; because day care is demanding of staff, staff turnover tends to be high. Parents who are employed may initially exhibit interest in the service and then, perhaps because adding the hours of transportation to the working hours of the parent makes an extremely long day for the child, decide not to use it.[62] At KLH, for example, thirty-nine parents indicated interest, but only seven actually used it.

Some hospitals with an acute need for nursing personnel are successfully

[58] Mary Dublin Keyserling, *Windows on Day Care* (New York: National Council of Jewish Women, 1972).

[59] Ellen Handler, "The Expectations of Day-Care Parents," *Social Service Review*, 47(2):266–277, June 1973.

[60] James L. Hymes, Jr., "The Kaiser Answer: Child Service Centers," in Samuel J. Braun and Esther P. Edwards, *History and Theory of Early Childhood Education* (Worthington, Ohio: Charles A. Jones Publishing Co., 1972), pp. 170–176.

[61] Joseph R. Curran and John W. Gordon, *The KLH Experience* (Cambridge, Mass.: KLH Child Development Center, Inc., 1970).

[62] In New York City, reportedly, a bank proposed to initiate a training program for minority women. Anticipating that many would have young children, it planned to open a day care center in its Times Square location. Eventually someone gave thought to the hazards of transporting infants and preschoolers on the subway during rush hour and the plan was abandoned.

operating day care centers.[63] Of 2,000 hospitals responding to a recent survey, 98 had child care facilities for staff, and 500 more expressed an interest in developing such facilities.

In occasional instances unions are responsible for the operation of child care centers.[64] A notable example is the Amalgamated Clothing Workers, with centers in several parts of the country.

Campus Day Care As the movement for women's liberation has made clear, day care is essential if women are to have the opportunity to pursue the education and training that are necessary for full participation in modern society. Recognition of this fact underlies the movement for campus day care. Although this movement has been led by students on many campuses, it has considerable support from faculty and staff. At least one high-ranking university administrator has observed that he thinks no university can divorce itself from discrimination on the basis of sex unless it meets the need for day care facilities. Nevertheless most campus centers have come into being only after considerable struggle on the part of the students. In many instances, lacking adequate financial support and being unable to meet licensing standards, campus centers have had a precarious existence.

Many issues relate to campus child care. One issue is that of control. As the handbook of one Canadian campus community day care center expresses it:

> We feel that a parent-controlled, cooperative day-care centre should be a community which, in a sense, becomes a family, with everyone in that community sharing responsibility for the children and the children relating freely as individuals to each other and to adults. . . .
>
> . . . It's our view that matters of staff and standards should be decided by parents and not arbitrarily imposed by ill-informed governments. Providing the children are not being treated badly *in clearly demonstrable ways,* we see no reason why parents of pre-school children should not be free to select the kind of school and the teachers they want, just as legally, parents of school-age children are allowed to place their children in the school of their choice.

Another issue has to do with the relationship of campus child care to the needs and services in the larger community. Failure to recognize the reality of the needs of people other than themselves has aggravated community hos-

---

[63] *Child Care Services Provided by Hospitals,* (Washington: Women's Bureau, U.S. Department of Labor, Child Care Services, Bulletin 295, 1970.)

[64] Irving Lazar and Mae E. Rosenberg, "Day Care in America," in Edith Grotberg, ed., *Day Care: Resources for Decisions* (Washington: Office of Economic Opportunity, 1971), pp. 59–107.

tility toward the campus in some instances. Furthermore, as Page notes,[65] on-campus programs may not be the most useful, especially when students live in many different areas. In that case, organization of day care services communitywide may be more appropriate.

A third issue, or concern, in campus day care arises from the fact that most of the students who need the care have very young children. As in group care in other settings, the problem is one of providing sufficient individual and consistent attention to the infant who is less than a year old. As one student, working in a campus "crib room," lamented, "There were only three babies there, but one on the floor was crying because his ball had rolled away, I was feeding one, and the third began to scream in his crib." She added later, "I don't think this care is for the babies. It helps the parents, but not the children."

FAMILY DAY CARE

Many people maintain that the solution to the situation just described lies in the provision of care in homes, rather than in centers. Perhaps the day care mother will avoid taking children too close in ages, so that she would not find herself pulled in three different directions as the student in the campus center did.

The majority of children in day care are in homes rather than center settings. Fewer than 5 percent of these homes, according to estimates,[66] are licensed or supervised. Nevertheless, family day care provides, at least potentially, a very advantageous setting for young children.[67] It can provide for a wide age range—from a few weeks to school age. Continuity in life styles and values is more easily assured in family care, which may be offered by a neighbor of the working mother, than in center care. Family day care is more suited to the convenience of the users since the hours of care are easily tailored to the work schedules of the parents, and children with illnesses are more easily accommodated.

In many instances the caregivers are "home-centered women who are in the business not of making much money but of filling their half-emptied nests because they find it gratifying to give child care."[68] They tend to be somewhat older than the mothers who need care, and to have children older than those

---

[65] Paula Page, "The Campus and the Day Care Movement," in *Campus Day Care* (Child Welfare League of America, 1971).

[66] Keyserling, p. 5.

[67] June Solnit Sale, "Family Day Care: One Alternative in the Delivery of Developmental Services in Early Childhood," *American Journal of Orthopsychiatry,* 43(1):37–55, January 1973.

[68] Arthur C. Emlen, "Slogans, Slots and Slander: The Myth of Day Care Need," *American Journal of Orthopsychiatry,* 43(1):23–36, January 1972.

to whom they provide day care. Their general concern for the well-being of children constitutes a source of satisfaction for the user.

· One project has demonstrated the feasibility of increasing the number of providers and at the same time improving the quality of the care. The Day Care Neighbors Service in Portland, Oregon[69] discovered and recruited neighborhood women who were giving child care and who were actively interested in helping parents to make appropriate child care arrangements. These mothers were provided with skilled social work consultation in their homes and by phone. They in turn recruited other caregivers and provided "matchmaking" help to parents in selecting appropriate caregivers. They also helped both caregivers and users to deal with problems that arose during care.[70]

Sale[71] describes another method of improving the quality of care. In the Community Family Day Care Project, day care mothers identified and recruited by local community members, participated in monthly meetings for which they were given token payment. These meetings provided a place for the mothers to discuss matters of mutual concern to them. In addition, the day care mothers were visited twice a month by students who on one day observed their methods of working with the children and on an ensuing day cared for the children while the mothers attended the project meeting. A toy library was established, and in some instances nursery school scholarships were provided, involving the day care mother in a cooperative relationship with other nursery school parents. The day care mothers requested a course in child development which was provided.

The experience of the Day Care Neighbor Service as well as the Community Family Day Care Service suggests that providing services to day care mothers is a more effective way to improve the quality of care than the usual licensing requirements. The relatively small number of licensed day care homes indicates that many qualified providers feel they cannot meet the requirements for licensing and so do not seek to be licensed.[72]

How does the experience of a child in a family day care setting compare

---

[69] Arthur C. Emlen and Eunice L. Watson, *Matchmaking in Neighborhood Day Care* (Corvallis: Continuing Education Publications, 1971).

[70] In many respects this project appears to offer promising solutions to the many problems involved in day care, especially for very young children. My enthusiasm has been somewhat dampened by the report of one colleague that an attempt at replication in a very different community did not work out well. Another colleague has reminded me of the difficulties involved in securing good foster homes for children and questions whether the problems are less acute in day care.

[71] Sale, op. cit.

[72] *Family Day Care West, A Working Conference,* III, Community Family Day Care Project of Pacific Oaks College, July 1972, pp. 19–28.

with his experience in the setting of a group center? A study by Prescott[73] provides some answers. This study involved observations of samples of children in "open" and "closed" structure group programs and in family day care homes. These observations were also compared with observations of children in a half-day nursery school and at home.

The closed structure offers high adult input, and relatively little individualized response to the children. Its cognitive emphasis takes the form of small muscle tasks to teach perceptual skills and eye-hand coordination. Sensory stimulation, such as might be provided by adults holding children, or by such materials as sand, pillows, or cuddly toys, is usually lacking.

Open structure day care provides children freedom to explore, to initiate activities, and to investigate the world through sensory channels. However, the teacher may not capitalize on these opportunities in ways that promote cognitive growth. Open structure offers children excellent opportunities to develop social skills with peers. Prescott notes that open structure promotes recognition of the individual needs of the children, but the pressures on the teachers at certain times of the day make actual meeting of those needs difficult if not impossible.

Family day care homes, according to Prescott, offer most of the components essential to individualized care—flexibility, high adult initiation, opportunities for sensory input, and creative exploring. It is especially good for infants and toddlers. Family day care offers rich opportunity for long adult-child conversations about people and events. Prescott notes that these are on a very different level from the more formal conversations typically heard in the group center. On the other hand, the family day care home may fail to supply the child with such materials as paper, pencils, crayons, paste, scissors.[74]

The home and half-day nursery school combination provides maximum child-centeredness. The child has opportunities at nursery school for peer interaction and an environment rich with possibilities for exploration com-

---

[73] Elizabeth Prescott, "Group and Family Day Care: A Comparative Assessment," II, *Family Day Care West,* pp. 1–21.

[74] Although Prescott's findings seem applicable to other centers and day care homes, they may give an impression of less variation among both centers and homes than actually occurs. Also, since Prescott's day care homes were participating in the Community Family Day Care Project described by Sale, they may not be representative. (However, Sale does note that she would not recommend one of the homes.) Margaret Zawadski, in a seminar paper at the University of California, Berkeley, made systematic observations in three classrooms in a child care center selected on the basis of convenience, and in three day care homes made available through an organization of day care providers. The caretakers in the homes tended to be "directive, and not particularly flexible," and their contacts with the children emphasized the correct way to do things. This was in marked contrast to the center, where the caretakers "used suggestions and questions to stimulate problem solving in both cognitive and emotional domains." Also, in two of the day care homes, the children were not permitted in the caretaker's living quarters. Clearly, parents selecting day care facilities are better advised to follow their impressions of each setting and their knowledge of their own children than to be guided by generalizations.

bined with opportunities for privacy in his own room and a one-to-one teaching relationship with his mother.

The effect of the day care setting on the child is in part a matter of the kind of child he is. Prescott, in a related study of group day care, defined a good fit for an individual child in a day care program: "The adults in the center and the activities which they provide enable a child to experience himself as competent and likeable and provide him with opportunities for enthusiastic and sustained involvement."[75] Her observations showed that some children thrive in a closed structure, and others in an open structure. And the quality of a center is indicated by its concern for its nonthrivers.

Unfortunately, the available options for most parents do not include the opportunity to choose the setting—group or family—in which their child will likely thrive best. Poor parents find that the waiting lists at most centers for which they are eligible are very long. So they must resort to family day care arrangements whether or not they prefer them. Middle-class parents often find that their income makes them ineligible for all-day center care. Like the poor mothers, they must make whatever arrangements they can. In their case these may include putting the child in a nursery school for part of the day and engaging a baby-sitter for the remainder. Whatever they do, it is often a compromise between what they would like and what they can find.

WORLD PERSPECTIVES

What significance does the diversity of settings for early childhood education and care and its patchwork availability have for the future development of our children and for our nation? This is a question that can only be answered with the passage of time. But it may be illuminating to compare our practices with those of other countries, particularly those that are similarly advanced industrially.

Such comparisons must not lose sight of the fact that practices with regard to children are deeply imbedded in cultural traditions and value systems that differ from one nation to another. What works well in one cultural context may not work in another, or it may undergo such transformation as to become unrecognizable.[76] Obviously, too, a brief consideration of a few of the many dimensions on which early childhood care and education in different countries may be compared grossly oversimplifies both the similarities and the differences.

---

[75] Elizabeth Prescott, *Who Thrives in Group Day Care?* (Pasadena, Calif.: Pacific Oaks College, March 1973), p. 94.
[76] In some instances attempts to replicate the British Infant School in the United States have resulted in classrooms completely different from the model.

National Policy and Administration

In the United States, the autonomy of local communities to provide for their children as they see fit in both education and care has gradually given way to an increasing number of programs that receive federal support, and hence are subject to federal regulation. Yet it would be difficult to say that there is a strong and well-articulated policy on children. The Federal Inter-Agency Requirements for Day Care, for example, are applicable only to federally funded programs. They set minimal standards for the ratio of children to caretakers, for the involvement of parents, and for health, nutrition, and safety. They do not prescribe the kind of program the children shall have.

This kind of national policy contrasts sharply with policy in countries which have national guidelines for the operation of early childhood education.

In the Soviet Union, the guidelines prescribe a collective rather than family-centered system of child rearing, and nursery-kindergartens for children from age two months to seven years are presumably available to all children.[77] The significance of this national involvement in the upbringing of children is highlighted in Bronfenbrenner's analysis[78] of child rearing in the Soviet Union as contrasted with child rearing in the United States. One observer of the Soviet scene notes, however, that the influence of Soviet policy is not as pervasive as Bronfenbrenner assumes. According to Jacoby,[79] only 10 percent of Soviet children under the age of two and 20 percent between the ages of three and seven are cared for in nursery-kindergartens. The rest of the children of working mothers (80 percent of Soviet women work outside their homes) are looked after by "babushkas" (grandmothers) or neighbors. Jacoby notes that the number of children in kindergartens is likely to increase, but doubts that Soviet parents want more state care for infants and toddlers.

The People's Republic of China contrasts sharply with both the United States and the Soviet Union.[80] In China there appears to be a general consensus regarding child-rearing goals. In the cities 50 percent of the children under the age of three are cared for in nurseries and 80 percent of the three-to-seven-year-olds attend kindergarten. However, the operation of these nurseries and kindergartens is decentralized, and policies are determined by local committees.

Other countries that compare with the Soviet Union in having highly centralized national administrations for early childhood education include

---

[77] Kitty Weaver, *Lenin's Grandchildren: Preschool Education in the Soviet Union* (New York: Simon & Schuster, 1971); Henry Chauncey, ed., *Soviet Preschool Education,* vols. 1 and 2 (New York: Holt, Rinehart and Winston, 1969).

[78] Urie Bronfenbrenner, *Two Worlds of Childhood* (New York: Russell Sage Foundation, 1970).

[79] Susan Jacoby, "Who Raises Russia's Children?" *Saturday Review,* August 21, 1971, pp. 40–53.

[80] Ruth Sidel, *China—Women and Child Care* (New York: Hill & Wang, 1972).

Belgium, France, the Netherlands, and Sweden.[81] They legislate requirements for safety, health, teacher certification, and the activities that should go on in the schools. In France and Belgium the inspectors who visit the schools have considerable authority. In the Netherlands and Sweden their role is more advisory. In all these countries support for the schools comes from the national government.

Countries with less centralization are Germany, Italy, and the United Kingdom. In Germany, guidelines are set forth nationally, but their enforcement is left up to regional political divisions. In Italy and in the United Kingdom, early childhood education is by law a local concern, but the national government provides guidelines. In the United Kingdom, Her Majesty's inspectors observe and provide counsel but are limited in authority.

In all these European countries, as in the United States, extensive early childhood programs operate privately. It is more difficult to get a complete picture of the services available to parents and their children than it is in the Communist nations.

Early childhood educators visiting abroad have long been impressed with the comprehensiveness of services in the Scandinavian countries. Pasantino, an American architect who studied child care provisions in Sweden, writes of "a total national commitment to the well being of young children."[82] Such commitment was well revealed in a child center that I visited in Stockholm. It enrolled children from the age of two months to seven years and also included an after-school program for seven- to twelve-year-olds. The infant program, which included a male teacher, adjoined the toddler program into which the infants, as they became toddlers, gradually moved. The toddlers in turn visited and were visited by the older children. As Pasantino emphasizes, there was no institutional feeling, but rather an atmosphere that was homelike, warm, and friendly. The building was organically integrated into the natural setting. The children moved freely in indoor and outdoor environments that presented both physical and intellectual challenge. Even more impressive was the evidence of planning and concern for the parents. For example, the mothers' work schedules are arranged around the needs of the children. Should a child become ill, a caretaker is sent to his home so that the mother can continue work. As the teachers get to know the children they share their understanding of the child and of effective child-rearing practices. Sharing, in this instance,

[81] Much of my information regarding early childhood education in the European countries mentioned here is derived from technical reports prepared for the Centre for Educational Research and Innovation of the Organization for Economic Cooperation and Development in Paris by Gilbert R. Austin. I am indebted to him for the opportunity to review these.

[82] Richard Pasantino, "Swedish Preschools: Environments of Sensitivity," *Childhood Education*, 47:406–411, May 1971.

does not mean that the teachers tell the parents what to do, but rather that they listen to them reflectively and come to develop mutual concerns and interests.

Age for Beginning Formal Schooling

In Sweden, as in the Soviet Union, the People's Republic of China, and the Netherlands, formal or academic schooling does not begin until the age of seven. In the United Kingdom, on the other hand, children enter the Infant School at the age of five.[83] In the other nations mentioned, formal schooling starts at age six.

It is interesting to consider how the age for the beginning of formal schooling relates to the kinds of programs provided in the nurseries and kindergartens. In Belgium, France, Sweden, and the United Kingdom, the emphasis in the preschools is on a safe and emotionally supportive atmosphere. In Belgium and France, where nearly 100 percent of five-year-olds are in nursery school, the program becomes more structured at age five and includes some reading instruction. In Sweden, where formal schooling does not begin until age seven the major emphasis throughout the preschool years is on the development of confidence, self-worth, and self-regulation rather than on academics. In England, the trend in the Infant Schools, beginning at age five, is toward informality. Reading instruction is, however, included.

In both the Soviet Union and the People's Republic of China, where formal schooling begins at age seven, the major emphasis is put on play, which is also the subject of much research. However, children receive some instruction in beginning reading and in counting in the kindergartens, and remedial speech lessons may be given those needing them before the age of six.

In China, at age seven the children are expected to read a little, to write simple characters, and to count. An interesting feature of early education in China is its direct teaching of Communist ideals with no diluting or sugar-coating of difficult ideas. Yee writes, "The [kindergarten] children learn about the oppression of the people before the 1949 'liberation' and about revolutionary traditions and heroes."[84] The concepts of "unification, fraternalism and productive labor" are stressed.

Effects of "Multiple Mothering"

As more and more women in countries all over the world move into work

---

[83] For discussion of the changing relationships between the infant schooling and later schooling, see Nanette Whitbread, *The Evolution of the Nursery-Infant School* (London: Routledge and Kegan Paul, 1972).

[84] Albert H. Yee, "Schools and Progress in the People's Republic of China," *Educational Researcher,* 2(7): 5–15, July 1973.

outside their home, there is increasing concern about the long-term effects that substitute caretakers may have on children, particularly infants. Interest in this problem, and also in observation of the ways other countries provide for infant care, has led to a number of studies of child care in other nations.[85] The results are not conclusive. In general, they highlight the nature of the relationship between the family and other societal institutions. For example, in the kibbutzim of Israel, often cited as an ideal example of multiple mothering, the families are self-selected and completely committed to communal social living. Furthermore, in the first year of life, the mother provides the major portion of the child's care and feeding. Similarly in China, where there is a clear commitment to the collective society, the feeding of the infants up to the age of eighteen months is often done by the mothers, who leave their work to return to the nursery. As Ruth Sidel points out in her study mentioned above, what is involved is not *serial* mothering in which the infant is subjected to a continual turnover of caretakers; rather, it is a supplementary kind of caretaking in a society in which everyone seems to be dedicated to the well-being of children.

From the experience of other countries, it is evident that good care can be provided for infants in either day care centers or day care homes.[86] It is equally evident that good care, particularly in centers, is costly. Furthermore, in many centers it appears to be difficult to recruit and retain child-care workers who continue over long periods of time to be maximally responsive to the infants in their charge.

Concern for the Disadvantaged Child

Although the Communist countries are presumed to provide equal opportunities for all children (Jacoby suggests that in the Soviet Union professional parents ask for and receive certain curricular modifications such as the inclusion of a foreign language), the other industrial nations are increasingly concerned about children who are at a disadvantage when they begin formal schooling. These children may be poor, recent immigrants, or children living in isolated families. In most of these countries the effects of experimental preschool programs are being investigated.

In Israel, where kindergarten attendance at age five has been compulsory since 1948, special attention has been given to the education of these children.

---

[85] Dale R. Meers and Allen E. Marans, "Group Care of Infants in Other Countries," in Laura L. Dittman, ed., *Early Child Care* (New York: Atherton Press, 1968); Dale R. Meers, "International Day Care"; Marsden G. Wagner and Mary Miles Wagner, "Day Care Programs in Denmark and Czechoslovakia"; and Hava Bonne Gewirtz, "Child Care Facilities and the Israeli Experience," all in Edith H. Grotberg, ed., *Day Care: Resources for Decisions* (Washington: Office of Economic Opportunity, 1971).

[86] Wagner and Wagner, op. cit.

Several experimental studies have been done.[87] Beginning in 1970 free kindergartens have been provided all children of disadvantaged background. In Israel, as in other countries, early childhood education is seen as a way of equalizing opportunity.

Looking at early childhood education and care from the perspective of other nations, the extent to which the problems and concerns and their solutions are similar is impressive. One gets no clear sense of direction from surveying what is done elsewhere, however, for it is clear that commitments to early childhood education and care differ enormously from country to country. If any conclusion is to be drawn regarding programs in the United States as contrasted with those in other countries, it is that we have greater diversity. The Robinsons comment on this:

> While coordination of programs in almost all countries is imperfect, the United States exemplifies near chaos, with narrowly conceived programs administered by public and private agencies at the federal, state and local level, often in ignorance of, and sometimes even in competition with one another. A count of public programs offering financial support to day care centers in 1969 revealed forty-two distinct programs administered by fifteen different agencies at the federal level alone![88]

We do not, it seems, lack either solutions or resources. The problem, much as Illich thinks about the schools, is to find ways to bring solutions to bear where they are most needed. The challenge is to match the inherent diversity in services to the diverse needs of parents and children.

---

[87] Sarah Smilansky and Moshe Smilansky, "The Role and Program of Preschool Education for Socially Disadvantaged Children," *International Review of Education,* 16:45–65, 1970.

[88] Nancy M. Robinson and Halbert B. Robinson, "A Cross-Cultural View of Early Education," in Ira J. Gordon, ed., *Early Childhood Education,* Seventy-first Yearbook of the National Society for the Study of Education (Chicago: University of Chicago Press, 1972), p. 297.

Chapter 6

Teaching Young Children

My own observations indicate that the elementary teacher may change the focus of his concerns as many as 1,000 times a day. [1]

The classroom is a remarkably busy place. . . . In the most active classroom a change of one sort or another occurs on an average once every five seconds. In the least active classroom there was a change every eighteen seconds. [2]

Child care and training are both rather simple, straightforward jobs. What is difficult and anomalous and what therefore seems to require a high level of sophistication is to do both jobs at once. [3]

This chapter, and those that follow, turn from consideration of the field of

---

[1] Philip W. Jackson, "The Way Teaching Is," in Ronald T. Hyman, *Contemporary Thought on Teaching* (Englewood Cliffs: Prentice-Hall, 1971), p. 8.
[2] Raymond S. Adams and Bruce J. Biddle, *Realities of Teaching: Explorations with Video Tape* (New Holt, Rinehart and Winston, 1970), p. 29.
[3] Carl Bereiter, "Schools without Education," *Harvard Educational Review,* 42:390–413, 1972, p. 408.

early childhood education—the issues that recur in it, the programs provided and the settings for them—to specific aspects of the role of the early childhood educator. The present chapter examines what may be described as the core function of the early childhood educator—teaching young children.

The teacher of young children does not need the researcher to demonstrate that hers is a demanding job. Nevertheless, were she to look at the studies that have recorded the activity of teachers in nursery schools,[4] day care centers,[5] Head Start, and prekindergartens, first, and second grades,[6] she might be intrigued both by the intricacies revealed and by the different ways researchers describe those intricacies. Perhaps she would derive some satisfaction from the report of one male researcher who took on the responsibilities of teaching a group of four-year-olds for a month. It was, he reported, an exhausting experience, demanding much more from him than his research endeavors.

What the teacher does in the classroom, the great variety of her interactions with the children, encompasses only part of her role as a teacher. As Jackson notes with regard to the elementary teachers he observed:

> Behavior relevant to the teaching task includes many things, such as preparing lesson plans, arranging furniture and equipment within the room, marking papers, studying test reports, reading sections of a textbook and thinking about the aberrant behavior of a particular student.[7]

Such activities, Jackson thinks, are so crucial to the rest of the teacher's performance that they should be specially designated as "preactive" teaching.

The teachers of the youngest children will, of course, not be marking papers, but they may spend considerable time planning activities and the materials needed for them, talking with parents and with others who know the children they are teaching, and reflecting on the children's behavior and development. In these preactive aspects of teaching the early childhood educator may provide special support to the teacher.

What the teacher plans and what the teacher does have their conse-

---

[4] For example, W. Reichenberg-Hackett, "Practices, Attitudes and Values in Nursery Group Education," *Psychological Reports,* 10:151–172, 1962.

[5] Elizabeth Prescott and Elizabeth Jones, *Day Care as a Child-Rearing Environment* (Washington: National Association for the Education of Young Children, 1972.)

[6] Lilian G. Katz et al., "Observing Behavior in Kindergarten and Preschool Classes," *Childhood Education,* 44:400–405, 1968. Robert S. and Ruth M. Soar, "An Empirical Analysis of Selected Follow Through Programs: An Example of a Process Approach to Evaluation," in Ira J. Gordon, ed., *Early Childhood Education,* Seventy-first Yearbook of the National Society for the Study of Education, Part 2 (Chicago: University of Chicago Press, 1972). J. S. Kounin, *Discipline and Group Management in the Classroom* (New York: Holt, Rinehart and Winston, 1970). R. L. Spaulding, *Classroom Behavior Analysis and Treatment* (Durham, N.C.: Duke University Education Improvement Program, 1969).

[7] Philip W. Jackson, "The Way Teaching Is," in Ronald T. Hyman, *Contemporary Thought on Teaching* (Englewood Cliffs, N.J.: Prentice-Hall, 1971), p. 7.

quences in the learning and the development of the children. Nevertheless, the precise nature of the relationships between teaching and learning is uncertain, and developmental consequences are obscured in a network of relationships yet to be untangled. Reviewing the research relating teaching behaviors to pupil achievement, at all levels from nursery school to college, Rosenshine[8] concludes that the results are not very clear. It is difficult to identify a single behavior or even a group of behaviors as a correlate of good teaching. Furthermore, in most of the studies employing systematic observation of classrooms, insufficient attention has been given such matters as the materials being used, the cognitive learning styles of the individual pupils, and the influence of the entire school environment on achievement.

Soar and Soar, reporting on their analysis of several Follow Through programs, are slightly more optimistic. They write:

> The most encouraging aspect of current work using systematic observation is the prospect that procedures are being developed and tested which will permit testing current theory, winnowing out portions that are in error, and extending the portions which are only partially developed. The likelihood seems great that as a result education for young children will be improved.[9]

The available studies of teaching at the early levels must be regarded somewhat critically. When a particular procedure is said to lead to a particular outcome, the teacher needs to consider both the immediate and the long-term consequences of using it. If, for example, she has taught the children that they should wait for her instructions before beginning any activity, the immediate consequences of expecting them to choose and carry through their own activities will very likely be disastrous. To avoid chaos, the teacher may decide to shift responsibility to the children more gradually, beginning perhaps with the opportunity to choose between two specified activities and moving by degrees toward the long-term goal—each child a self-propelling learner.

Concern for consequences, and particularly for those that are long-term, represents a concern for the development of the individual child. Such concern enormously complicates the business of teaching. Bereiter, commenting on the complexity, says, "It is one thing for an adult to recognize his potentiality for biasing the course of child development and try to minimize this effect and another thing for him to regard such biasing as his mission."[10] The first, he

---

[8] Barak Rosenshine, "Teaching Behavior Related to Pupil Achievement: A Review of Research," in Ian Westbury and Arno A. Bellack, eds., *Research into Classroom Processes* (New York: Teachers College Press, 1971), pp. 96–97.

[9] Soar and Soar, op. cit., p. 257.

[10] Carl Bereiter, "Schools without Education," *Harvard Educational Review,* 42:403, August 1972.

believes, is responsible child care; the second, education, and they had better not be combined. Bereiter considers attempts to influence the development of the child an imposition on the rights of the child and his family.[11] Education should be the prerogative of the parents. He also questions the effectiveness of the school's efforts in this direction.

Combining child care and education, Bereiter thinks, results in ineffective training in academic skills. For example, "a reading lesson and a science lesson thus come to have much the same ingredients—a mishmash of memorization, drill, procedure learning, inquiry, question-and-answer recitation, factual exposition, craft projects, and free-floating discussion."[12] The teachers try to do too many things at the same time. Rather than concentrating on the training procedures that would ensure the acquisition of the basic skills (such acquisition is the only legitimate justification for public schooling, according to Bereiter), they bring all kinds of extraneous matters into the instruction.

On the other hand, Kohlberg maintains that development should not be separated from instruction but rather should be the aim of education. For him, "developmental criteria are the best ones for defining educationally important behavior changes."[13] These developmental criteria are based on the principle that development is "not just any behavior change, but a change toward greater differentiation, integration and adaptation." Such changes are "irreversible, general over a field of responses, sequential and hierarchical."[14] Changes in cognitive development are inherent in changes in personality, or ego development, and are reflected in social, moral, and esthetic areas as well.

Kohlberg's reply to Bereiter's assertion of imposition on the freedom of the child notes that education for development "relies on open methods of stimulation through a sequence of stages, a direction of movement which is universal for all children."[15] It is, in this view, the child himself who constructs his own logical and ethical principles.

The position I take in this book accords fairly well with that taken by Kohlberg. It is a position that demands a great deal from the teacher. It recognizes that the available developmental criteria provide only general guidelines for the teacher. Teachers may misread those guidelines. Not wishing to impose themselves on the children, they may fail to provide instruction when it is needed. For example, children quickly lose interest in potentially productive projects that require reading or mathematical skills beyond their

---

[11] For an expansion of this argument, see Carl Bereiter, "Education: An Affront to Personal Liberty?" *Learning,* 2(2):90–95, October 1973.
[12] Bereiter, "Schools without Education," p. 405.
[13] Lawrence Kohlberg and Rochelle Mayer, "Development as the Aim of Education," *Harvard Educational Review,* 42:449–496, November 1972, p. 485.
[14] Kohlberg and Mayer, pp. 483, 486.
[15] Kohlberg and Mayer, p. 494.

level of competence. Without instruction and practice in the necessary skills they cannot progress. On the other hand, unwilling to accept as valid the ideas the children have, the teacher may subtly manipulate them. These are possibilities that must be faced. They underscore the need for providing support and counsel to the teachers. The risks in expecting teachers to be knowledgeable and competent seem no greater than those involved in the assumption that the teacher's role consists only in the application of training procedures. Such procedures may or may not be developmentally appropriate for a particular child.

Education to promote the development of the child is inconceivable if the teacher is not free to use her intelligence. Only through her own active investigation will she develop the knowledge of children, and the knowledge about children, that is essential for effective teaching.

KNOWLEDGE OF YOUNG CHILDREN[16]

The early childhood years cover a wide span of development and encompass obvious changes in the children. Teachers who have worked with all these ages often express a preference for, or greater insight into, the earlier or the later part of the span. In any event, those teachers who are open to young children, and who have the desire, the patience, and the intuitive sensitivity to attend to what the children do and say and are, know of many of their characteristics that must be taken into consideration in guiding and teaching them.

The first of these characteristics is simply and profoundly the uniqueness of each individual. More attention often seems to be given such individuality in the earlier span of years, but teachers of older children, when they are not pressed by too large groups or too rigid standards for achievement, are also aware that children categorized as alike on the basis of some testing device differ in important respects. John, for example, plods slowly and carefully through the first grade reading-achievement test, making no mistakes as far as he goes. His best friend tackles the same test in slapdash fashion, goes through more items, misses several, and comes out with the same score as John. His teacher cannot effectively teach the two in exactly the same manner.

When teachers are able to use their knowledge of the ways children differ, the value the early childhood teacher has traditionally placed on the uniqueness of each child becomes something more than the mere sentimentality of which they have sometimes been accused.[17]

---

[16]Major portions of this and the following section were originally published in "Guiding Children for Life in Tomorrow's World," in Robert H. Anderson, ed., *Education in Anticipation of Tomorrow* (Worthington, Ohio: Charles A. Jones Publishing Co., 1973), Chapter 2, pp. 28–51.

[17] Lilian G. Katz, "Sentimentality in Preschool Teachers: Some Interpretations," *Peabody Journal of Education*, 48:96–105, January 1971.

Teachers know also that the child's life outside the school shapes his interests and his concerns within the school. Yet one of the major tragedies of present-day education has been the failure to find ways for teachers to build on children's interests and concerns, and whatever strengths and resources they have. In too many ghetto classrooms, for example, children have been seen as different from their middle-class peers, but not as different among themselves, each with his own repertory of language and information, his own learning style, his own uniqueness.

Sensitive teachers who are aware of and responsive to the individuality of children soon learn that age, although often a fallible predictor of what a child is likely to do, *does* provide some guidelines. They begin to relate to the similarities that characterize children who are approximately the same age and who come from similar backgrounds.

The younger the child, the more likely he is to give outward and sometimes vivid expression to his feelings, to want his own way in relating to other children, to interpret instructions and explanations in ways that seem idiosyncratic, to investigate actively the world around him, and to become caught up in sequences of behavior that have no apparent end, that are, indeed, completely playful. Yet with all this, it is strikingly apparent that the younger child, be he three or four or five, learns a great deal. He continually manifests new ideas, new skills. On the other hand, despite his suggestibility, he seems relatively impervious to certain concepts, revealing some beginning grasp of them only when the total environment has been carefully arranged so as to program his understanding.

At many points the teacher of the young child may confront the fact that a child's experience is not what she, as the teacher, had anticipated. The paper bag masks for Halloween set off paroxysms of fear in a usually tranquil three-year-old; the six-year-old who has been reading with increasing competence evades the opportunity to read aloud, and when specifically requested to do so brings his book with dragging feet; some seemingly sophisticated seven-year-olds, apparently forgetting the purpose of their experimentation with differing types of soil, are making mud pies; the committee of nine-year-old best friends is beset with aggressive dissension.

Through incidents such as these runs a common thread. The reality to which the child responded and the motives that directed his behavior were not those the teacher envisioned. Although some degree of mismatch between the teacher's expectation and the child's actualization is probably inevitable, there is an ever-increasing body of knowledge about children and their development that the teacher can draw on to increase her understanding of the child's perception of reality.

KNOWLEDGE ABOUT YOUNG CHILDREN

Exponents of early education have long maintained that programs were or should be based on the findings of research. They have not always explained how the applications are best made, and sometimes have engaged in what Sheldon White[18] has referred to as "a slightly overheated rhetoric" in which evidence supporting a particular point of view has been emphasized, while evidence to the contrary has been deemphasized or not much discussed.

Research regarding Child Development and Learning

While the field of knowledge having to do with child development and learning has expanded at a rapid rate, there are many obvious gaps in the currently available literature. Several years ago Siegel[19] pointed to some of these gaps when she noted that the bulk of the research then appearing in *Child Development* had to do with children of elementary school age and with adolescents. Four-year-olds and neonates were the next most frequently studied. Despite the title of the journal, less than 15 percent of the studies printed therein dealt with information covering an extended period of time. A large portion of the studies used descriptive-correlational methods and imposed no experimental controls. A quick review of the same journal for the years that have passed since Siegel's criticism suggests that there has been little change in the proportion of longitudinal studies. Although there are more studies of an experimental nature, relatively few of them relate directly to the setting of school or center. Other journals dealing with child development and learning have also appeared more recently but they do not seem to differ in the kind of research reported.

Perhaps too much is expected from developmental research. Lipsitt and Eimas,[20] in reviewing the literature of a single year, comment on the lack of a unifying theory—a system for getting the "whole child" back together. They note, however, that there is increasing evidence about the various processes involved in development and learning. These processes "get themselves together in diverse and fascinating ways in different people over the course of development," highlighting the importance of individual differences. Similarly, Gollin and Moody,[21] in the course of reviewing the next year's accumulation of literature, comment on the contribution of developmental theory to

---

[18] Sheldon White, "Plausibilities and Possibilities in Early Education," *Pediatrics,* 44:901–904, December 1969.

[19] Alberta E. Siegel, "Editorial," *Child Development,* 38:901–907, 1967.

[20] Lewis P. Lipsitt and Peter D. Eimas, "Developmental Psychology," in Paul Mussen and Mark Rosenzweig, eds., *Annual Review of Psychology,* 23:40 (Palo Alto: Annual Reviews, Inc., 1972).

[21] Eugene S. Gollin and Mark Moody, "Developmental Pyschology," in Paul Mussen and Mark Rosenzweig, eds., *Annual Review of Psychology,* 24:37 (Palo Alto: Annual Reviews, Inc., 1973).

training programs for disadvantaged children. They caution that "unless theoretical considerations are closely adapted to individual differences, programs will continue to be addressed to ages, stages, or statistical averages and not to human learners." Developmental theory can inform the teacher but it cannot substitute for her knowledge of the individual child.

In considering the limitations of the available research, we should also note that to the extent it is based on theory, that theory most often has to do with the development and learning of children as individuals. One important source of individual difference is sex. Boys and girls respond differently to instruction and guidance. But the extent to which "such differences are inherent or culturally determined is uncertain."[22] This is a matter currently receiving more attention. A further limitation of the available research is that relatively little has had to do with the behavior of young children in groups, and still less with teaching them in groups.

Theories of Child Development

In recent years several books comparing theories of development have been published,[23] and several authors have written articles[24] dealing with the theory from which early childhood education programs are or could be derived. The authors do not agree as to what constitutes a viable theory, nor as to which theories are sufficiently alike to be categorized together. Kohlberg[25] identifies three broad streams of thought that have influenced early education. The first, or "maturationist," stemming from Rousseau, includes the followers of Freud and Gesell. The second stream, "cultural training," stems from Locke and includes Thorndike, Skinner, and the behavior shapers. The third, "cognitive-developmental" or interactional stream, includes Dewey and Piaget.

The normative-maturational view taken by itself seems to offer extremely tenuous guidelines for the teacher in early childhood programs. Normative data, and particularly that which is longitudinal in nature, provide an important, although limited, backdrop of information about developmental sequences, to be kept in view as teachers and others consider the provisions to be made for the young child's learning. But to determine the nature and

[22] Eleanor E. Maccoby, ed., *The Development of Sex Differences* (Stanford: Stanford University Press, 1966).
[23] A. L. Baldwin, *Theories of Child Development* (New York: John Wiley & Sons, 1966); Jonas Langer, *Theories of Development* (New York: Holt, Rinehart and Winston, 1969).
[24] Milly Cowles, "Four Views of Learning and Development," *Educational Leadership,* 28:790–795, 1971; Lawrence Kohlberg, "Early Education: A Cognitive-Developmental View," *Child Development,* 39:1013–1062, 1968.
[25] Kohlberg, "Early Education: A Cognitive-Developmental View."

conditions of that learning we need to draw on theories that predict the consequences of certain kinds of experience, as well as data supporting the theory.

Psychoanalytic theory, particularly as represented in the work of John Bowlby, Erik Erickson, Anna Freud, and Susan Isaacs, has had a considerable influence on early education in the United States, especially as applied to the child under the age of five. Psychoanalytic theory provides a rich source of insight into the emotional and fantasy life of the child and offers many clues for supporting his efforts to cope effectively and realistically.

Cultural training, behavior or learning theories, have been influential in early education since E. L. Thorndike elucidated the significance of his connectionism for teaching kindergarten children and John B. Watson set forth his techniques for conditioning children. Social-learning theories, derived from the work of Clark L. Hull, with inspiration from Sigmund Freud and espoused by such researchers as Robert R. Sears, Neal Miller, John Dollard, and Albert Bandura, have also made their contribution. Currently behavior theory as applied to early education is represented in the work of such people as Carl Bereiter, Wesley Becker, Siegfried Engelmann, Donald Bushell, Jr., and Arthur W. Staats.[26]

In an analysis of the learning theory tradition and child psychology, White[27] writes that the learning theory tradition "offers no articulated learning theory of child development." It is, however, "insistent on environment, learning, reinforcement, and peripheralism, against others who contend for maturation, stages, development, and central structures as causative agents." From the standpoint of early childhood education, those in the learning theory tradition who have addressed themselves to children in the classroom have clearly demonstrated behavior modification techniques that work. Two critical questions have, however, not been answered. The first, as White notes in "The Learning Theory Tradition and Child Psychology," is whether their success is based on the reinforcement schedules or on other presently unidentified factors inherent in the situation and the child. The second question has to do with the long-term effects of such techniques. Are they merely facilitators, getting the child started on a path in which he can eventually become autonomous, or do they encourage passivity and conformity? Langer[28] suggests the latter when he terms this stream of theory the "mechanical mirror" theory.

---

[26] For a review of recent studies of learning, see Harold W. Stevenson, "Learning in Children," in Paul H. Mussen, ed., *Carmichael's Manual of Child Psychology* (New York: John Wiley & Sons, 1970), pp. 849–938.

[27] Sheldon White, "The Learning Theory Tradition and Child Psychology," in Paul H. Mussen, ed., *Carmichael's Manual of Child Psychology* (New York: John Wiley & Sons, 1970), p. 685.

[28] Langer, *Theories of Development.*

Longitudinal research, not yet undertaken, seems essential if these questions are to be answered satisfactorily.

Unlike behavior theory and like psychoanalytic theory, the cognitive-developmental or interaction theory does take a long-term view. It too needs to be bolstered by longitudinal data. Langer has labeled this stream of theory, dominated by the work of Piaget and those who were inspired by him, the "organic lamp" theory. This theory "assumes that development is a process of interaction between organismic and environmental factors, but it focuses upon the individual's self-generative rather than upon the environment's socializing part in the developmental process. . . . The environment . . . is merely the occasion for, or scene of, and not the cause or agent of, development."[29]

Current State of Knowledge of Development and Learning

Much of what is now known about learning and development is not yet reflected in the literature that is readily available to educators. As White points out,[30] what may be termed "micro-theories" relating to the nature of learning are becoming more specific and more detailed as laboratory studies relating to attention, perception, memory, emotion, and language accumulate. At the same time, and on a different time scale, "macrotheories" relating to the orderliness of development, building on the work of Freud and Piaget, are taking clearer form.

In this context learning is no longer seen as additive. The child constructs his own reality, and the teacher can no longer be seen as the agent of change; rather, she serves more as a clarifier of the child's knowledge.

That knowledge, in turn, is plural in nature. Consider, for example, the knowledge based on language, compared with knowledge based on action or on intuition. In contrast to older analogies viewing the brain as a telephone switchboard, or as a computer, the appropriate modern analogy is that of a *set* of computers each handling a different knowledge system and interacting with the others.

These new conceptions of the nature of development and learning have implications for the conception of personality. As White puts it, the unity of personality is gone. The personality that is revealed at any time is specific to the context in which it occurs. It is not clear whether this adaptive characteristic of the person, illustrated in the fact that children enrolled in the Bereiter-

---

[29] Langer, *Theories of Development,* p. 157.
[30] Sheldon White, paper presented at the Minnesota Round Table on Early Childhood Education, Minneapolis, June 1973. Taped by Child Care Information Center, The Presbyterian Center for Human Development, Hampton, Virginia.

Englemann program acquired "new" voices for the program setting, refutes the notion of the "whole" child. Presumably the child had some awareness that the expectations of the program were different from expectations for them elsewhere. Presumably also there are limitations to the number of adaptive maneuvers the person can make and still retain a sense of his own identity and integrity. Nevertheless, the new conception does call into question many commonly held notions about the effects of a few hours of school five days a week in training children to be honest, or creative, or to have positive self-concepts.

Finally, White emphasizes, learning can no longer be taken as an explanation for development. Rather, development explains learning.

THE CHILD'S PERCEPTION OF REALITY

Present knowledge about child development and learning offers few, if any, prescriptions for teaching. However, it seems reasonable to use it to inform and amplify the intuitive, commonsense knowledge of children that comes from close association with them. What then does the teacher need to know about children in order to understand the reality with which they are presently coping and to deal with them in ways that seem likely to promote further development?

Development is used here in the sense of movement toward greater adaptation, differentiation, and integration, and draws most heavily on cognitive-developmental theory. The long-term goal is competence in logical thinking, eventually at the level, in Piaget's words, of "formal operations." In personality development, the long-term goal, in Erikson's words, is "realization of a sense of identity." In moral development, the goal is to act on values and principles which have validity and application apart from the authority of the groups or individuals holding them and apart from the individual's group identification.[31] Such goals are ordinarily not reached until the period of adolescence,[32] but they are preceded by a sequence of substages that can serve as markers for the progress made. These substages are most clearly delineated in the development of thinking, less so for personality.

The Filters of Individuality

Progress through the developmental stages reflects the dynamic intertwining of the organismic and experiential factors that make up the child's individual-

[31] Elliot Turiel, "Stage Transition in Moral Development," in Robert M. W. Travers, ed., *Second Handbook of Research on Teaching* (Chicago: Rand McNally, 1973), p. 734.

[32] All the goals described by Turiel are derived from experience in Western culture, although it can be argued that they are all universally applicable.

ity. Although the general direction of development is forward, and gains made are usually maintained, development is also marked by periods of disruption or even of apparent regression. In personality development, for example, the youngster who on the whole has shown considerable initiative and accomplishment in most areas of his life may revert to a more doubtful and less confident attitude when confronted with a situation having many unfamiliar elements. Or, in cognitive development, when he becomes aware of new possibilities, the child may become confused about matters that had previously been quite clear to him.

It may be useful for the teacher to think of the child's individuality as providing him with different kinds of filters through which he takes in and responds to the program provided him. What gets through the filter depends on what has happened to him previously. Stored in his memory are representations of his actions, of objects he has perceived and events that have occurred. The object or event currently confronting him is appraised against that stored experience. In the light of his appraisal the child responds with interest, or reluctance, or perhaps not at all. Responses appear to be selected on the basis of their congruity with previous experience. Given sufficient opportunity for feedback from whatever he confronts, he may alter his perception of the situation. The responses he makes, in their turn, have consequences with representations that are also stored in memory and serve to alter the nature of the filter.[33]

Some "filters" may change relatively little with development. They represent such factors as the child's greater openness to visual or to auditory stimulation, his preference for expressing himself in motoric as opposed to verbal ways, his inclination toward the mechanical rather than the social, or his tendency to be impulsive or deliberate. The teacher's knowledge of the nature of the child's ways of filtering his experience provides her with information as to how he is likely to confront new ideas or experiences.

We do not know to what extent the groundwork for some of these differences in individuals is established even before the age of three. A growing body of research highlights the extent of behavioral individuality in infancy, and some work suggests that such individuality to some extent shapes the caretaking behavior of the parent.[34] There is also evidence that the responses teachers

[33] D. B. Gardner, "The Child as an Open System," in Georgianna Engstrom, ed., *Play: The Child Strives toward Self-Realization* (Washington: National Association for the Education of Young Children, 1971); Jean Piaget, "The General Problems of the Psychobiological Development of the Child," in J. M. Tanner and Bärbel Inhelder, eds., *Discussions on Child Development*, vol. 4 (New York: International Universities Press, 1955), pp. 3–27, 77–83.

[34] R. Q. Bell, "Stimulus Control of Parent or Caretaker Behavior by Offspring," *Developmental Psychology*, 4:63–72, 1971. L. V. Harper, "The Young as a Source of Stimuli Controlling Caretaker Behavior," *Developmental Psychology*, 4:73–88, 1971. A. Thomas et al., *Behavioral Individuality in Early Childhood* (New York: New York University Press, 1963).

make to young children are modified in accord with the characteristics of each child.[35]

In the past decade psychological studies dealing with individual variation, as it is revealed in cognitive processes, have proliferated. According to Kagan and Kogan, "few systematic conclusions flow easily from [a] review" of this research. Nonetheless, "The psychological distance between investigations of perception, language and thought, on the one hand, and studies of personality dynamics, on the other, has shortened." Furthermore, Kagan and Kogan note, "It is clear that an individual's preferred fashion of interpreting, transforming and reporting information will have to be a variable in any equation that seeks to explain him."[36] The individual's preferences may also need to be taken into more specific account in his early education. Doing so would add an important dimension to the tradition of respect for individual differences long given lip service in early education. In the nursery school such respect was manifested in the limitation of activities demanding the participation of the whole group. In the kindergarten, where the number of children was larger, and the pressure for reading readiness greater, individualization was less apparent. Group instruction, except for reading (in smaller groups), often characterized the first grade. In the past decade, however, with the advent of aides and assistants and of programmed instruction, the tendency to bend the child to the group rather than adapting the instruction to the child has received some correction. It is not clear, however, whether the eventual goal should be to fit instruction to the child's preferred ways of processing information, or to introduce him to other ways, with the goal being flexibility and the modification of style to fit the task at hand.

The Filters of Cognitive Structure

In contrast to the "filters" derived from individuality are those that are clearly developmental, changing as the child grows older. These have been much studied, although not often by repeated observations of the same children over a period of years. It is Piaget, of course, who has provided insight into the cognitive structures of children and adolescents and who has described the sequence of qualitative changes that may be expected as the child moves from infancy to adolescence. Other investigators[37] have verified the sequences in other countries and among different socioeconomic groups.

[35] M. R. Yarrow et al., "Child Effects on Adult Behavior," *Developmental Psychology*, 5:300–312, 1971.
[36] J. Kagan and N. Kogan, "Individual Variation in Cognitive Processes," in P. H. Mussen, ed., *Carmichael's Manual of Child Psychology* (New York: John Wiley & Sons, 1970), pp. 1352, 1353. See also Jack C. Westman, ed., *Individual Differences in Children* (New York: John Wiley & Sons, 1973).
[37] For example, P. R. Dasen, "Cross-Cultural Piagetian Research: A Summary," in J. W. Berry and P. R. Dasen, *Culture and Cognition: Readings in Cross-Cultural Psychology* (London: Methuen, 1973).

Unfortunately, some parts of the sequence have been studied more carefully than others, so that more is known, for example, about the transition that occurs somewhere between the ages of five and seven when the child acquires a stable concept of number, than is known about the thinking of three- and four-year-olds, or the shifts that occur after the attainment of number conservation. Also, considerably more attention has been given to the child's responses in the interview situation than to the kind of thinking he may display in the classroom situation. However, teachers and others who have come to know through their own interviewing how the child's responses to conservation, or classification, or seriation tasks tend to shift as they grow older often find that they have a new grasp of the way the child filters reality that is applicable in the classroom.

Elkind,[38] drawing his insights from Piaget, points out how the child's questions mirror the development of his mind. At about age three he begins to use language to acquire information, to learn the names of things. The first, and for a time seemingly perpetual, "why" questions are often the source of some frustration or annoyance; for example, "Why is it time to go home?" or "Why do I have to wear a sweater?" At age four or so, questioning expands as though the child believes that everything in the world is there to be understood. Origins, death, the purposefulness of things (Why does the giraffe have a long neck?), questions of these sorts, particularly in the context of modern technology, can mislead the adult into giving the child much more information than he can assimilate. At the age of five or so, questions begin turning to the physical world, to amounts and space and time; and by six or seven take on more adult form and deal more with distant time and space and the "how" of things. The shift corresponds to the transition that occurs in the child's thinking when he becomes able to conserve.

Looked at from a different stance, the child's questions also reflect the changing character of his concerns as a developing person. The "why" questions that initially have to do with whatever seems to impede his expression of his own autonomy give way to those that express his readiness and initiative for exploration. He projects himself actually and imaginatively into all kinds of roles and possibilities. This exuberance again gives way to a more sober, reflective, earthbound desire for real accomplishment.

According to Piaget, "the affective and social development of the child follows the same general process as the cognitive, since the affective, social and cognitive aspects of behavior are in fact inseparable."[39] Following this line of

---

[38] David Elkind, *Children and Adolescents: Interpretive Essays on Jean Piaget* (New York: Oxford University Press, 1970).
[39] Jean Piaget and B. Inhelder, *The Psychology of the Child* (New York: Basic Books, 1969), p. 114.

thought, several investigators, for example Harvey [40] and Loevinger, [41] have proposed stage theories in which personality or ego development can be viewed in the context of cognitive development. Kohlberg[42] has drawn on Piaget's theory to formulate stages of moral development. The bulk of the empirical work related to these formulations has been done with adolescents and children older than seven. However, the close meshing of the beginnings of cognitive development, as seen by Piaget, with the beginnings of ego development, as seen by psychoanalytic ego theorists, has been demonstrated at the infancy level.[43] For the age span from two to five, Lois Murphy's *Widening World of Childhood,* [44] although not so deliberately focused on validating the Piagetian theory, nonetheless provides clear evidence of shifts in the child's thinking as he moves toward mastery of his impulses and increasingly effective coping with the world of things and people.

The Filters of Emotional Concern

The emotional concerns that are focal at succeeding stages of personality development, or that may persist throughout the stages, constitute another filter through which the child responds to the program provided for him. The child who does not trust people or things does not see the world as a place to be investigated. The child with little sense of his own self-worth lacks the courage to try for himself. Children who are filled with guilt, whether over real or imagined transgressions, tend to confront learning defensively rather than openly. Such concerns may be so basic and so pervasive as to make teaching a child difficult, if not impossible. On the other hand, for most children school experience has the potential, not always realized, and sometimes exaggerated, for alleviating some of the child's concerns and strengthening his ability to cope effectively.

Getting through to the Child

The analogy of the filters emphasizes the complexities of the child's view of things and the importance of the teacher's understanding of how that view often differs from hers. When the teacher understands she is in a better position to alter the environment or her teaching strategies in ways helpful to him.

[40] O. J. Harvey et al., *Conceptual Systems and Personality Organization* (New York: John Wiley & Sons, 1961).

[41] Jane Loevinger and R. Wessler, *Measuring Ego Development* (San Francisco: Jossey-Bass, 1970).

[42] L. Kohlberg, "Stage and Sequence: The Cognitive Approach to Socialization," in D. E. Goslin, ed., *Handbook of Socialization Theory and Research* (Chicago: Rand McNally, 1969), pp. 347–480.

[43] Therese G. DeCarie, *Intelligence and Affectivity in Early Childhood* (New York: International University Press, 1965).

[44] Lois Murphy, *The Widening World of Childhood* (New York: Basic Books, 1962).

There are some dangers here. In a sense, teaching is a matter of hypothesizing about the way the child's filters are operating, choosing strategies in line with the hypothesis and then accepting, modifying, or rejecting it in line with the way the child responds. Even the most intuitive teacher may misinterpret what the child says or does.[45] But the greatest danger comes when the hypothesis is wrong and the teacher is insensitive to the evidence.

Erroneous assumptions about the child's perceptions are easily and tragically made when the teacher looks at the child, not as an individual but merely as a member of some group. How many children never have a chance because their teacher thinks of them only as "physically handicapped" or "disadvantaged" or "Black" or "Indian" or "nonverbal" or "hyperactive" or "spoiled"?

Situations like these, where the teachers operate on untested assumptions, responding little if at all to the reality of each child's individuality, led Bereiter and others to contend that teachers had better not meddle with development. Unfortunately, however, the mere assertion that the teaching is not directed to development provides no guarantee that it may not also create developmental havoc. Since teachers can hardly avoid some contribution to development, it seems better to expect them to be knowledgeable and to provide them the kind of colleagueship that enables them to share and check their perceptions with others.

EDUCATION FOR DEVELOPMENT

If early childhood education takes as its major goal the promotion of the child's development, with a particular but not exclusive emphasis on the development of cognitive structures, what will be the essential elements in its programs? What propels the child from the sensorimotor intelligence of infancy toward the more systematic and critical thinking of which the eight- and nine-year-old is capable? How does the teacher support such development?

Piaget[46] specifies four factors in the transition: maturation, experience of the physical environment, the action of the social environment, and equilibration or self-regulation, the factor that serves to coordinate the others. The school program has no influence on the first factor, although it cannot ignore it. The school and the teacher contribute directly to the second and third factors, but this contribution is not the only one the child receives. The fourth factor rests with the child, although it is in a sense the product of the other three.

---

[45] Selma H. Fraiberg, *The Magic Years* (New York: Scribner's, 1959), drawing on psychoanalytic and Piagetian insight, provides numerous examples of the difficulty adults have understanding young children, and vice versa!

[46] J. Piaget, "Piaget's Theory," in P. H. Mussen, ed., *Carmichael's Manual of Child Psychology* (New York: John Wiley & Sons, 1970), pp. 703–732.

The goal, it should be noted, is not to accelerate the child's progress from one level of development to another, but rather to provide a wide range of possibilities at each level. The concern is for the child "as a constructor of reality"—as one who puts together all sorts of things in a variety of ways. The important dimension here is not the level of logical goodness of these constructions, but rather the extent to which they testify to the child's breadth of experience and his ability to build upon it.[47]

Put another way, the goal is for the child to develop increasing competence. Participation in the program ought to increase the child's ability to solve problems, that is, to find different ways to reach a goal. It ought to increase both his understanding of his immediate and larger environment and increase his options for participation in both.[48]

Providing for the Physical Environment

According to Piaget, the child's actions on his physical environment contribute to two kinds of knowledge. He derives physical knowledge of the properties of objects as he acts on them in different ways. He constructs mathematicological knowledge as he becomes aware that a set of objects can be grouped in different ways. He can, for example, sort on the basis of color and sort again on the basis of form or function. He can order the same objects on the basis of the difference in some property. Hierarchical classification, seriation, and conservation thus evolve from action. In addition, as he acts on his environment, the child structures space and time, and develops notions of causality.

One may ask why the child needs any particular kind of environment in order to build the rudiments of scientific and mathematical knowledge. Might not a natural setting with space for exploration, rocks, soils, water, and a variety of plants and animals provide as effectively for action as the artificial classroom, no matter how elaborately equipped?

Adequate provision for the child's activity on his environment certainly includes variety not only in the classroom, but also expansion beyond its four walls. Furthermore, variety needs consideration not only over space but through time. There are classrooms where the possibilities in some materials are never fully explored by the children. Unlike natural settings which constantly change, even though subtly, some classrooms are basically static.

Variety, it may be added, does not necessarily call for a different material,

---

[47] Anne Bussis and Edward Chittenden, "The Horizontal Dimension of Learning," in *Evaluation Reconsidered* (New York: Workshop Center for Open Education, City College, 1973).

[48] For a review of the elements involved in the development of competence, see M. Brewster Smith, "Competence and Socialization," in John A. Clausen, ed., *Socialization and Society* (Boston: Little, Brown, 1968), pp. 70–320. Competence is discussed further in Chapter 7.

or a new piece of equipment. Variety comes, and new cognitive structures emerge, when the child is encouraged to vary his repertory of actions, behavioral and cognitive. Unit blocks, for example, that staple of the traditional nursery school, are spread and stacked by the youngest children, and serve as vehicles for the imagination of the four- and five-year-olds, but become scale representations in the hands of seven- and eight-year-olds.

If the child's body is seen as the instrument through which cognitive structures are developed, it becomes clear that the environment needs to provide for a wide range of possibilities. Climbing, jumping, running, dancing, singing, playing an instrument, painting—all have their place in a program focused on development.

Providing for the Social Environment

Traditionally, the teacher has had a large, if not major, social influence on the child's knowledge. To teach was to tell and to explain. In the school focused on development the teacher has a more complex role. She contributes directly to the child's knowledge by giving him information, but she also contributes indirectly through her arrangement of the physical environment, through her questioning strategies, and through the provision she makes for his collaboration with his peers.

Young children learn a great deal simply by being told. For the youngest children, names and labels, the rules of group living must be given directly. Older children similarly acquire from the teacher much of the information they need, particularly that relating to the customs of social living, precautions for safety, and arbitrary conventions such as the use of capital letters or reading from left to right. Even when children are encouraged to investigate and discover for themselves, they need the teacher's help in organizing their findings and in relating them to larger structures of knowledge. As Karplus[49] has shown in developing his science curriculum, children may not be expected to discover all the concepts they need. Rather, given the teacher's "invention" of a concept they can then apply it in their further investigations.

The teacher of young children is, however, wary of providing instruction that is so remote from the child's present level of understanding as to be either confused or ignored by him. Accordingly, she not only listens to and observes him in the general run of the class activities, but from time to time explores his thinking in relation to a particular task or situation. The questions she poses are not designed to elicit a correct answer so much as to reveal the kinds of consideration he can give to the problem. The child's responses are clues to the further information or perhaps "invention" he needs.

---

[49] R. Karplus and H. Thier, *A New Look at Elementary School Science* (Chicago: Rand McNally, 1967).

The importance of the teacher's role in instruction of this sort has been noted by Piaget, who comments on "the necessity for a rational deductive activity to give a meaning to scientific experiment, and the necessity also, in order to establish such a reasoning activity in the child, for a social structure entailing not merely cooperation among the children but also cooperation with adults."[50]

Cooperation among the children, in Piaget's view, serves cognitive development as well as social development. Collaboration with his peers helps the child to "decenter," that is, to understand the world from the view of the other as well as from his own view, and hence to become more objective and more flexible in his thinking.

It is ironic that the cognitive in early education has so often been accompanied by lessened emphasis on social cooperation. The traditional nursery school encouraged the children to develop common purposes in their play. Many of the innovative programs provided little time for this sort of exchange. The traditional elementary school emphasized social conformity, and except for the playground and, in some instances, classes for "slow" children, provided little opportunity for social give-and-take among the children.[51] Individualized programmed instruction, intended to promote individual progress without invidious comparison and competition, has not always realized its intent. As one eight-year-old, selected to explain to a visitor how individual programming worked, remarked, "There's only one other kid in this room I have to worry about. Sometimes he's ahead and sometimes I am. The other kids aren't so smart, and they don't go as fast as we do."

Perhaps this child's self-appraisal was realistic. Yet the visitor could only regret that the child, in that particular school, had little if any opportunity to find out what those "slower" children might know or be able to do. In a world where ultimate survival seems dependent on cooperation, one would expect social development to be a major goal for the school.

In helping children to move toward greater social collaboration, the teacher is guided in part by understanding of the child's view of the situation. She does not expect the child to become a cooperative member of a total class project without seeing that he has first successfully negotiated smaller group enterprises. For example, rather early in the school year, a teacher of a mixed age group of fives, sixes, and sevens decided to have a brief daily evaluative period, in which the group of twenty-five youngsters discussed how things were going, made suggestions for new or revised activities, and so on. All went well

[50] J. Piaget, *Science of Education and the Psychology of the Child* (New York: Orion Press, 1970).
[51] See Edith W. King, *Educating Young Children: Sociological Resources* (Dubuque, Iowa: Wm. C. Brown, 1973), for examples of typical ways schools deal with the social relationships of young children.

with the six- and seven-year-olds, but the fives clearly could not long sustain interest in a discussion that demanded that they consider so many other points of view. They might learn to listen, or perhaps to seem to listen, but they needed considerably more practice in smaller and more definitely task-oriented groups before they would develop a good grasp of the cognitive elements of the situation.

The teacher's provisions for the children's socialization reveal certain moral commitments. The young child interprets right and wrong, good and bad in terms of the physical or hedonistic consequences for him, not in terms of principles. Nevertheless, his moral development appears to be influenced both by the rationality of the adults who care for him and by his experiences in taking both authority and subordinate roles with his peers.[52] Thus, the network of rules and interpersonal relationships that are built up in the classroom need to be examined for the values they represent. What acts are considered good—helping another child, exhibiting curiosity, being inventive, or being quiet, staying in line, and knowing the right answer? What would our friend from outer space (see Chapter 3) infer as he watches the interactions between the teacher and the children with different skin coloring, children who speak differently, children who are slower than most, children who are clumsy?[53] Such a network represents the "hidden curriculum" of the school, a curriculum which may have greater long-term consequences than the one outlined in the curriculum guides.

Providing for Self-Regulation

Within the early childhood period the child makes great strides in his development. His view of himself and the world changes from predominant subjectivity to the kind of objectivity underlying logical reasoning. He can think about things and about relationships between things, keeping track of which aspects change and which stay the same when transformations occur. His knowledge is increasingly organized in a systematic fashion.

These changes are brought about as the child interacts with the physical and social environment. Piaget comments:

> In the realm of education, this equilibration through self-regulation means that school children and students should be allowed a *maximum* of activity of their own, directed by means of materials which permit their activities to be cognitively

---

[52] Martin L. Hoffman, "Moral Development," in P. H. Mussen, ed., *Carmichael's Manual of Child Psychology* (New York: John Wiley & Sons, 1970).

[53] See King, *Educating Young Children: Sociological Resources,* for an analysis of the moral implications of certain early childhood education practices.

useful. In the area of logico-mathematical structures, children have real under-standing only of that which they invent themselves, and each time that we try to teach them something too quickly, we keep them from reinventing it themselves. Thus, there is no good reason to try to accelerate this development too much; the time which seems to be wasted in personal investigation is really gained in the construction of methods.[54]

In essence, Piaget proposes that the child needs time for his development —the three-year-old cannot be made into the five, or the five into the seven —but he is not proposing a laissez faire approach in which the children do whatever pleases them. The teacher's knowledge of sequences in development and of the concepts that are basic to an understanding of the modern world provides some guide to the kinds of activities that will be most productive.

However, Piaget's theory, grand though it is, does not encompass all that may go into education for the early childhood years. It is, after all, not a pedagogical but an epistemological theory. It offers few specific guides to the teacher beyond that of being respectful of the child's inherent ability to develop his own cognitive structures. As Elkind has noted, "in the long run, we will benefit most from Piaget's contribution if we accept him on his own terms and if we do not attempt to make his ideas conform to our own preconceived notions."[55] Accordingly, the teacher must turn to other sources for assistance with some of the problems that are faced in instructing and guiding young children.

Providing for Many Ways of Knowing

While the eventual development of logical thinking is a major goal for early childhood education, it is not the only goal. There are many kinds of knowl-edge, and many kinds of cognitive and affective structures, in addition to those investigated by Piaget.

The child's play, his chants, his dances, and his art[56] all have elements that may contribute to his eventual ability to think logically, but thinking of this sort, thinking to which Piaget can apply his method of analysis, represents only one aspect of thought. It does not take into account reverie, fantasy, or those aspects of thought that are attributed to unconscious processes by psy-choanalytic theorists. There is every reason to value the child's expressions of this personal knowledge for its own sake.

---

[54] Jean Piaget, "Foreword," in Millie Almy, *Young Children's Thinking* (New York: Teachers College Press, 1966), p. vi.

[55] Elkind, p. 135.

[56] For an analysis of the contributions of the arts to the child's development, see Howard Gardner, *The Arts and Human Development* (New York: John Wiley & Sons, 1973).

While the teacher needs to be clear about long-term developmental goals and how best to facilitate the child's reaching them, she is also responsible for helping the child with learning that is of a different order. There are shorter-term goals including the acquisition of certain perceptual-motor and language skills and learning the routines that order group living. For such goals she may draw on behavior and social learning theories as well as on cognitive-developmental or interaction theory.

SOME SELECTED TEACHING STRATEGIES

The programs for poor children that were developed in the 1960s varied in the role they gave the teacher. In some programs the major emphasis was on instruction, in others on facilitation. Some made specific provision for the guidance role; others assumed that if the instruction were well done, guidance would largely take care of itself. Since most of the programs at the preschool level were for half-days only, the teacher's caretaking function received relatively little attention.

A number of programs emphasized specific strategies for carrying out the various teaching functions. The functions of the teacher of young children have been set forth in Chapter 2 but are also reviewed here. In the section that follows, several strategies are briefly described to illustrate the range of possibilities available. Some strategies are applicable to only one of the functions of the teacher; others may apply in all of them. Their appropriateness to a particular teaching situation depends on the goals of the program and, of course, on the teacher's ability to use the strategy effectively.

The Functions of the Teacher of Young Children

Different programs place major emphasis on different functions, but the nature of the young child is such that within every program a measure of caretaking, of guidance, and of instructing and facilitating will be apparent. The strategies teachers use in carrying out these functions may differ.

Katherine Read's description of the role of the nursery school teacher reveals some of the overlapping of the functions. She emphasizes the facilitating functions of the teacher—creating a climate for learning, extending and enriching children's own interests, providing blocks of time, adapting activities to the needs of the group. She also stresses the guidance functions—helping the child feel confident, avoiding comparisons, reinforcing what the child does, positively or negatively depending on the content of his behavior, and being a good model. In describing the role of the teacher she does not specifically address the caretaking functions, yet her book includes a long section on guiding children in "experiences common to everyone," and adjusting to new experiences and routines. Although she clearly does not put much reliance on direct verbal instruction in curriculum areas, particularly where all the children are involved, it is clear that the teacher's facilitation and guidance also involve considerable instruction.[57]

Prescott and Jones, in a study of the behavior of teachers in child care centers, identified two "alternative convictions concerning effective child-rearing" that were reflected in the behavior of the teachers. On the one hand were the teachers who believed that the children should be provided with the prescribed forms of behavior. They tended to teach factual information and give generous feedback for right or wrong answers. On the other hand were the teachers who believed that individualized forms of social behavior can be developed from within the child himself if they are recognized by the child and confirmed by adults. These teachers "attempt to foster general attitudes of consideration for others and an experimental, questioning approach to the environment."[58] It appears, then, that the strategies the teacher uses in part are a product of what she believes.

Prescott and Jones's work also suggests that the way the teacher sees herself as an active force in the child's environment is also a factor in the way she functions. Those who see themselves as most powerful encourage more, or restrict more, and teach more "lessons." Presumably the strategies teachers use comfortably and effectively depend on their beliefs and attitudes, including those having to do with self.[59]

In this connection it may be noted that the modern British Infant School movement, and also the Education Development Center program developed as a Follow Through model in this country, assume that each teacher must work out the ways of teaching that are appropriate for her as well as for the children with whom she works. This point of view is reflected in the literature describing the role of the teacher. The research of Gardner and Cass, for example, reports in considerable detail on the observed teaching of forty-eight nursery and infant school teachers.[60] In addition, it includes descriptions of some of the teachers, giving a sense of their individuality. Brearley completes

---

[57] Katherine H. Read, *The Nursery School: A Human Relations Laboratory* (Philadelphia: W. B. Saunders, 1971).

[58] Elizabeth Prescott and Elizabeth Jones, *Day Care as a Child-Rearing Environment* (Washington: National Association for the Education of Young Children, 1972), p. 20.

[59] This possibility has been given some consideration in research at the preschool level, but the results are not clear. The matter is discussed in an unpublished manuscript by Lilian G. Katz, "Teacher-Child Relationships in Day Care Centers," 1972. ERIC document no. 046 494.

[60] Dorothy E. M. Gardner and Joan E. Cass, *The Role of the Teacher in the Infant and Nursery School* (Oxford: Pergamon Press, 1965).

her book, *The Teaching of Young Children,* with a detailed observation of one teacher at work. *The Teacher's Role,* in the Citation Press series on informal schools in Britain, presents the role through interviews with four teachers, each one of whom is individually described.[61]

Although the most effective teachers modify their teaching strategies to fit particular children or groups of children, they may not always be aware of all the possibilities that are appropriate for them and the children. Less effective teachers have special need to develop more versatility in their teaching.

Most of the strategies described below have been identified with one or more of the programs for young children that were developed during the sixties. None of them can be regarded as completely innovative, even at the preschool level, for they have their roots either in the pedagogical practice of an earlier day, or in psychological theory formulated before the sixties. Nor is the list exhaustive, for the intent is only to illustrate the range of possibilities.

The Responsive or "Prepared" Environment[62]

The importance to the child's development of his encounters with his environment has been emphasized earlier in this chapter. Kindergarten, first grade, and at a later date, nursery school teachers who were influenced by John Dewey early accepted this as a pedagogical principle. But it was Maria Montessori who placed major emphasis on individual instruction through the medium of autoeducative materials.[63]

In 1964, Glen Nimnicht and his colleagues began a nursery school program for poor children that was to evolve into the Responsive Environment Model for preschool, kindergarten, and primary (Follow Through) grades. The program combined elements of the traditional nursery school and of Montessori programs, but also based its theory on the work of O. K. Moore.[64]

The Responsive Program places considerable emphasis on materials— toys, games, records, blocks—that have inherent possibilities for the child's

[61] Ann Cook and Herb Mack, *The Teacher's Role* (New York: Citation Press, 1971).

[62] Chapter 7 includes further discussion of the preparation of the environment.

[63] Evelyn Weber, *The Kindergarten* (New York: Teachers College Press, 1969), p. 5. For descriptions of the prepared environment and its related teaching strategies from Montessori's view, see Maria Montessori, *The Montessori Method* (New York: Schocken Books, 1964; 1st ed., 1912) and *Dr. Montessori's Own Handbook* (New York: Schocken Books, 1965; 1st ed., 1932). For a description and evaluation of the Montessori materials in an early nursery school, see Susan Isaacs, *Intellectual Growth in Young Children* (New York: Schocken Books, 1966; 1st ed.,1932). For a recent description of the teacher role and strategies together with a report on recent research, see Thomas J. Banta, "Montessori, Myth or Reality?" in Ronald K. Parker, ed., *The Preschool in Action: Exploring Early Childhood Programs* (Boston: Allyn and Bacon, 1972), pp. 216–244.

[64] O. K. Moore and A. R. Anderson, "The Responsive Environment Project," in R. D. Hess and R. M. Bear, *Early Education: Current Theory, Research and Practice* (Chicago: Aldine, 1968).

learning from his involvement in them (printed materials such as workbooks are not featured). The teacher not only selects the materials to foster the development of certain skills, concepts, and attitudes, but she also responds to the child's activities with them. She may give hints or prompts in order to guide the child toward his own discoveries.[65]

"Teach Teaching, Not Correcting"[66]

Montessori's materials were designed to be self-correcting. In the case of the boxes of cylinders, for example, there is only one way in which the ten cylinders can be fitted into their proper places. Montessori's lessons, directed, it should be remembered, to the individual child, were also designed to eliminate failure. To teach the child to use the terms "large" and "small" she would at an opportune moment after the child had sucessfully built and rebuilt the pink tower confront him with the extreme cubes, the largest and the smallest. "This is large," she would say, and "This is small." Then after several clear repetitions, "Give me the small one," and finally, "What is this?"[67] Montessori's critics ask whether there may not be other, more imaginative uses for the self-correcting materials. They also ask whether the teaching may not be more a matter of ritual than of understanding. Nevertheless, the aphorism "Teach teaching, not correcting" suggests a strategy appropriate to those situations where the child needs to know a particular answer or to follow a particular direction. It suggests clarity on the teacher's part, not only as to what the child is to learn or do, but also as to the complexity of the task, and how the child is likely to perceive it.

Behavior Modification

Several of the early childhood programs developed in the sixties based their teaching strategies on behavior theory. An example is the Behavior Analysis Model directed by Bushell. The first step in the basic strategy for the program is to "define in precise terms the behavior which a student must be able to display at the completion of each grade level," then to determine the precise skills the student already has, and finally to establish a system of effective reinforcement procedures. Activities that are preferred by the students, such as "free time, attention of the teacher, diet supplements, or opportunity to work with preferred materials," are used as reinforcers. Since such reinforcers are difficult to deliver immediately, a token reinforcement system is established

---

[65] "The Responsive Environment Model," in S. Chow and P. Elmore, *Early Childhood Information Unit* (New York: Educational Products Information Exchange, 1973).

[66] E. M. Standing, *Maria Montessori, Her Life and Work* (New York: Mentor Omega Books, 1962).

[67] *Dr. Montessori's Own Handbook*, p. 125.

whereby the child accumulates tokens (plastic chips) that may be exchanged for opportunity to engage in a preferred activity. [68]

The use of behavioral modification techniques has greatly expanded in the last decade, in both classroom and clinic. [69] Those who espouse their use in the classroom, or by parents, note that teachers and parents have always been behavior shapers. Their responses to the child's behavior determine the direction it takes. With greater awareness of their influence they can change and schedule their responses so that the child's behavior is less disruptive or more focused on particular learning tasks.

Critics of behavior modification strategies acknowledge that they "work." However, they question whether the child necessarily perceives the situation in the way the behavior shaper seems to assume. They assert that the whole situation is more than the sum of its parts. The analysis of the behavior of both child and adults into bits, and the establishment of an apparent relationship between those bits overlooks many of the inherent realities of the situation.

Katz points to some of these when she suggests that teachers "condition with caution." [70] What lies behind the child's behavior that the adult proposes to modify? Is it attributable to his immaturity? Does it represent a means for coping with his anxiety? If so, will the proposed substitute serve the same purpose, or will a new and unforeseen behavior function in that way? Is it a behavior that can be modified by a simple explanation to the child of a behavior that is preferable?

One of the many manuals describing behavior modification techniques quotes on its frontispiece an African proverb, "The best way to eat the elephant standing in your path is to cut him up in little pieces." [71] To which the critics of behavioral analysis may respond, "Okay, but you no longer have an elephant."

Pattern Drill

This strategy, in which the teacher establishes with the children a series of correct responses, somewhat in the manner of the Montessori *teach teaching* strategy described above, has long been used in the teaching of foreign lan-

[68] "The Behavior Analysis Model," in S. Chow and P. Elmore, *Early Childhood Education Information Unit* (New York: Educational Products Information Exchange, 1973).

[69] The National Institute of Mental Health in 1971 published *Behavior Modification in Child and School Mental Health,* an annotated bibliography by Daniel G. Brown (HEW Publication # (HSM 71-9043). Nearly half of the items deal with the use of the techniques by teachers. See also Wesley Becker et al., *Reducing Behavior Problems: An Operant Conditioning Guide for Teachers* (Urbana, Ill.: ERIC/ECE, 1969).

[70] Lilian G. Katz, "Condition with Caution," *Young Children,* 27:277–280, June 1972.

[71] Albert Mehrabian, *Tactics of Social Influence* (Englewood Cliffs, N.J.: Prentice-Hall, 1970).

guages. Bereiter and Engelmann[72] applied it to the teaching of disadvantaged preschoolers. Some of their assumptions regarding the nature of these children's cognitive and language development are open to serious question. However, the teacher who masters the strategy may apply it effectively in situations where much practice of quick responses is in order. When drill of this sort is well-paced and done by an enthusiastic teacher, it may take on the quality of a game for the children.

Landreth comments:

> Such games, in small doses, adapted or spontaneously invented to help a learning process, can be a useful supplement to a child's learning numbers, letters, directions, or other bits of information. Advertising agencies would not set such store by singing commercials if their captive audiences did not learn something from them. But, as an educational curriculum with enforced participation by all children, regardless of their needs or interests, educational games could turn young children off games and gamesy teachers forever.[73]

Questioning

As in pattern drill, the questions the teacher asks in any area of the curriculum determine the kinds of thinking to be elicited. The match between the kinds of questions asked and the level of the child's thinking is important.

With the younger children especially, the teacher's questions may be needed to focus and extend the children's observation. Curiosity and an urge to investigate are supported by the teacher's queries: "Does the rabbit have a tail?" "Which bell makes the louder noise, the little one or the big one?" Asking children is often a better strategy than telling them![74]

Some teachers are so intent on imparting information to children that they forget to assess the ways it may be assimilated. Thus, answers to open-ended questions—"Can you tell me about . . . ?" "What do you think about . . . ?"—are often more revealing than answers to questions with a more specific focus. They can be followed by "Tell me more," "How do you explain that?" "Some people think that . . . " "What do you think?" Learning to ask questions that do not provide children with clues for the expected answer takes both verbal and facial control. Children learn early to watch for the teacher's

---

[72] Carl Bereiter and Siegfried Engelmann, *Teaching Disadvantaged Children in the Preschool* (Englewood Cliffs, N.J.: Prentice-Hall, 1966).

[73] Catherine Landreth, *Preschool Learning and Teaching* (New York: Harper & Row, 1972), p. 185.

[74] A basic reference on questions is N. M. Sanders, *Classroom Questions, What Kinds?* (New York: Harper & Row, 1966). E. Paul Torrance and R. E. Myers, *Creative Learning and Teaching* (New York: Dodd, Mead, 1972), has two chapters on questioning that include some illustrations with younger children. Helen Collantes Mills and Ralph Anslee Mills, *Designing Instructional Strategies for Young Children* (Dubuque, Iowa: Wm. C. Brown, 1972), has a section of readings on questions.

expression of approval or disapproval in response to their first comment. They shape the remainder of their response accordingly.

Piaget's clinical methods of questioning children have been adapted for use in several early childhood programs.[75] Practice in conducting Piagetian interviews with children is one way that teachers can gain confidence and skill in questioning techniques. The insights the teacher gains into the ways the children think, and her ability to apply these insights in all areas of the curriculum, have value over and above the particular experiments she does with the children.

Tutorial Approach

The one-to-one relationship of the interview takes on new dimensions in the tutorial approach developed by Blank.[76] According to her analysis, preschool children from poverty areas, in contrast to their middle-class peers, often lack the "ability to assume a definite mental set, to shift reflectively from one aspect of a situation to another, to voluntarily evoke previous experiences, and to keep in mind various aspects of a task." This analysis accords in some respects with that made by other investigators.[77] Blank believes that the problem arises when the child has insufficient opportunity for dialogue with adults whose responses to him tend to correct the egocentric aspects of his speech.

Blank developed a program in which children are tutored individually. Within the sustained and intimate relationship developed with the child, the tutor engages him in tasks about which he can be questioned in ways calculated to focus and shift his attention appropriately and selectively. In her book *Teaching Learning in the Preschool,* Blank analyzes the dialogue between teacher and child, showing how tasks (often derived from activities encountered in the nursery school) can be posed, how both correct and incorrect responses can be handled, and demonstrates the ways the child grows in competence as the tutoring progresses.

This strategy is complex, and mastery requires much practice and analysis. Critics maintain that it may be less appropriate for preschool than for older children. They also emphasize that the child does not lack the necessary abilities; they believe the apparent limitations in the child's functioning are tied

---

[75] For example, Constance Kamii, "An Application of Piaget's Theory to the Conceptualization of a Preschool Curriculum," in Ronald Parker, ed., *The Preschool in Action,* pp. 36–58; and Celia Stendler Lavatelli, *Piaget's Theory Applied to an Early Childhood Curriculum* (Boston: American Science and Engineering, Inc., 1970).

[76] Marion Blank, *Teaching Learning in the Preschool: A Dialogue Approach* (Columbus, Ohio: Charles Merrill, 1973), p. 10.

[77] See, for example, I. E. Sigel et al., "Categorization of Behavior of Lower and Middle Class Negro Preschool Children: Differences in Dealing with Representation of Familiar Objects," *Journal of Negro Education,* 35:218–219, 1966.

to the unfamiliar cultural setting. For example, Gleason[78] reports on a study in which preschool children from backgrounds similar to those of the children Blank taught learned in a few hours of training to give effectively organized and nonegocentric responses in communication games. She does not think that the children were taught a new language. Rather, they had a variety of descriptive styles available and the training sessions facilitated that style.

Facilitation is also the aim of Blank's strategy. There seems to be little question that the teacher who has command of the strategy will approach her instructional role in the classroom with new insight and greater skill.

Discovery

Discovery, more than instruction, is what early childhood education is about, say those who see the teacher's role primarily as that of facilitator. From that point of view, preparation of the responsive environment and certain questioning strategies are involved in teaching for discovery. Others note that when the world is new, as it is to young children, discovery is indeed the order of the day. But if discovery is to be more than trivial, it needs to be tied in some way to the knowledge that other people possess. Thus, for example, in the Science Curriculum Improvement Study, *invention* parallels *discovery.*[79] The children explore and experiment independently with a variety of materials and objects. Then the teacher provides, through demonstration and discussion, an *invention,* a concept such as interaction, for which the child, returning to his exploration, can *discover* a variety of examples.

Supporting and Extending Children's Play

Many nursery school and kindergarten teachers, while acknowledging the maxim "They learn through their play," take what can only be described as a "hands off" attitude toward it. This attitude was challenged when observers began to study the play of children living in poverty. They noted that in their spontaneous play, at least in the school or center, these children did not develop the variety of roles and plots that appeared in the play of their middle-class peers.

In Israel, Smilansky[80] developed a strategy for extending and improving

---

[78] Jean B. Gleason, "An Experimental Approach to Improving Children's Communicative Ability," in Courtney B. Cazden, ed., *Language in Early Childhood Education* (Washington: National Association for the Education of Young Children, 1972), pp. 101–106. This volume contains many practical suggestions for working with young children, as well as an analysis of some of the issues involved in the teaching of language. For a more detailed analysis, see Courtney B. Cazden, *Child Language and Education* (New York: Holt, Rinehart and Winston, 1972).

[79] Robert Karplus and Herbert D. Thier, *A New Look at Elementary School Science* (Chicago: Rand McNally, 1967).

[80] Sara Smilansky, *The Effects of Sociodramatic Play on Disadvantaged Preschool Children* (New York:

the quality of the sociodramatic play of kindergarten children. This strategy had three major elements. The first of these was an assessment of the individual child's play. Factors considered in the assessment included the child's apparent understanding of make-believe roles, his use of make-believe with objects, his verbal description of the actions and situations, his persistence in the role, and his interaction with the other players. The second step was to provide an experience for the group, such as a visit to a health clinic, from which play themes could be expected to emerge. Finally, the teacher, assuming an appropriate role, intervened in the play of those children whose assessment had suggested a need to develop or extend the make-believe play.

In this country, similar strategies were incorporated into the Piagetian curriculum developed by Kamii.[81] Project CHILD, under the direction of Robison,[82] also incorporated sociodramatic play in its curriculum, but apparently with less emphasis on teacher intervention. More recently, several experimental studies dealing with various aspects of children's play have emphasized the importance of supporting and extending the child's make-believe play.[83]

Children Teach Children

Piaget's emphasis on the role of the child's collaboration with other children in the development of his intelligence adds support to current concerns for informality and openness in early education. The fact that children can effectively teach other children with gains on both sides has been demonstrated many times.[84]

Profitable interchanges among children do not happen simply because they share the same classroom. Rather, teachers plan time schedules, organize space, assign tasks, discuss the matter of living together in ways that help children to relate to one another. Classes with mixed ages have a built-in opportunity for older children to teach younger children. Even in classes where children are approximately the same age, a wide range of activities provides many possibilities for children to learn from one another.

Older children, participating in a class of younger children, can fill many needed roles. They may, for example, read to them individually or in groups, listen to them read, help out on trips, or supervise the workbench. In so doing, they gain in both skills and poise.

John Wiley & Sons, 1968).

[81] Constance Kamii, "An Application of Piaget's Theory to the Conceptualization of a Preschool Curriculum," in Parker, ed., *The Preschool in Action.*

[82] Helen F. Robison, "Rationale for the CHILD Curriculum," in Parker, ed., *The Preschool in Action.*

[83] Jerome L. Singer, *The Child's World of Make-Believe, Experimental Studies of Imaginative Play* (New York: Academic Press, 1973).

[84] Alan Gartner et al., *Children Teach Children: Learning by Teaching* (New York: Harper & Row, 1971).

Discipline

Any consideration of teaching strategies must include some attention to the perennial problem of discipline. The involvement of individual children in activities that they find challenging and satisfying obviates many discipline problems. In those work and play situations where children can interact freely with one another, one sees the beginning of the collaboration that Piaget values for its contribution to the development of intelligence. But the interchange is sometimes charged more with affect than with intellect. The teacher must often draw a fine line between the give-and-take of children relating to one another constructively, if not always peacefully, and the chaos that signals the loss of control.

The understanding of individual children, the setting of rational limits that are made explicit at the child's level of understanding, firm and consistent intervention when a child goes beyond the limits—all these contribute to the kind of discipline that helps children to develop their own inner controls. In addition, teachers need a firm grasp of the dynamics involved in groups, even when group members are only three- or four-year-olds. This involves knowing the relationships among the children as a group—who are the leaders, who are the followers, who sets off whom, and how these relationships are changing over time.[85] Teachers also need skill in preventive tactics including the organization of space and materials to avoid unnecessary confrontations and the planning of a schedule that enables children to invest their energies appropriately.

Teaching Strategies and Development

The inclusion of teaching strategies derived from different theories is deliberate. The long-term view of development sometimes requires short-term use of such strategies as behavior modification or pattern drill. Some youngsters need to savor a considerable amount of success before they can begin to develop a broader, self-regulated competence.

Unfortunately, the relationships between development and instruction have received little investigation. There are, however, some promising beginnings.

In Geneva, Piaget's colleagues, Inhelder, Bovet, and Sinclair, have conducted a number of experiments to determine whether providing the child with

---

[85] For a classic reference related to the dynamics of groups, see Fritz Redl and David Wineman, *Controls from Within* (Glencoe: The Free Press, 1952). Although this describes a residential treatment center for highly aggressive nine- and ten-year-old boys, the strategies and tactics the staff used with them provide valuable information for the teacher of younger children.

Hermine H. Marshall, *Positive Discipline and Classroom Interaction* (Springfield, Ill.: Charles C Thomas, 1972), puts discipline in the context of learning and development.

certain kinds of information would change his reasoning in some of the typical Piagetian experiments. Sinclair notes, "Learning is dependent on development, not only in the sense that certain things can be learned only at certain levels of development, but also in the sense that in learning—that is, in situations specifically constructed so that the subject has active encounters with environment—the same mechanisms as in development are at work to make for progress, and, if there is progress the same structures result."[86]

Sinclair and her colleagues did not attempt to devise strategies to teach the concepts they investigated. However, the kinds of training they gave the children and their analysis of the changes in the children's thinking as the training sessions progressed provide useful insights for those who are concerned with instructional strategies.

Another series of studies that illuminates the role of instruction in the child's development is reported by Olson.[87] Olson's work constitutes an excellent illustration of the careful systematic research needed to illuminate the child's acquisition of a single concept—in this case, that of the diagonal. Given a "checkerboard" on which the checkers of one color have been used to construct a diagonal across the board, what is involved when the child is asked, with the original board no longer visible, to construct a similar diagonal on another checkerboard? This is a task in which all six-year-olds in a socioeconomically varied sample succeed. But only 28.5 percent of three-year-olds, 37.5 percent of four-year-olds, and 77.5 percent of five-year-olds can do the task. It is, accordingly, a good task with which to examine a variety of developmental problems, and also to consider how instruction may affect the acquisition of the concept.

Olson examined three instructional strategies, using two of them in experimental studies. The first was an educational toy, designed to direct the child's activity in copying patterns, including the diagonal. The second, and more powerful, strategy involved giving the children verbal clues as to how to differentiate nondiagonal from diagonal—"The criss-cross starts at a corner and goes straight across the middle to the other corner." The third strategy, used by a Montessori teacher, was a nonverbal demonstration of the wrong moves and correct moves in constructing the diagonal. Olson's analysis of his results in these and other experiments clarifies the roles of both language and action in the construction of knowledge. It deserves careful reading by all who are concerned with instruction for development.

Promising work relating to instruction also stems from the formulations

[86] Hermina Sinclair, "Recent Piagetian Research in Learning Studies," in Milton Schwebel and Jane Raph, eds., *Piaget in the Classroom* (New York: Basic Books, 1973), p. 58.

[87] David R. Olson, *Cognitive Development: The Child's Acquisition of Diagonality* (New York: Academic Press, 1970).

of Pascual-Leone,[88] a student of Piaget. Pascual-Leone has analyzed the kinds and numbers of schemes (operational activities, or sets of reactions) that are involved in solutions of the tasks that Piaget has studied. The number of schemes that children appear to coordinate as they try to solve a task correlates with age. Pascual-Leone refers to the increasing capacity to coordinate more schemes as an increase in "mental space." Using Pascual-Leone's model, Case has designed instructional strategies that enable children with a given mental space to handle problems that, under ordinary circumstances, demand more than the mental space available at their age. As Case notes, Pascual-Leone's formulation involves both learning and developmental perspectives.[89] Accordingly, it may serve as a conceptual bridge between learning and developmental theorists, and ultimately provide much-needed information on the relationships between instruction and development.

The Question of the Match

J. McV. Hunt, in the early 1960s when the work of Piaget was just beginning to come to the attention of educators, formulated what he called the principle of the "match." As he put it, "At each age level the environmental circumstances must supply encounters for the child which permit him to use the repertoire of schemata that he has already developed and which force him to accommodate them if the rate of development and motivational interest are to be maintained."[90] He recognized this as a more precise formulation of the educator's adage that "teaching must start where the learner is."[91]

The experience of the past decade has not demonstrated that governing the child's encounters with his environment accelerates development of his intelligence, but it has underlined the many ways children differ and the variety of ways they may be taught.

The essential problem now is to provide as appropriate matches as possible between the individuality of the children and the teaching strategies used with them. The goal, to repeat, is not the acceleration of development; rather it is as much realization as possible of the child's potential at each succeeding level of development.

The complexities of modern living and the frailties of human nature being what they are, such a goal may prove to be illusory, but I think that we cannot, in good conscience, aspire to less. The burden of realization, of course, rests

[88] J. Pascual-Leone, "A Mathematical Model for the Transition Rule in Piaget's Developmental Stages," *Acta Psychologica*, 32:301–334, 1970.

[89] R. Case, "Learning and Development: A Neo-Piagetian Interpretation," *Human Development*, 15:339–358, 1972.

[90] J. McV. Hunt, *Intelligence and Experience*, Copyright © 1961 (New York: The Ronald Press Co.).

[91] Hunt, p. 268.

not alone with the teacher, but also with the other adults who are influential in the lives of children. One of these adults is the early childhood educator, part of whose role is to support the efforts of the teacher. In the conception of early childhood education presented here, the teacher (and the early childhood educator) never cease developing. For them, as for the child, learning is a continuous process.

Chapter 7

Provisioning for Development and Learning

"How-to-do-it" manuals have no faith in us, therefore we can have no faith in them. They are unconvincing because they concentrate on a sterile process and do not venture into the complex and subtle area of human relevance which must be the first reason for any process. Human relevance is the single issue which unites us, the children, the teachers, the parents and the professional specialists. We have to dedicate ourselves to the simple idea that we all count. We count because it is only with each other that we can grow. Our reciprocating ideas and actions have to be encouraged. [1]

This chapter deals with the way the role of the early childhood educator builds upon and extends the stage-setting and facilitating function of the teacher. It looks at the kinds of environments that are needed for the care and education of young children and goes beyond the classroom to consider the variety of services that are needed to support their development. It describes briefly some of the administrative functions the early childhood educator may have. These

---

[1] Peter Prangnell, "The Friendly Object," *Harvard Educational Review,* 39(4):40, 1969.

functions, although often remote from the program as the children experience it, are nevertheless essential to its operation.

Although certain kinds of provisions must be made for all programs whatever their setting, others vary. All programs must be administered, but each kind of program has its own special requirements. Programs involving infants cannot be equipped in the same way as those for older children. Home-based programs use already-available space, but that does not lessen concern for the effective use of that space, nor for the availability of certain kinds of equipment and materials. Already-established programs operate under constraints that differ from those affecting programs that are in the process of planning. Programs using public funds differ from those that are established independently, but all are, to some degree, restricted by finances and by regulatory codes.

THE PREPARED AND EXTENDIBLE ENVIRONMENT

Montessori, according to Standing, saw the "prepared environment" for children age two-and-a-half to six or seven years as an "enclosed space," a place specially created for the purpose of assisting development. But Montessori recognized that the time would come when the child would begin to look toward the larger world, no longer fully satisfied with his special environment.[2] Today, the environment for early childhood education is not so tightly limited to the confines of the school or center—children explore the neighborhood and beyond—but Montessori's principle of preparation still holds. Since Montessori, not only educators but psychologists, anthropologists, sociologists, and architects have studied the ways the environment may affect the behavior of children.

Moore and Anderson, drawing on sociological theory, propose four principles that should guide the design of an environment within which "even very young children can acquire complex symbolic skills with ease." The first principle states that "one environment is more conducive to learning than another if it permits and facilitates the taking of more perspectives toward whatever is to be learned."[3] Thus, an environment might provide opportunity for the child to function as explorer and investigator, and to be active in creating his own effects, as well as some situations in which he would take a more passive role. There should also be opportunities for the child to engage

[2] E. M. Standing, *Montessori, Her Life and Work* (New York: New America Library of World Literature, 1962), p. 279.

[3] Omar Khayyam Moore and Alan Ross Anderson, "Some Principles for the Design of Clarifying Educational Environments," in David Goslin, ed., *Handbook of Socialization Theory and Research* (Chicago: Rand McNally, 1969), pp. 571–613, quotes on p. 571 and p. 585.

in reciprocal relationships where he must assume the viewpoint of another person. Another perspective is that involved in assessment, evaluating, and judging. Moore and Anderson term it the "referee" perspective. It occurs when an individual considers the totality of a situation such as a game, taking into consideration the probable viewpoints of all participants in the interaction.

A second principle is that an environment is more conducive to learning when it is autotelic. Such an environment provides activities that are inherently rewarding and noncompetitive.

A third principle is identified as the productive principle. Of two learning activities, the more productive one is that which permits the learner to deduce things about it, or to make probable inferences.

The fourth principle states that the learning environment that is more conducive to learning is more responsive to the learner's activities, and is so structured that the individual can learn about himself as a learner.

Early childhood educators may question whether most three- and four-year-olds will often be able to take the perspective of the other person, let alone the referee perspective. They would suggest that principles taking into account the developmental levels of the children, and the nature of their previous experience, should also guide the planning of the children's environment.[4] These questions and reservations do not invalidate the principles. The planners of environments for even the youngest children can ask what their effect will be. Will the environment perpetuate the single perspective of passive learning, or will it enhance both the child's activity and his growing ability to view the world and himself from a variety of perspectives?

The question of the ways different aspects of the environment affect children's development and learning receives ever-increasing attention from psychologists. Craik, reviewing the broad field of environmental psychology, notes that "a broad, thin, but rapidly expanding layer of empirical research underlies current knowledge in environmental psychology."[5] Drew, looking at research on the effects of the physical environment on psychological behavior, pleads for a more systematic examination of the full range of parameters of the physical environment.[6] Neither reviewer offers the early childhood educator any specific guidelines, but both cite research that may have eventual, if not immediate, significance for her.

---

[4] Elizabeth S. Hirsch, "What Are Good Responsive Environments for Young Children?" *Young Children,* 28(2):75–80, December 1972.

[5] Kenneth H. Craik, "Environmental Psychology," in Paul H. Mussen and Mark R. Rosenzweig, eds., *Annual Review of Psychology,* vol. 24 (Palo Alto: Annual Reviews, Inc., 1973), pp. 403–422.

[6] Clifford J. Drew, "Research on the Psychological-Behavioral Effects of the Physical Environment," *Review of Educational Research,* 41(5):447–465, December 1971.

Space

Without space, whether relatively permanent as in the case of the school or center, or borrowed, or "mobile," as in home-based programs, it is difficult to conceive a program for young children. Furthermore, as Kritchevsky demonstrates, the organization of space affects the behavior of both children and the teachers. It would seem, then, that concern for the arrangement of space would be a major feature of the preparation of the environment. However, in her study of fifty child care centers, Kritchevsky[7] found little awareness of either the way space influences behavior or the way space itself is influenced by other factors. One such factor is the size of the center. Medium-size centers had the highest quality space. Another factor is the center's sponsorship. Public centers had more interesting and less-crowded space than did proprietary centers. A third factor is the socioeconomic level of the families served. Space was better used in centers where the parents belonged to a higher socioeconomic group.

Assuming that the centers Kritchevsky studied were not atypical (informal observation suggests that the space problems she observed can be readily matched in schools and centers in many parts of the country), the early childhood educator will find much that needs to be done about space. Perhaps the major part of her efforts will go into the arrangmement of equipment and furniture. Usually, she will find herself confronting space that is already fixed by walls and fences. She may, however, also be involved in planning a new building. An opportunity to discuss the planning of space with architects can open new vistas for her.[8]

Hall, an anthropologist, says, "Space speaks."[9] For the early childhood educator the questions are: What do we want this space to say? How can we arrange it so that an appropriate message gets through to our clients? The way the space is organized can reflect the program goals or in various ways negate them. Thus, a first step to space arrangements is clarity about goals, not only in general but with reference to specific aspects of the program. A second step is to find ways of looking at space from the viewpoint of the individuals who will be using it.

The latter step requires consciousness of the aspects of space to which people of varying cultures and varying ages may respond differently. Hall notes that "space is organized differently in each culture. The associations and

[7] Sybil Kritchevsky, "Physical Settings in Day Care Centers: Teachers, Program and Space," in Elizabeth Prescott and Elizabeth Jones, *Day Care as a Child Rearing Environment* (Washington: National Association for the Education of Young Children, 1972).

[8] See, for example, Fred Linn Osman, *Patterns for Designing Children's Centers* (New York: Educational Facilities Laboratories, 1971).

[9] Edward T. Hall, *The Silent Language* (New York: Fawcett World Library, 1968), p. 146.

feelings that are released in one culture almost invariably are something else in the next."[10]

Space for Adults Osman's *Patterns for Designing Children's Centers* suggests the variety of questions that need to be asked if space is to serve the center and its clients effectively. As far as the parents are concerned, some of these questions are: Does the center entrance welcome the parent? Does it provide an easy transition for the child, thus facilitating the parent's arrival and departure? Does the space within the center invite the parent to stay awhile, to observe the children, to participate in various ways? Space arrangements play a large part in determining whether or not parental roles in the school or center are enacted in line with its goals.

Much the same kinds of questions need to be asked with regard to home-based programs. The home visitor must sense the organization of the space as used by the family and consider how she can introduce materials and activities without infringing on it.[11]

In the school or center, the organization of exterior space speaks directly to the community. Does it permit community members to have a glimpse of what goes on, or is it walled off? The reality of vandalism cannot be ignored. However, Osman's experience suggests that an acknowledgment of the presence of community members, and provision for them to look on from the periphery, would be less likely to result in destruction than a more closed approach.[12]

What does space say to the staff? Is there a place for them to have moments of relaxation? For them to plan together? To meet with parents in a comfortable setting? Many long day programs owe the relative serenity of their staff to the existence of a quiet spot where the teachers may have a cup of coffee and "put their feet up" for awhile.

Space for Children Space may speak appropriately to the adults and not be well adapted to the children. A realm for children must be created in such a way that the teacher's realm, although functional for her, also complements

---

[10] Hall, p. 149.

[11] The widespread assumption that the homes of the poor are necessarily disorganized is likely erroneous. In retrospect, I think that some of the differences I observed in visiting home-based programs may be attributed to the home visitor's sensitivity to space and its significance to the parents. One visitor seated herself and laid out her materials with no evident regard for the probable play space of the infant in the family, nor did she consider where the mother might sit. The lesson with the older child went on amid constant interruptions. In another observation the comments of a different home visitor and another mother indicated that space arrangements had received mutual consideration. The baby was settled with a string of spools, outside the half-circle created by mother and visitor's chairs turned toward the older child and his materials. In this case the lesson proceeded smoothly and without interruption.

[12] Osman, pp. 24–25.

the children's realm. The teacher needs to be able to see the child's activities in order to supervise him, but the vertical dimensions of the space should deemphasize her presence, just as the horizontal arrangements should keep her off the circulation paths used by the children.[13]

To plan space adequately for children requires knowledge of the child's perspective. Werner notes that "space is originally one aspect of the child's consciousness of his body."[14] As he grows, the infant's space is bounded by what he can reach and touch. "Space continually expands into more and more distant regions" but "the space of the child remains closely bound up with the ego for a long time."[15] The child's response to spatial arrangements changes with age, dependent on what he can do. Werner cites an early study of a city area involving, for the adult, a street, a path sloping down, and a landing place. The area next to the street is fenced. For the child, the fence beckons to be climbed and the slope invites running. The functional meaning of the setting depends on the age of the child. For the two-to-three-year-old, it provides an opportunity for independence—to escape briefly from the attention of the adult. Older children see the same setting as a challenge to their gymnastic abilities.[16]

Coles reports an elementary school child's perspective on the school building: "The corridors they're just too long and you should have a car to travel from one part of the bulding to the next." Her brother, old enough to be in high school, comments, "The windows, no one ever looks in them or out of them." He describes the bathrooms as "a mile away" and big—"you can get lost in it and by the time you get back you've missed everything they are talking about."[17] Younger children do not often comment so explicitly on their environment, but their behavior usually reveals when they find the space overwhelming or overcrowded.

Information about children's reactions to various space arrangements and to other aspects of their environment is only beginning to accumulate. Accordingly, the early childhood educator will likely find that many decisions regarding the environment are best made tentatively, subject to testing with the group of children for whom the plans are made.

In dealing with the question of how a particular space arrangement affects the behavior of the children, it is clear that not space alone, but other factors as well are influential. These include the kinds of objects in the space, the

[13] Osman, pp. 19–21.

[14] Heinz Werner, *Comparative Psychology of Mental Development* (New York: International Universities Press, 1957), p. 172.

[15] Werner, p. 173.

[16] Werner, pp. 387–388.

[17] Robert Coles, "Those Places They Call Schools," *Harvard Educational Review,* 39(4):46–57, 1969.

number of children, and the kind of adult control. To appraise this influence, the approach that has been used by Barker [18] and Wright [19] in studying the ecology of human behavior is useful. Shure, following this method, investigated the different patterns of behavior associated with five indoor areas (art, books, dolls, games, blocks) in a nursery school. [20] Children spent most time in the block and art areas, least with books. Although materials were used constructively in all areas, the most constructive use occurred in the art and book areas, the least in the block area. The block area, which was the largest, attracted the most children and served as the center for much social interaction, although the children did not necessarily use the materials that were available there.

This finding raises what has been called the question of "critical density." [21] What is the appropriate amount of space for a given number of children to provide for security and constructiveness? (In a study of preschool children McGrew found that social density—the number of persons available for interaction—had more consequences on behavior than spatial density.) [22] Related to the question of density is the question of location. For example, how can space be arranged for young children so that it does not isolate them from the life of other groups and from exploration beyond its boundaries?

Other questions have to do with the sense of place, the awareness of landmarks, and the identity of a particular setting. How much stability in these does the young child need? Can the large, completely open space such as that found in the "pod" school serving as many as ninety children provide the child with sufficient sense of place? Is it the case that in such a setting the child sees the various activity areas as a cluster? Does he anchor himself to the total cluster, or to a particular area? Does the teacher herself serve to orient the child, or do some children simply follow others? [23]

These questions should be pursued. Current trends toward open classrooms, team teaching, and the enrollment of children younger than five may combine to bring younger and younger children into very complex space and

---

[18] Roger C. Barker, *Ecological Psychology* (Stanford: Stanford University Press, 1968).

[19] Herbert F. Wright, *Recording and Analyzing Child Behavior* (New York: Harper & Row, 1967).

[20] Myrna Beth Shure, "Psychological Ecology of a Nursery School," *Child Development,* 34(4):979–992, December 1963.

[21] Osman, p. 16.

[22] W. C. McGrew, "Interpersonal Spacing of Preschool Children," cited by Kenneth Craik, "Environmental Psychology," in Mussen and Rosenzweig, eds., *Annual Review of Psychology* (Palo Alto: Annual Reviews, Inc., 1973).

[23] Edward A. Chittenden, "The Territorial Imperative," in Charles E. Silberman, *The Open Classroom Reader* (New York: Vintage Books, 1973), notes that the British Primary Schools find most satisfactory a three-walled classroom that is open to interaction with other groups or has a movable partition on the fourth side. He also notes that few of the English schools enroll more than 350 children, although class size may run to 40.

time arrangments. The problem, as Prangnell observes,[24] may lie less in the size of the space or the variety of learning centers than in the lack of opportunity for the child to explore and become familiar with them at his own pace.

Neither size nor complexity need be overwhelming if the environment provides the child some opportunities to pause, to withdraw from the ongoing activity of the group, to become a watcher or a dreamer. Such opportunity is crucially important for the child who spends a long day in a group setting. Some architects are sensitive to this need and some teachers create comfortable nooks for children, but the observer in too many schools and centers can see no place where a child can withdraw.

For young children outdoor space is no less important than indoor space and may provide as many, or more, occasions for learning. Ideally, the outdoor space adjoins the classroom and the children move easily from one area to the other. The outdoors extends the indoors and, in addition, offers opportunities for running, climbing, digging, building, collecting, gardening, and a variety of imaginative adventures.[25]

Materials and Equipment

With almost no exceptions,[26] those who are interested in the care and education of young children agree that certain materials and equipment are essential for their work and play. None would quarrel with the principle that the selection of such equipment and materials should be guided by the goals of the program, but an ever-increasing variety of equipment and materials makes selection no easy task.

The 1972 survey of early childhood education materials conducted by Educational Products Information Exchange (EPIE) located 42 producers and distributors of instructional materials assembled in kits. They found 92 such kits ranging in price from three to 500 dollars. They also identified more than 50 catalogs describing other materials that would be appropriate for use in early childhood education.[27] A 1970 EPIE survey of playground equipment listed nearly 40 "innovative" pieces and over 45 producers of "traditional equipment."[28]

---

[24] Prangnell, *The Friendly Object.*
[25] Two volumes that are helpful in planning for outdoor space are Lady Allen of Hurtwood, *Planning for Play* (London: Thames & Hudson, 1968), and Jeannette G. Stone and Nancy Rudolph, *Play and Playgrounds* (Wasington: National Association for the Education of Young Children, 1970).
[26] The Bereiter and Engelmann program, as originally introduced (Carl Bereiter and Siegfried Engelmann, *Teaching Disadvantaged Children in the Preschool,* Englewood Cliffs, N.J.: Prentice-Hall, 1966), required very little in the way of either materials or equipment.
[27] Educational Product Report No. 42, *Early Childhood Education: How to Select and Evaluate Materials* (New York: EPIE, 1972).
[28] Educational Product Report, *Playground Equipment* (New York: EPIE, May-June 1970), vol. 3, nos. 8 and 9.

In her role as provisioner of materials and equipment, the early childhood educator makes, or helps teachers and, in some instances, parents make, innumerable decisions. The EPIE report suggests that such decisions should be guided by an analysis of the views of human development espoused by those planning the program, together with their preferences about type of program and consideration of available local resources. In the light of the values revealed in the analysis, the possibilities for equipment and materials can be examined and choices made.

The discussion that follows examines some of the values that may guide the selection of equipment and materials. It considers equipment, the semi-fixed and more permanent features of the environment first, and then turns to instructional materials. In considering materials, we look upon values as polarities, although it is unlikely that any program would choose either of the extremes for all kinds of materials.

Equipment   Time was when any observer in a first grade classroom could predict in advance of opening the door the rows of seats and desks, the teacher's desk and chair, the chalkboard and reading charts. Nowadays the equipment has changed and so has its arrangement. Movable tables and chairs replace the fixed desks and seats (in many classrooms they are seldom moved, however). The teacher's desk no longer fronts the room. Depending on the affluence of the school, or the ingenuity of the teacher, there is much more equipment and an abundance of materials.

Despite these changes, in only a few classrooms will the knowledgeable observer fail to make a moderately accurate prediction of the classroom's major contents. The variety of equipment that goes into classrooms these days is quite standard, varying little from California to Colorado to Connecticut.

Nor is the situation very different in programs for young children, whether they be in schools or in child care centers. Now and then a not-very-affluent group of parents and teachers will see the floor as the fundamental equipment it is, and save the money they might spend on chairs and tables for books and art materials. Sturdy trees may serve the place of the ubiquitous jungle gym.

The point is not that small children should not have chairs or climbers. Rather, it seems that too often equipment is purchased because it appears on some list of requirements. Too seldom does anyone think about how each piece of equipment will be used, or consider whether something else could serve the same function as well or better. The availability of so much equipment, so many catalogs, so many kinds of tables and chairs, so many versions of the jungle gym, such a variety of arrangements for water and sand play and for the use of clay and paint—all this makes it seem that the major equipment questions are those of choice among pieces that serve the same function.

A more important prior question asks, "Are the activities this equipment makes possible the activities we want in this classroom?" If this question were asked more searchingly and more often, there would be fewer instances of rather expensive equipment receiving little use in a particular classroom.

Those who choose equipment for programs need to understand not only the goals of the program and how the use of a contemplated piece of equipment will serve a particular goal, but also whether it may serve additional goals. How will it respond to the explorations of the children? As Prangnell puts it, "Flexibility can be gained when each object has not only its obvious function but also a certain ambiguity, so that, in different circumstances it can be used in a variety of different ways."[29]

This principle cannot be applied indefinitely. Phonographs and tape recorders, for example, are extremely useful pieces of equipment—the materials they can bring to or elicit from children are infinitely varied—but each has its own function and does not readily serve others. They are essential to the technology that will be considered in a later section of the chapter.

Instructional Materials Like the equipment with which they may be used, instructional materials should serve the goals of the program. To determine the extent to which a particular material has the desired function, certain questions may be raised.

1 *Direct or vicarious experience?* Children can be taught and do learn in the course of their own direct experience with the animate and inanimate world. As they participate in that world they encounter it directly. They also encounter representations of it, as they themselves imitate, and remember, and as they listen to others and watch them express themselves. They are, in addition, surrounded by signs and other printed material so that they begin early to observe symbols.

The child's direct experience is limited in time and space. To extend it, and also to highlight and organize it, educators, book publishers, and manufacturers have collaborated, making available toys, models, replicas, pictures, maps, films, records, tapes, books, and workbooks. All these provide vicarious experience.

The EPIE report on materials shows how the experience the child has with various kinds of instructional materials may be scaled according to its directness.[30]

A Scale of Experience Referents for Instructional Materials

Direct Experience

---

[29] Prangnell, *The Friendly Object,* pp. 39–40.
[30] EPIE Report No. 42, p. 44.

with objects, people, events, processes, qualities, and patterns of relationships:

- Children can operate on, manipulate, these things directly.
- Children can watch while someone else manipulates these things.
- Children operate on, manipulate representations of phenomena which they have previously experienced directly.
- Children watch someone else manipulate objects representing their own direct experience, or analogous experiences.

Vicarious Experience
with objects, materials representing phenomena the children have never experienced directly:

- Children manipulate these materials directly.
- Children observe while someone else manipulates these materials.
- Children manipulate verbal representations.
- Children listen to someone else manipulate verbal representations.

In the "traditional" nursery school most of the materials provided direct experience. Books and stories offered vicarious experience but they were frequently selected for the parallels they provided to the children's direct experience.

In contrast, the elementary school traditionally has leaned more on vicarious than direct experiences. In many cases the textbooks and other materials provided represented phenomena that middle-class children had experienced directly. This was often not the case where poor children were concerned.

It is difficult to appraise where schools now stand with regard to the mixture of direct and vicarious experience. As a result of the emphasis on cognitive development in the 1960s, many preschools began to use more materials that were representational rather than natural. Many curricula focused on the properties of color, form, and size, and these, it seems, were as often represented in pictures as in objects. In the elementary schools, the innovative science curricula emphasized direct experience, but many schools use science textbooks more as readers than as a departure for experimentation. The influence of the British Primary School may be to restore direct experience to the preschool and to encourage it in the elementary school. In any event, the early childhood educator will want to consider the question of the kind of experience the children will have in the programs for which she has responsibility.

2　*Self-directed or programmed?* Are the materials to be such that the child is expected to "mess about" and make his own discoveries? Or are they to take him through a series of steps designed to ensure the "correct" discovery?

The proponents of open education, and those of Piagetian persuasion, generally opt for leaving control of the material with the learner, but others raise some important questions.

Resnick points out that learning is likely to take longer under learner control than when the materials are programmed for use in specified ways.[31] The child may explore a number of false avenues, cannot sequence the material for himself, nor diagnose his moment-to-moment successes and difficulties. Accordingly, to ensure the learning of specific content objectives before the learner's interest and the instructor's resources run out, learner control may sometimes have to be abandoned.

Resnick further suggests that the decision to abandon learner control should depend on the "generativity" of the content toward which instruction is directed. Is the skill or knowledge crucial to the learner's ability to control his environment and to continue to learn? "Is the short-term loss of self-controlled activity worth the long-term gain in self-control that can be realized through temporary engagement in efficient externally directed instruction?"[32]

Many programs have to face and decide this question. If the goal of the program is the facilitation of development, the long-term view will prevail. But the decision will include reckoning of the efficiency of the proposed externally directed instruction in terms of knowledge of the individual child for whom it is proposed. Nor should it overlook the fact that certain kinds of learning are more easily acquired through direct instruction. The open educator's concern with externally directed instruction is not necessarily that it should be eliminated but rather that it should not dominate the child's school experience as it so often does.

Resnick raises her question in the larger context of the place of technology in an open society. She indicates her belief that the open society requires an educational technology that is "highly efficient when necessary and yet finely responsive to the interests, current abilities and stylistic preferences of the individual."[33]

Although current technology may be evolving in the direction Resnick describes,[34] at present it seems better adapted to the learning rate of the child than to his learning style or interests. For the present, it is the teacher primarily who responds to the individual. As Resnick observes, little empirical research is available to testify either to the ability of the child, left on his own, to find

[31] Lauren Resnick, "Open Education: Some Tasks for Technology," *Educational Technology*, 22:70–76, January 1972.
[32] Resnick, p. 74.
[33] Resnick, p. 76.
[34] The question of technology in early childhood education receives further consideration in Chapter 10.

the right match for his own interests and abilities, or to the average teacher's intuitive skill in helping him to make that match. On the other hand, a good argument, based on the experience of an increasing number of teachers, can be made for the notion that the child, assisted by an *informed* teacher, can make good progress in learning that is largely self-directed.

3 *Teacher-involved or teacher-proofed?* Many of the materials for teaching preschoolers as well as those for teaching reading, mathematics, science, and social studies to older children are designed to counteract assumed teacher mediocrity. Materials are packaged and the strategies for using them so carefully prescribed that, providing the teacher can read the directions, she can teach the program. Some teachers do exactly that—they instruct the children directly from the teacher's manual.[35]

Hawkins, an exponent of open education, discusses the critical role of the teacher in relation to the child's direct experience with materials. As he sees it, the child as he explores materials gets "feedback" from them. He is not able to analyze all this for himself, so the teacher's function is to provide "a kind of external loop, or selective feedback."[36]

An example of this is the six-year-old who was using structured rods in mathematics. He was asked to find all the pairs of rods which together were the same length as a given rod. He soon discovered that when he had found one pair, he could reverse their order and so obtain a second appropriate pair. He then proceeded to match up all the possible pairs and reversed pairs equivalent to the given rod. But only when the teacher asked him to name each numbered pair was he able to articulate his discovery of the commutative law $(6 + 1 = 1 + 6)$.[37]

Hawkins believes that the child should learn to internalize the function the adult provides so that eventually he no longer needs the teacher. Growth involves "the incorporation of conjoint information from the natural world and of things which only other human beings are able to provide." Merely providing the child a "rich, manipulable and responsive environment" is insufficient.[38] When the child has a range of choices, what he does gives the teacher basis for deciding what should come next, "what the provisioning should be for him."[39] The relationship between the child and the teacher

---

[35] Someone has commented that teachers in the English Primary Schools do not expect textbook manuals to give other than the most general kinds of directions. They assume that they know "how to do it."

[36] David Hawkins, "The Triangular Relationship of Teacher, Student, and Materials," in Charles Silberman, ed., *The Open Classroom Reader* (New York: Vintage Books, 1973), p. 366.

[37] Edith Biggs, "Why We Teach Mathematics," in Silberman, ed., *The Open Classroom Reader,* pp. 635, 636.

[38] Hawkins, p. 369.

[39] Hawkins, p. 370.

develops through their mutual interest in a "third thing"—the materials that the teacher makes available.

Kallett, taking a view similar to that of Hawkins, describes a kind of dialogue that goes on between the child and materials. Some of it is overt, some covert, "an interplay of images or unverbalized thoughts." The teacher, in order to join the child-material and child-self "conversations" needs to know what it feels like to work with materials.[40]

Thus, from the view of an open approach to the education of young children, materials ought not to be teacher-proofed. Rather, the teacher's involvement (which must be supported by her own training, including participation in workshops) is essential to the child's effective use of materials.

4 *Packaged or "found"?* Assuming that the emphasis in a given program is to be toward direct more than toward vicarious experience, the question arises as to the kinds of materials that are most appropriate. How much is to be purchased and how much scrounged? It takes only a quick review of the catalogs put out by school supply houses, toy manufacturers, and publishers who provide kits of materials for instructional programs to conclude that anything that is needed can be purchased.

Nevertheless, something can be said for the materials that teachers find, beg, or borrow in addition to the fact that they are usually free or inexpensive. Not only do such materials provide needed variety, but the activity involved in their collection implies an important attitude of mind on the part of the teacher. The teacher looks at objects with a sense of their varied properties and the ways those properties relate to the developing ideas of the children. This is not mindless scavenging; rather, it reflects the same process of inquiry that is to be encouraged in the children.

5 *Teacher responsibility or child responsibility?* If a program intends to nurture the inquiring attitude of the children, the responsibility for materials must be shared by children and teacher. As they are increasingly involved in the question of what is needed, children see new possibilities in the world around them. They no longer merely exploit the environment created by the teacher, but are themselves involved in its creation and in the exploitation of its possibilities.

6 *The child alone or the child with other children?* Many of the available instructional materials are designed for the use of the individual child. Others, often in the form of games, encourage the collaboration of two or more children. An important consideration in the selection of materials has to do with the kinds of opportunities they create for children to learn from one

[40] Anthony Kallett, "Communications with and through Materials," in Silberman, ed., *The Open Classroom Reader,* p. 381.

another. Such learning may be direct, as when one child tells or shows another something he had not known. It may also be indirect, as when one child's way of doing things or of approaching a problem provides a model for another.

7 *The whole curriculum or a part of it?* Although the discussion so far has emphasized concrete as opposed to vicarious experience, it should be clear that no one kind of material is sufficient for a good program. Children need direct contact with phenomena, but vicarious experience extends their knowledge. Books, films, and records all have their proper place. Children need to become self-directed, but instruction is sometimes required to facilitate the child's readiness to move on his own. The need for variety, for materials appropriate to particular learning tasks and to particular children, together with an appreciation for the resources and limitations of particular teachers —these are all factors that guide the early childhood educator in the provisioning of materials.

Cost Considerations

Since few budgets are limitless, the early childhood educator and the staff, and sometimes the parents, must make choices with regard to equipment and materials as well as space. They have to ask whether a particular item is dispensable or indispensable. If the program does not have this piece of equipment or these materials, what will the consequences be? Can something else serve as well? Short- and long-term cost is also a consideration. Particularly with regard to equipment, the cheaper but less sturdy piece, or the one with a single purpose may be more expensive than something with a higher initial cost.

Some Unanswered Questions

As an observer who believes that the environment is a critical factor in children's learning and development and who also visits many schools and centers for young children, I am often puzzled at what I see. Sometimes the environment seems to give children mixed messages.

Safety   Children should be protected from hazards, but the range of such protection runs from none to precautions that completely inhibit the child's freedom and initiative. On the one hand, some children in their own homes are subject to such hazards as lead poisoning, rat bites, serious burns, and fractures. On the other hand, in schools, children as old as six are often prohibited from using any but the least challenging apparatus. They cannot venture into the playground or go on an errand without the attendance of an adult. Heinicke notes that "in the interests of safety, many day care centers have chosen to eliminate swings, climbing apparatus, tools such as saws and hammers, and innovative play such as riding tricycles backward."[41] Observers in schools and centers in England have long observed that children there have a much greater measure of independence than is the case here. Perhaps cultural differences are reflected in the behavior of the children, or perhaps high insurance rates are responsible for the kinds of anxiety that seem to permeate many programs in this country.

Children, Media, and Machines   The questions Resnick raises about the role of technology in open education extend beyond programmed learning. What is the role of TV, films, tape recorders, cameras, and other audiovisual materials and devices in the program for the young children? Some programs in day care homes and centers are built around the TV schedule. Considering the present paucity of programs intended for children, the quality of children's experience in such programs probably needs examination. On the other hand, there are schools and centers that do not sufficiently use available technology to extend and clarify the children's experience.[42]

The Role of Novelty in Materials   As discussed in Chapter 6, novelty plays an important role in stimulating the child's interest and in modifying his cognitive structures. But the child also needs time to repeat and to exploit the familiar. In some programs novelty appears to have become the major goal. Teachers continuously introduce new materials. An art program for preschoolers serves as an illustration. In contrast to the traditional nursery school where paint, clay, and fingerpaint served as staple materials to which the child brought increasingly refined skills and new ideas, these programs emphasize novel materials and teach novel uses. The traditional nursery school often failed to recognize signals that the children needed new challenge, But today's child, who receives a barrage of new experiences outside of school, may have more need to investigate, to explore, and to come to terms with some basic media than he has to rush from macaroni to macramé in a single week.

Conspicuous Consumption   Is there a limit to the variety of experience and hence the number and variety of materials a group of children needs? Judging from the sheer number of things that are found in some classrooms,

[41] Christoph M. Heinicke, "The Organization of Day Care: Considerations Relating to the Mental Health of Child and Family," *American Journal of Orthopsychiatry,* 43(1):19, January 1973.

[42] See Bruce R. Joyce, *Alternative Models of Elementary Education* (Waltham, Mass.: Blaisdell Publishing Co., 1969). Chapter 5, on the technical support systems of the school, provides an excellent analysis of the possibilities for data storage and retrieval systems on specific topics, for example, "A New England Town," that can be used with children as young as six.

the answer would seem to be "No." Longer observation and more careful consideration of what children are doing, however, suggest a different answer. Many classrooms accumulate quantities of materials, store them casually, and use relatively few of them. In other programs, an amazing amount of material is expended by the children, with little regard to whether its use is appropriate or even necessary. Implicit in both kinds of programs is the notion that the worth of the children's experiences is somehow measured by the variety of things available to them. The conservation of resources, both man-made and natural, is basically the problem of the adults, but it makes little sense to run classrooms as though such problems were nonexistent.

The Esthetic Environment   Not all classrooms are well designed for the kinds of activities that go on in them, and some are basically drab and dreary. Regardless of the setting, however, some teachers manage to organize the room and display the children's work in ways that are pleasing to the eye. Even when many activities are going on at the same time, the effect is agreeable. It seems that it is possible to create and maintain an environment that is both attractive and functional. Just as the sound of a classroom—the hum of conversation broken by the occasional bursts of excitement that occur when children are deeply involved in their work and play—reveals something of the quality of the living in it, so too does its appearance. Absorbing activity for young children is often not tidy as it flows in and out of the various learning centers—but neither is it chaotic. One senses that both teachers and children have a sense of order. That quality goes a long way toward the creation of an esthetically pleasing environment.

HEALTH, NUTRITION, AND SOCIAL SERVICES

The early childhood educator's responsibility with regard to needed health, nutrition, and social services varies greatly depending on the settings in which education and care are provided. In some instances, when she is affiliated with the public schools, the services available to older children may also be used by the younger children. In most instances, however, such services are insufficient for younger children, and supplementary or substitute arrangements must be made. Any program that involves day care poses the problem of securing comprehensive services.

> Well-functioning families, both internally and by utilization of community agents, provide for the nutritional, medical, psychological, social and physical needs of their members. Working-parent families, no matter how well they function, cannot personally provide for all these needs: parents are away for most of the young

child's waking hours, and the procurement of services after-hours becomes increasingly difficult in our bureaucratic, 9 to 5 society. So parents must rely on day care centers to help them meet the comprehensive (not just educational) needs of their children.[43]

Head Start intended to provide comprehensive services to very poor families, but numerous problems prevented the realization of the plan. Peters, reviewing the Head Start experience in comparison with that of certain model day care programs, concludes that new approaches are needed. It is time, she thinks, to "stop beating the old dead horse of traditional services and get on with the work of finding out how, and if, health-care and social services can be made truly relevant to daytime programs for children in our modern society."[44]

The early childhood educator may find that her agency has secured and maintains services that are minimal. A portion of her work may be devoted to improving or changing services.

Health and Social Services

Minimal provision of health services assumes that the health of the child is the responsibility of the parents. The center assumes responsibility for knowing the health services that are used by the parents, for ongoing observation of the child, for providing emergency care when necessary, and for simple first aid. It also sees that its staff members are in good health and that sanitary procedures are followed in caring for the children.[45]

As far as social services are concerned, at the minimal level the parent is responsible for locating the center and informing the center staff of any developments at home that may affect the child in the center. The center screens applications, interviews parents and children at the time of entrance, obtaining information about the parent and the child, including his developmental history, explains the service to the parents, and keeps them informed about the child. Any problems that cannot be settled by parent or center are referred to some other agency.

Maximal health and social services as described by Peters would be an inherent part of the total program, correlating and integrating the preventive and curative aspects of health care, with maximal communication between

[43] Peggy Daly Pizzo, *Operational Difficulties of Group Day Care* (Washington: Day Care and Child Development Council of America, 1972).

[44] Ann DeHuff Peters, "The Delivery of Health and Social Service to Child and Family in a Daytime Program," in Dennis N. McFadden, ed., *Early Childhood Development Programs and Services: Planning for Action* (Washington: National Association for the Education of Young Children, 1972).

[45] E. Belle Evans et al., *Day Care* (Boston: Beacon Press, 1971), pp. 91–101.

staff and parents. Many aspects of health care, Peters believes, can be delivered by other than professionally trained individuals, provided they are given training and continuing consultation. All programs should have methods for screening and identifying problems and handicaps and provision for follow-up with the family.[46] Ill children should be cared for at the center, and adequate staff and space should be available for this.

Peters proposes two alternative models for developing these kinds of services. The first model includes three types of health personnel: a part-time pediatrician, a pediatric nurse practitioner or an equivalently trained public health nurse, and licensed practical nurses. The first two would serve several centers, each of which would have its own licensed practical nurse.[47] The second model takes the form of a consultation team consisting of a physician, a public health nurse or nurse practitioner, and a social worker. Such a team would provide regular service to a number of programs, but would do so on a consultation basis. Both models are intended to establish services that operate in the centers, not in distance offices or clinics.[48]

In addition to meeting the health needs of the children, the models proposed by Peters would provide for activities sometimes carried exclusively by the social worker. These include "parent participation groups, agency advocacy on behalf of families with common problems, referral services and crisis intervention."[49] Although the models were developed for centers serving infants and toddlers, they can be extended to older children and can function in connection with home-based programs.

In occasional centers and in many school settings psychologists may also serve as members of the team providing services to children and their parents. They may administer developmental inventories, conduct tests of speech, hearing, and other aspects of the child's functioning, and serve as consultants to teachers and parents regarding children who appear to have difficulties.

Nutrition Services

Any school or center serving young children for even a short period of the day must make provision for the nutrition of the child. Minimally, children bring a snack or lunch from home. When the school or center has its own food services, it not only provides hot meals for the children but also an opportunity to educate children and parents about nutrition. As some programs have

[46] Peters, pp. 67–69.

[47] Peters, "Health Support in Day Care," in Edith H. Grotberg, ed., *Day Care Resources for Decisions* (Washington: Office of Economic Opportunity, n.d.), pp. 328–330.

[48] Peters, in McFadden, ed., pp. 72–73.

[49] Enolia B. Archinard, "Social Work and Supplementary Service," in Grotberg, ed., *Day Care Resources for Decisions,* pp. 373–392.

shown, such education can begin while the children are still infants. The caretakers' gentle encouragement helps the babies to enjoy a variety of foods.

Birch, whose work emphasizes the importance of adequate nutrition to the growth and development of healthy and intelligent children (see Chapter 6), also stresses parent education with regard to nutrition. "The enlistment of cooperation and the education of the parent can have effects which are beneficial not only to the child who is in the care, but to all children in the families, born and as yet unborn."[50]

Provisioning an adequate nutrition program involves the early childhood educator and the staff in nutrition education and also in some very practical questions. For example, is the food to be prepared on the premises or is it to be catered elsewhere? Most early childhood educators believe that learning for the children is enriched when the food is prepared in the center. Such preparation does mean that the responsibilities of the director expand to include decisions on kitchen equipment, on purchasing, and on food preparation, together with supervision of an additional set of workers.

Supplementary Services

Although few centers are at present able to provide much more than minimal services, many boards, particularly where parents are deeply involved, believe that a variety of services might be added. Some think that any service that enables the parents to have more time to spend with their children, or that improves the quality of the family living, is a legitimate function for the center. Precedent for this idea can be found in the operation of the Kaiser Child Service Centers during World War II. There the parents, both of whom were working long shifts, could arrange to have shopping done and appointments with dentists made; they could purchase prepared food for home consumption and borrow toys and books for the children.[51] Currently some centers are trying to establish cooperative buying services and organizing to work for improved housing and better recreational services.

ADMINISTRATION[52]

Adequate provisioning for children, whether in schools, centers, or home-

---

[50] Herbert G. Birch, "Malnutrition and Early Development," in Grotberg, ed., *Day Care Resources for Decisions,* p. 360.

[51] Gwen Morgan, "The Kaiser Child Service Centers," in Samuel J. Braun and Esther P. Edwards, *History and Theory of Early Childhood Education* (Worthington, Ohio: Charles A. Jones Publishing Co., 1972), pp. 368–372.

[52] Although administration could have been discussed as a function involving other adults, I have chosen to regard it as a supporting or providing function.

based programs, has to be managed and directed. Someone must take responsibility for seeing that the kind of program that has been planned operates as intended. This means recruiting and hiring the teachers and other staff members, seeing that they are supported in their work and that they receive appropriate remuneration and benefits. It also means fund-raising, budgeting, and accounting. These are the functions of the administrator, a role that the early childhood educator sometimes holds. Under this title she may be responsible for several programs, or as director, she may work with a single program. Titles vary, as does the extent of her responsibility.

Many of the functions of the administrator will be discussed in Chapter 9 on working with adults and need not be elaborated here. Essentially they are directed toward keeping channels of communication open so that everyone in the organization feels himself to be part of a team in which each person makes a special and essential contribution. The goal is to avoid the kind of compartmentalization ironically described by one teacher in a large city school system:

> Life in school is carefully compartmentalized. There is the box of the classroom with its smaller boxes for gym and cluster teachers and library. There is the box of staff relations, with small boxes inside for different grades and groupings. There are the authority boxes, supervisory and union, and it is becoming increasingly difficult to tell them apart. There are the boxes of relations with custodians, school aides and paraprofessionals, parents, community people, and other such lesser forms of life.[53]

Some of the functions of the administrator require considerable specialized knowledge. In large programs these functions are sometimes carried out by someone with responsibility for other programs, not necessarily involving early childhood, as well. The early childhood educator works with that person to inform him of the special needs and circumstances of the early childhood program.

Legal Aspects

The administrator contracts with a governing board to carry out their policies. In so doing, she assumes responsibility for seeing that contractual relationships are maintained with other staff members and the parents. Contractual relations with the parents include responsibility for the safety and protection of the children. The administrator also sees that the program operates within the applicable codes.

---

[53] Gloria Channon, *Homework, Required Reading for Teachers and Parents* (New York: Outerbridge and Dienstfrey, 1970), p. 41.

In situations where the parents who use the school or center are also its owners, the lines of responsibility need special clarification. Carmichael and her colleagues provide a helpful analogy.[54] In the analogy the parent board stands in the position of the owners of a large ship. They invest in and own the ship, determining where they want it to go, what kind of cargo it is to carry, and what kind of crew and how many passengers it is to have. They hire the captain, whose functions parallel those of the administrator-director. He plots the course by the most advantageous route, sees that the cargo is properly stowed, cares for the health and safety of the passengers, and manages the crew. He is in charge during the voyage. "Even if those ship owners decide to sign on as members of the crew, while they are underway the captain is in command."

Business Aspects

The administrator may be involved in fund-raising as well as in the preparation of budgets. She is also responsible for fee collection, the preparation of payrolls and tax reports, insurance, purchasing, the maintenance of plant and equipment, and the accounting and record-keeping systems.

These aspects of the early childhood educator's work as an administrator tend to be those for which she is least well prepared, and in which she is often least interested. They are also aspects for which specific preparation is difficult to obtain. For example, a professor in a university department of business administration who has worked closely with the director of a child care center observes that many of the business aspects of operating a center can only be learned on the job. This is because the diversity of requirements for accounting, depending in part on the source of funding, is so great.

On the other hand, a study of several centers and day care homes indicates that a knowledge of "break-even" accounting might make considerable difference in the eventual success or failure of many child care operations.[55] It appears that there are some basic business principles that the administrator should understand, and training or consultation on these is essential.

Most early childhood educators seem likely to disavow an interest in business, and especially in the inevitable paperwork involved in the operation of a center. However, in some centers more of the administrator's time goes into these aspects than into those more directly influencing the program and its support. Ironically, the administrator may come to prefer the business

[54] Viola S. Carmichael et al., *Administration of Schools for Young Children* (Los Angeles: Southern California Association for the Education of Young Children, 1972), p. 43.

[55] Bill O'Connell, "A Break-even Analysis of Twelve East Bay Child Care Services," unpublished paper, April 1973.

aspects to the other aspects of her work. In one large city, for example, a move to separate the business functions of child care centers directors from their supervisory and training functions met with considerable opposition from some of the more experienced directors. It appeared that they derived more satisfaction from sitting in the office with papers and telephone than from direct involvement with the children and the teachers.

Community Aspects

The community aspects of the administrator's work have a considerable influence on the long-term success of a program. In these aspects she works collaboratively with members of other community agencies, seeks resources for support, receives guidance that is useful in policy formulation, and provides information about her own agency.

Program and Staffing

The administrator translates policy into action through recruiting, selecting, supervising, and training staff members. Although these functions will be given detailed consideration in Chapter 9, it may be well to emphasize here the close connection between the quality of administration and supervision and the effectiveness of the program.

Heinicke and his colleagues, in discussing the ways the organization of day care can support the mental health of children and families, suggest several guiding principles for administration. One such principle is that "administrative practices support autonomy in decision making on the part of the staff responsible for decision making."[56] Children need adults who can serve as models for decision making. Unless the staff has freedom to make decisions, accept failures, and innovate, their relationships to the children will reflect the uncertainty and ambivalence they experience. This principle underlines the need for clarity in communication and for the team approach to authority that is discussed in other chapters.

Heinicke and his colleagues set forth another guiding principle that has been implied in earlier discussion. The staff working with children must receive stimulation and support from their administrator.[57]

The need for such support is also highlighted by Pizzo, who comments that everyone laments the plight of the young mother who is housebound with two preschoolers. Should we give less attention to the situation of the child care worker who may be "centerbound" in one room with fifteen or twenty active

---

[56] Heinicke, p. 18.
[57] Heinicke, pp. 18, 19.

preschoolers for as long as eight hours? Such schedules are hardly "conducive to warm, consistent, creative, adult-child relationships.[58] Nor do they allow time for planning and reflection.

Working with young children is physically demanding. The teacher of preschoolers rarely sits at her desk. Working with young children is also emotionally demanding. Children conceal their feelings much less than older people. The teacher must deal with the gamut of emotional expression, including hostility and anxiety as well as love and pleasure. Finally, working with young children, although intellectually demanding in regard to understanding the child's cognition, is not intellectually stimulating. From all these views, the teacher of young children needs support. She must have relaxation and a change of pace to protect her from physical fatigue. She needs emotional satisfaction as an adult so that she can in turn provide emotional support to the children. Similarly, she needs adult intellectual stimulation so that she does not become fixed at the level of the children.

SUMMARY

To provision is to supply, or to fit out. I chose this term to describe functions of the early childhood educator that might have been labeled "maintaining a technical support system" or "management." The term does not, of course, change the reality of what must be done to ensure that the necessary resources, both human and physical, are available for the child's development and learning. Perhaps, however, it emphasizes somewhat better than the more technical terms the purpose of all the arrangements that are made.

The provisioning is for the children and their parents, and its purpose is the facilitation of the children's development and learning. Since children and their parents differ, the prescriptions of the bureaucratic "how-to-do-it manuals" are often inappropriate for them.

Efficiency *is* a consideration. Some ways of doing things waste time and energy and duplicate the efforts of others. Technology effectively supports many human efforts, but those who develop procedures and provide technical support must never forget that these are but means to ends. The early childhood educator as provisioner and administrator is in a good position to see that the environment provided for the children, and the services made available to them and their parents, are organized in ways to promote the development and learning of all concerned.

[58] Pizzo, p. 11.

Working with Adults: Parents

The relationship between parents and teachers can best be described as a mutual assistance pact for the good of the child. Of course, the cooperative effort is often invalidated by mutual fear and resentment. *

The circle of adults surrounding the teacher of young children has grown larger as society has become more complex. The first grade teacher, for example, whose work at one time involved few adults other than the principal and the parents of the children, now relates to school psychologist, nurse, social worker, librarian, and reading specialist. She may be a member of a teaching team and she may have one or more aides. At the preschool level the network of relations is often equally complex.

The focus of all these relationships is, or ought to be, the child, and the most crucial relationship is that between the teacher and the parent. When the teacher and the parent share their understanding of the child and agree on the direction for his learning and development, his chances for a good start in his education are greatly increased.

* Robert Coles and Maria Piers, *Wages of Neglect* (Chicago: Quadrangle Books, 1949), p. 59.

Although everyone acknowledges the importance of the parent-teacher relationship, it is often taken for granted. Not much is done to prepare teachers for it.

In some countries, the early childhood teacher-to-be is required to spend some time living in a family with young children in order to get a sense of the demands of the parental role. More generally, it seems, the teacher learns ways of working with parents only from her later experience.

As far as working with other adults is concerned, the situation is not much different. Preservice education for the early childhood level has tended to give some attention to the question of parents, but little to the matter of working with other adults.[1]

Perhaps such neglect has stemmed from the fact that the student's initial concern about how she is doing with the children is so pervasive. Perhaps the teacher educators think such concern precludes any focus on how she is doing with adults. Some teacher education programs do, however, emphasize self-understanding, attempting to widen the student's interest and insight into all of her relationships from the beginning of her training.

Privately, some who are responsible for the training of teachers for early childhood education assert, "When it comes to working effectively with other adults, some students have the necessary qualities, and some don't. There's not much one can do to change them."

Clearly not all those who chose to work with young children are equally enthusiastic about working with adults. Those who are appear to be the most ready to learn the necessary skills. The early childhood educator role calls for as much, and probably, more, contact with adults than with children. The present chapter, and the one that follows, are concerned with the ways the early childhood educator functions with other adults.

In the present chapter the focus is on working with parents. In certain respects this chapter parallels the earlier chapter on teaching young children. Just as it is essential for the early childhood educator to be an effective teacher of young children, it is equally important for her to be skilled and understanding in her relationships with their parents.

---

[1] For example, *Characteristics of Early Childhood Teacher Education* (Washington: Association for Childhood Education International, 1968) provides an analysis of ten exemplary programs but makes no specific mention of preparation for working with either parents or other adults. However, some shift seems to be under way. A later publication, *Preliminary Report of the Ad Hoc Joint Committee on the Preparation of Nursery and Kindergarten Teachers* (Washington: National Education Association, n.d.), says: "The team approach to instruction is vital to the operation of programs for young children, and should be covered in the preparation of personnel." Also, Joyce, reviewing ten "model" teacher-education programs developed under the aegis of the Office of Education in 1968, notes that all provide for the teacher as a "team member," that is, as a colleague and a specialist. See Bruce Joyce and Marsha Weil, eds., *Perspectives for Reform in Teacher Education* (Englewood Cliffs, N.J.: Prentice-Hall, 1972).

PERSONAL CHARACTERISTICS

What are the qualities deemed essential for working with other adults?

Effectiveness stems from a strong sense of self. The adult who is in touch with his own feelings, who knows his own strengths, weaknesses, concerns, and values maintains an integrity in working with others. He is not easily manipulated and he does not try to manipulate others.

Respecting himself, tolerant of his own idiosyncrasies, he treats others with equal human dignity, regardless of position or background. He is wary of stereotypes and lets the other person come through to him as an individual, not merely as the representative of some group.

To work with other adults in ways that facilitate mutuality of purpose, a person also needs to be able to listen not only to what is said but also to what may be conveyed in omission or in gesture. He must also be able to validate his understanding of what is said with the other person. As Sullivan notes:

> An enormous amount of difficulty all through life arises from the fact that communicative behavior miscarries because words do not carry meaning but evoke meaning. And if a word evokes in the hearer something quite different from that it was intended to evoke, communication is not a success.[2]

Words evoke unintended meanings when the hearer has established certain expectations about the other person. For example, the fact that all teachers have had parents, and that parents have had teachers, colors their perceptions. Accordingly, a young teacher may see in the parent's concern for the child's achievement the demand for perfection that she experienced in relation to her own parents. Also, many parents approach their child's teacher in trepidation based either on specific recollections of their own schooling or on a general unease with authority figures. Other feelings, as for example, envy of the other's position, also distort perceptions. A mother, feeling tied to her home with her young children, sees the teacher as liberated. If she is poor, she may think of the teacher as rich. The teacher, in turn, may see the parent as someone who has, in contrast to herself, more limited responsibilities and freedom to arrange her own schedule.

Finally, in a time when everyone is a specialist in something, the person who works effectively with other adults needs a sense of the nature and limits of his own expertise and similar regard for that of others. The teacher, for example, knows better than anyone what the child does in school, but when it comes to what he is like at home the parents become the experts.

---

[2] Harry Stack Sullivan, *The Interpersonal Theory of Psychiatry* (New York: W. W. Norton, 1953), p. 184.

WORKING WITH PARENTS

In today's early childhood programs teachers encounter parents in a variety of roles, in addition to those of "Johnny's mother" or "Rachel's father." Parents may participate in the classroom as volunteers or as paid aides. Occasionally their role is that of student, as they learn to teach children in school or center, or in the case of some home programs, in their own homes. They may serve on advisory councils to the school or center, or they may, in the case of cooperatives or "alternative" schools, be the teacher's employers.

In the early years of childhood, the parents' roles seem to overlap somewhat with the role of teacher. After all, the traditional role of the school has been to stand *in loco parentis.* Psychologically, however, the parental and teacher relationships to the child differ in several respects. Clarity in this regard helps the teacher of the young child in fulfilling her role in relation to both child and parent.

Comparison of Teacher and Parent Roles

All the functions ascribed to the teacher role—caretaking, guiding, instructing, facilitating, and serving as a model—can also be observed in the parental role. The proportion of time devoted to these functions usually differs, however, depending in part on the ages of the children. But the parent-child relationship is bound by an emotional intensity that is, or should be, lacking in the teacher-child relationship.[3] The parental tie is the tie that binds, and it is accordingly the parent who is the person the very young child wants most when he is hurt, upset, confused, or tired. Furthermore, the child is, in a sense, an extension of parental ego. No parent regards his child with the same objectivity as the child's affectionate teacher.

For the child, his relationship with the teacher provides entry into a world that is rich with possibilities for peer companionship, for exploration, and for learning. He needs the teacher's warm emotional support for these endeavors, but not a replica of the family's situation. The point was succinctly made by a mother's response to a teacher who suggested that a child having difficulty in beginning reading might be feeling unloved. The mother said, "We love him. You teach him."

Just as the parent role differs from the teacher role, so too do the settings in which they are typically enacted. Here the advantage seems to rest with the teacher, who most of the time works in an environment specially designed for children. In contrast, the parent's role requires great versatility in adapting settings designed for adults—kitchens, automobiles, supermarkets—to the

---

[3] Anna Freud, "The Role of the Teacher," *Harvard Educational Review,* 22:229–234, 1952.

needs of children. It is true that the teacher must cope with more children than the parent. However, the fact that each child usually wishes to participate in the activities of the group gives the teacher a set of incentives and sanctions not usually available to parents.

Perhaps the best way to emphasize the difference between the home and the school or center setting and the demands of the parental role is to let a father who became a "househusband" for a summer describe a typical day with his three- and five-year-olds:

> After six to eight hours of responding to demands for food, drink, toys, tied shoelaces; after endless requests to go to the park, to go to the swimming pool, to eat in a restaurant, after cleaning up spilled food and drink, discarded clothing, abandoned toys, after pouring out orange juice and being told it should be milk, after being asked for hot dogs, then being told peanut butter sandwiches would be better, after vacuuming the house only to find mud tracked on the rug minutes later, after cleaning up the three year old only to find him minutes later rolling in the dusty gravel of the driveway, I found myself screaming in rage at the kids out of all proportion to a given offense. I found I spanked them more than I wanted to, and often simply as an expression of my personhood. After all I was not their slave. . . . [4]

When the teacher is clear on the differences between the parent-child and teacher-child relationships, she is better able to avoid putting herself in a position of rivalry with the parent. The temptation to make up to the child for something that seems to be missing in his relationship to his parents is replaced by an effort to provide greater support to the parents.

All these matters are complicated by current child-caring realities. Increased mobility, the high rate of separation and divorce, and the employment of mothers outside their homes for major portions of the day are all factors that make the parental role increasingly difficult to fill.

Danger, it seems, lies in the possibility that to an increasing extent the roles—teacher, caretaker, therapist—that should be only supplementary to the central parental role will serve as substitutes for it. Gerzon, in *A Childhood for Every Child,* sees trouble ahead if the parent is held "only marginally accountable for his child's growth." He writes:

> Obstetricians take charge at birth; pediatricians are responsible for a child's ailments and cures; the teacher for his intelligence; the coach for his physique; the supermarket and food industry for his food; television for his myths; the minister

---

[4] John C. Lovas, "Trials of a Househusband," *California Living, San Francisco Sunday Examiner and Chronicle,* June 6, 1973, pp. 40–44.

for his soul; and the psychiatrist, if necessary, for the feelings wedged in between. Technical parenthood is narrowed to housing and clothing these various component parts so that they hang together in a legally coherent form which can be identified as John or Mary.[5]

Gerzon goes on to say that "a father or mother cannot view life as a mass of disconnected technical questions which must be left up to the experts." He urges parents to assume their own responsibilities. By the same token, it behooves the "experts" to fill their roles in ways that encourage such assumption.

If the teacher is to support and not diminish the role of the parent, she needs to understand how parents influence their children. The literature relating to this question is voluminous. In the last quarter century, a number of studies have pinpointed clusters of parental characteristics that appear to be associated with specific aspects of the child's development. As concern for competence and achievement, particularly among children coming from poverty areas, has increased, studies suggesting that certain parental behaviors affect the course of a child's cognitive development have been highlighted.[6] Some studies have focused on the ways mothers teach their children.[7]

The Parent as Teacher

In general, studies comparing middle-class mothers with those from less-privileged homes show that middle-class mothers tend to give more detailed and specific directions to their children, supply more reasons and explanations regarding expected behaviors, and use more positive reinforcement.[8] There are, of course, differences within classes as well as between them.

One study, by White and Watts,[9] is of special interest because it has followed parents and their children in the home setting. White and Watts began their work with a study of three- to six-year-olds in school settings in

---

[5] From the book *A Childhood for Every Child,* by Mark Gerzon, Copyright © 1973 by Mark Gerzon. Published by E. P. Dutton & Co. (Outerbridge & Lazard, Inc.), and used with their permission.

[6] For a comprehensive review of these studies in the years from 1945 to 1969, see Robert D. Hess, "Parental Behavior and Children's School Behavior: Implications for Head Start," in Edith Grotberg, ed., *Critical Issues in Research Related to Disadvantaged Children* (Princeton: Educational Testing Service, September 1969). Many other studies have appeared more recently. For example, Maxine Schoggen and Phil Schoggen, *Environmental Forces in the Home Lives of Three-Year-Old Children in Three Population Subgroups* (Nashville: Demonstration and Research Center for Early Education, George Peabody College for Teachers, January 1971) (Mimeographed).

[7] Robert D. Hess and Virginia Shipman, *The Cognitive Environments of Urban Preschool Children* (Chicago: University of Chicago, 1968).

[8] Helen L. Bee et al., "Social Class Differences in Maternal Teaching Strategies and Speech Patterns," *Developmental Psychology,* 1:726–734, 1969.

[9] Burton L. White and Jean C. Watts, *Experience and Environment,* vol. 1 (Englewood Cliffs, N.J.: Prentice-Hall, 1973).

an effort to define the nature of competence in that age period. They found that such manifestations as getting and maintaining the attention of adults in socially acceptable ways; planning and carrying out multistep activities; attending to two things simultaneously or in rapid succession appeared as early as age three in some children. These three-year-old manifestations of competence were so similar to the qualities that had been observed in very competent six-year-olds that it appeared likely the sixes would also have manifested them at age three. White and Watts accordingly decided to look at one- to three-year-olds to see how such competence developed. They observed children in their homes and concluded (tentatively, since their sample was limited to 31 children who were, however, studied intensively) that the mother's "direct and indirect actions with regard to her one-to-three-year-old child are the most powerful formative factors in the development of a preschool child." They found effective mothers at all socioeconomic levels.[10] "A mother need not necessarily have even a high school education . . . nor . . . very substantial economic assets." Further, "a good job can be accomplished without a father in the home."[11]

The mothers of the most competent children, in contrast to those who are least competent, "interact more with them, engage in more intellectually stimulating activities with them, teach them more often, encourage them more often, initiate activities for them more often, and are more successful in controlling their children."[12]

These findings raise many questions regarding the mother-child relationship and also regarding the role of the school and teacher in supporting it. Are some mothers "naturally" good mothers, or does the match between the baby's characteristics and the mother's child-rearing style play a part in the mother's effectiveness?[13] If the important interaction between mother and child takes place in the ten-to-eighteen-month period of life, as White and Watts believe, is not that the period when support is most needed? Might those who are having problems be most open to assistance in changing the character of the interaction? Would the effort the teacher may put into teaching the less competent three-year-olds be better spent with their mothers?

Regardless of how these questions are answered, it is obvious that the child coming to school after he is two already has a history of learning. His mother is part of that history. The nature of that history is an important factor to consider when the teacher and parent try to arrive at common goals for furthering the development, learning, and well-being of the child.

---

[10] The very poor were represented in their sample by a single child.
[11] White and Watts, p. 242.
[12] White and Watts, p. 199.
[13] Alexander Thomas et al., *Behavioral Individuality in Early Childhood* (New York: New York University Press, 1963).

In certain situations such agreement has not been achieved without confrontation. Where programs provided in schools or centers have, in effect,
atrophied and are no longer responsive to parents and children, parents have
found it neccessary to demand change.

An institutional lack of responsiveness to parents runs deeper than the
failure of the teachers to recognize the unique background of experience of
each child. Nevertheless, the teacher's awareness of how the child may have
been taught, and of what his parents regard as important, does facilitate
coming to a mutual understanding.

Parental Background and Values

Are there any shortcuts to finding out about children and their parents? If a
teacher could know only one thing about a child's parents, what would give
her the most information? Where they live? What their work is? Their ethnic
origin? Their religion?

The effects of socioeconomic status, usually marked by occupation and
place of residence, on child-rearing practices and family values have long been
studied. At least two decades ago several studies[14] challenged the pervasive
emphasis on middle-class ways and values that characterized the schools,
textbooks, and commercial television.

In the next decade increasing numbers of children from the lower socioeconomic groups found the public school curriculum meaningless and did not
achieve in school. As was described in Chapter 5, interest in studies of the poor
grew. From some of these studies, a picture of child-rearing practices among
the poor emerged.[15] They described the attention given to children as incon-
sistent, depending more on the wishes of the mother than on the needs of the
child, often punitive, and restricted in verbalization. Home environments were
seen as noisy and confusing to the developing child, while parents were described as uninterested in the children's schooling.

From the beginning, the researchers cautioned that their findings might
not be applicable to all poor families. Deutsch wrote:

---

[14] For example, Allison Davis and Robert J. Havighurst, *Father of the Man: How Your Child Gets His Personality* (Boston: Houghton Mifflin, 1947); August deB. Hollingshead, *Elmtown's Youth: The Impact of Social Classes on Adolescents* (New York: John Wiley & Sons, 1949).

[15] Literature describing these studies and the programs that were developed is plentiful. See, for example, Jerome Hellmuth, ed., *Disadvantaged Child,* vols. 1, 2, and 3 (New York: Brunner/Mazel, 1967, 1968, 1970); Ronald K. Parker, ed., *The Preschool in Action: Exploring Early Childhood Programs* (Boston: Allyn and Bacon, 1972); R. D. Hess and R. M. Bear, *Early Education: Current Theory, Research and Practice* (Chicago: Aldine, 1968); and two books edited by Joe L. Frost: *Early Childhood Education Rediscovered* (New York: Holt, Rinehart and Winston, 1968) and *Revisiting Early Childhood Education* (New York: Holt, Rinehart and Winston, 1973).

It is easy to refer to the population as "The Disadvantaged" and through our language . . . come to regard the individuals described as constituting a homogeneous group. This, of course, is not true: there are wide and vast variations between subgroups—and between individuals—of the population labeled "disadvantaged." These variations have to do not only with broad ethnic and racial differences, with geographical and urban-rural differences, but also with the more specific and individually applicable familial differences.[16]

Deutsch's caution was too often not heeded, and too many teachers too often assumed that poor parents would fit the textbook description of the "disadvantaged."

The eagerness with which many poor parents sent their children to Head Start and other preschool programs, and the numbers of them who became volunteers and aides should have broken through the stereotyped picture of child-rearing in poverty. A pervasive ethnocentrism often serves to blind teachers and others to the fact that child-rearing patterns in poor homes are often not inadequate but, rather, different from those in the middle-class nuclear family. When, for example, the poor child is a member of an extended family, he has access to a network of affectional support that is usually lacking for his middle-class peer. Furthermore, the supposed language deficits in the case of many poor children cannot be attributed to a lack of experience with language. Rather, two languages are often involved, that of the particular ethnic group to which the child belongs, and standard English.[17]

Teachers, if they are to work effectively with parents and children, need to understand the variety of cultural backgrounds from which they come. With regard to the poor, it is important to recognize that poverty in this country is poverty where "the poor are less than poor. They are poor while others are rich and they do not have the power to demand their 'fair share.'"[18] This fact has led some investigators to conclude that programs designed to improve the educational opportunities for the poor are doomed to failure. As they see it, the changes needed to eradicate the "culture of poverty" are political, not educational.[19]

There are many complexities involved in understanding the behavior of people who differ from us, culturally, financially, or any other way. Tulkin comments:

[16] Martin Deutsch, in Jerome Hellmuth, ed., *Disadvantaged Child,* vol. 1, p. 7.
[17] Stephen S. Baratz and Joan C. Baratz, "Early Childhood Intervention: The Social Science Basis of Institutional Racism," *Harvard Educational Review,* 40:29–50, Winter 1970; Charles A. Valentine, "Deficit, Difference and Bicultural Models of Afro-American Behavior," *Harvard Educational Review,* 51:137–157, May 1971.
[18] Steven R. Tulkin, "An Analysis of the Concept of Cultural Deprivation," *Developmental Psychology,* 6:326–339, March 1972.
[19] Christopher Jencks et al., *Inequality: A Reassessment of the Effect of Family and Schooling in America* (New York: Basic Books, 1972).

It is easier to think of these other people as "groups" and more difficult to think of them as individuals who differ a great deal among themselves—just as members of our own group do. It is easier to think of them as wanting to be like us and needing us to help them; it is more difficult to reject the philosophy of the "white man's burden" and allow people the freedom to retain life styles which differ from the ones we know. It is easy to blame people for what we have defined as their "deficits" but more difficult to consider how we as a society might have contributed to the problems we have defined as "theirs."[20]

The teacher's need to understand differences in cultural backgrounds and life styles if she is middle-class, as Tulkin implies, is not limited to understanding the poor. Blue-collar families, for example, are reported to emphasize the "'traditional' values of obedience, neatness and respect for adults" in contrast to middle-class families who want their children to be happy, to confide in them, and to be eager to learn[21] Despite their middle-class background, a generation of college- and university-educated young parents are bringing their children up with a new set of values emphasizing spontaneity, self-expression, nondifferentiated sex roles, and in some instances communal living.[22]

Generalizations about groups of people can be helpful to the teacher. Knowing that the father is likely to be the source of authority in the Puerto Rican or Mexican-American family, or that the Indian family values cooperation over competition provides the teacher with needed background for meeting the parent. It helps her understand why so many of the traditional middle-class goals such as obedience to a female teacher, or achievement at the expense of one's peers, are not readily accepted as goals by certain minority groups. It provides a base for planning programs that respect the values of the parents and keep a variety of options for competence open to the child.

Generalizations can also be dangerous, however, when the teacher views the parent only as a representation of a generalization and fails to listen to him or her as a unique person with a particular set of values and concerns.

Parents with Special Needs

In the sense that every parent is different from every other parent, all have unique needs. However, some kinds of needs recur frequently. They cut across cultural groups, and are, or should be, of some concern to the teacher.

One group of parents receiving considerable attention as their number has grown are the single parents. Research does not support the commonly held

---

[20] Tulkin, p. 334.

[21] Mirra Komarovsky, *Blue Collar Marriage* (New York: Vintage Books, 1967), p. 76.

[22] David E. Smith and James Sternfield, "The Hippie Communal Movement: Effects on Child Birth and Development," *American Journal of Orthopsychiatry,* 40:527–530, April 1970.

notions that children from one-parent families do less well in school, are more prone to delinquency, or that fatherless boys have difficulty developing masculine identification. It does, however, point to the crucial role of the single parent. That role is complex and difficult.[23]

Teachers, to be effective in working with single parents, need to be realistic about the responsibilities the parent carries. They also need to guard against assuming there are problems when none exist.

Parents of handicapped children are another group that early childhood teachers are encountering more frequently as schools and centers expand to include a wider range of youngsters. Many of these parents carry a heavy burden, not only of responsibility for the child's proper care, but sometimes of guilt and unacknowledged anger. Although reason tells them the child's problem is not of their doing and that they are not being punished, their emotions often say otherwise. Again, however, like other groups of parents, they vary greatly, and the teacher needs to know each individually, rather than taking their concerns for granted.

To caution against a hasty and presumptuous reading of the parent's problems or anxieties is not to deny that many parents are deeply troubled. Indeed, as her knowledge of parent and child grows, the teacher and the early childhood educator especially should be able to distinguish between those merely in need of support from the teacher and other parents and those in more serious trouble, for whom more specialized help is needed.

Current statistics on child neglect and abuse,[24] which in all probability underestimate their extent, underscore the parental need for relief from some of the pressures of child rearing and the need for a variety of kinds of support. The teacher's sensitivity to the problem, and her knowledge of resources for dealing with it, are crucial.

Another group of parents often in need of support, but difficult to reach, are the migrants. Society's response to those who work in the fields has been, until recently, minimal. Since 1966 some programs have been devised for the children and, in a few instances, for their parents.[25] They seem only to begin to confront the need.

Not economically disadvantaged but similarly rootless,[26] many middle-

[23] Elizabeth Herzog and Cecelia Sudia, "Families without Fathers," *Childhood Education,* 48:175–181, 1972.

[24] Report of the Joint Commission on Mental Health of Children, *Crisis in Mental Health: Challenge for the 1970's* (New York: Harper & Row, 1970), pp. 344–345. See also Leontine Young, *Wednesday's Children: A Study of Child Neglect and Abuse* (New York: McGraw-Hill, 1964).

[25] Gloria Mattera, "Migrant Education in the United States: Some Significant Developments," in *Migrant Children, Their Education* (Washington: Association for Childhood Education International, 1971).

[26] Perhaps the term "rootless" is more applicable to the middle-class workers who seldom return to the places they leave than to the agricultural migrants who follow the crops in the same areas, often returning to the same home-base community.

class families rarely spend two consecutive years in the same community. Toffler suggests that their children may need to be "trained for turnover."[27] Clearly the fact of turnover greatly complicates the relationship of parent and child to the teacher. If each thinks of the other as "here today, gone tomorrow," does it matter how they relate to one another? Or can we hope to build so pervasive an understanding of caring for children and caring about parents that they can move from one school or center to another as though in an extended family? This is another area where there are many questions and, as yet, few answers.

Differing Points of View

Considering the diversity of backgrounds of parents and teachers, and the differences in their needs, perhaps one should remark more on the many instances where they work amicably together for the good of the children than on the instances where their points of view differ. These points of view are rarely irreconcilable, but it may take considerable time, discussion, and reflection for each to understand the other, and for that understanding to be reflected in their planning for the child.

The early childhood educator, whose background may be as limited as that of many teachers, has much to gain from a deliberate effort to confront and understand the pluralism in our society. When she becomes able to respect and empathize with people whose cultural roots and values differ from hers, she will be in a better position to support both the teachers and the parents.

Some areas of difference between parents and teachers arise so often as to be predictable. Among these are discipline, play, and beginning reading. In each area parents and teachers often have different beliefs, different knowledge of the child, and sometimes different goals for him.

The teacher, according to old stereotypes, demands strict conformity to her rules, and the parent often finds these ill-adapted to the particular needs of the child. At the early childhood level, however, the parental complaint seems more likely to relate to too much "permissiveness." When the teacher fails to establish and maintain consistent, rational, and explicit limits, parental concern seems justified. In other situations the problem lies in different goals and different notions of how to reach them. Some parents value conformity. Their experience has taught them that the best way to get along is to do as you are told. They expect the same from their children. The teacher, on the other hand, seeks a more active role for the child. She wants him to understand the limits and within those limits weigh choices and their consequences. Differ-

[27] Alvin Toffler, *Future Shock* (New York: Bantam Books, 1971), p. 121.

ences of these kinds need thorough exploration if they are to be resolved. Consideration must be given the possible predicament of the child. Fortunately, most children can adapt to the requirements of different settings. There is no doubt, however, that many parents would prefer to have the option to select a school or center where the convictions about discipline are in accord with their own.

Some parents feel as strongly about the place of play in the curriculum as they do about the nature of discipline. The work ethic is strong in our tradition, so strong that these parents feel cheated if the program does not emphasize what they regard as work-oriented activities. When the teacher is articulate about the contribution that play makes to the child's development, and the parent can see for himself what goes on in play and how it progresses, his concerns may be alleviated. Parents need to understand that ample provision for play need not indicate a disregard for the child's intellectual development or for his achievement.

Just as many parents are concerned that their children "only play" at the center or school, they wish their children to begin early to learn to read. Some of their concerns undoubtedly stem from the insistence during the past decade that "earlier is better." In the case of parents who are poor, their concern also stems from the hard evidence that many of their children have been going through elementary school and into high school without acquiring effective reading skills.

This is a tough problem. On the one hand, experience clearly indicates that children can be taught simple decoding skills as early as five, or even four, but there is also evidence that, as the complexity of the material to be decoded increases, children who have not yet attained the level of operational thinking have difficulty. This raises the question of whether anything has been gained by beginning the instruction at an early age. Equal effort to facilitate intellectual development generally might be just as efficacious. Indeed, several investigators have proposed postponement of beginning reading instruction beyond the age of six.[28]

The problem with postponement is that it fails to take into account the reality of cultural expectation for beginning reading to start no later than age six. Perhaps when there is more general awareness of the beginning reading process and the nature of its precursors, and more appreciation of individual differences in rate of development, these expectations will change. My own view inclines to an environment that is rich with reading opportunities and a

---

[28] Hans G. Furth, *Piaget for Teachers* (Englewood Cliffs, N.J.: Prentice-Hall, 1970); William D. Rohwer, Jr., "Prime Time for Education: Early Childhood or Adolescence," *Harvard Educational Review,* 41(3), 1971; Louise B. Ames et al., *Stop School Failure* (New York: Harper & Row, 1972).

teacher who is knowledgeable about the processes involved in learning to read as well as about methods of instruction. Such a teacher can communicate to parents the nature of the progress the child is making toward beginning reading and the ways she is promoting that progress. I suspect that what worries most parents is not that the teacher has not begun systematic instruction of the four- or five-year-old, but rather that she fails to do so out of ignorance of what to do or out of lack of concern for the child.

PARENT INVOLVEMENT

The extent of parental involvement in planning, implementing, and evaluating the education of young children ranges widely. At one extreme parents do, or are expected to do, what the professionals tell them. At the other extreme the parents tell the professionals what needs to be done.[29]

At the extreme of least involvement, some public schools and some private and commercial schools and centers meet the parent with a "take it or leave it" attitude. Since school attendance is required for older children and many parents of younger children are hard-pressed to find schools and centers that are conveniently located and within their ability to pay, many parents have little choice but to "take it."

"Taking it" may involve any number of meaningless rituals—receiving reports on the child's progress, or lack thereof, possibly visiting the child's class, conferring with the teacher, and attending parents' meetings. On the other hand, in some schools and centers, even where the parents are given little choice regarding their child's activities, these rituals seem significant. The difference undoubtedly rests with the genuineness of concern and depth of interest manifested by the school and center staffs.

At the extreme of greatest involvement, such as that found in many cooperative nursery schools, in Head Start programs with strong parent advisory councils, and in many alternative schools, parents determine policy. Some of the same rituals are engaged in but take on additional meaning when parents view the school or center as theirs.

In considering the various ways schools and centers provide for parent involvement, it may be well to note again the fact of individual difference. Not all parents want to be involved in the same ways. Some do not care to serve on boards, although all want to know that their opinion counts in decision making. Some do not care to participate in the classroom, although all want to feel welcome there.

---

[29] For an analysis of the differences in parent power vis-à-vis teachers in relation to types of preschools, see Ellen Handler, "Teacher-Parent Relations in Preschool," *Urban Education,* 6:215–232, 1971.

A list of the ways parents may be involved underscores the importance of the teacher's ability to work with other adults. The nature of the relationship to the parent varies somewhat, depending on the situation, but all call for openness, insight, and considerable knowledge.

Informal Contacts

The way the teacher and other staff members greet the child and the parent, the quick comment on his interests, a concern for what has been happening at home, all contribute to the parent's sense that his child is known as a person. In the day care center, where schedules are often arranged so that one person is on duty when a child arrives and another when he leaves, the problem of managing these informal contacts so that the parent has a sense of continuity is especially important. The mother who, for example, warns the morning staff person that her child has not slept well and may need extra rest can only be aggravated when the afternoon person reports that she cannot understand why the child has been fighting and crying so much.

As children move into kindergarten and first grade, notes may serve as the communicative bridge between school and home. Here, as in other contacts with parents, teachers need a sense of the way the parent will read the note (or have difficulty reading it) and how the parent is likely to feel about the contents.

A good criterion for decisions about formal reporting to parents is the significance such reporting is likely to have for them. The public school report-card tradition has permeated many early childhood programs, especially those that emphasize preacademic work. There is no question that parents should be informed about their child's development and learning in whatever program he attends, but whether a formal report card is the most effective means for accomplishing this is debatable. The old quip about the child receiving an "A in sandpile" suggests some of the problems.

Many programs at both preschool and kindergarten-primary levels are struggling with the question of how they can most effectively share with parents the progress the child is making. Some, tying their program to a set of behavioral objectives, are satisfied to report which ones the child has attained. Others, concerned that parents have an understanding of the totality of the child's experience, are experimenting with narrative reports, photos and films, and the child's own products.[30] Many rely more on conferences with parents than on formal reports.

[30] The question of evaluation is discussed further in Chapter 10.

Conferences

The parent-teacher conference may be seen by the teacher and the early childhood educator as an opportunity to get to know the parent, to share goals, report progress, and make plans. The parent's expectation for the conference may be as much determined by the kind and quality of informal contacts she has with the teacher as by anything else.

If the parent has had opportunity to observe or participate in the child's program, or if he has not taken advantage of these but feels welcome, conferences are likely to be productive. Where conferences are the norm, rather than occurring only when problems arise, they are also more effective.

Good conferences—conferences where a mutual sharing between partners goes on, and from which a sense of direction emerges for both—do not just happen. They require planning. Teachers cannot be expected to do them well if they must be sandwiched into an already full schedule.

Planning involves thinking about what is to be reported about the child and how it will be shown. Anecdotal observations of the child's behavior and samples of his work may be selected. These are particularly important when the parent has not been an observer.

In another aspect of planning, the teacher may anticipate how she might respond in the role of the parent. Here the teacher draws on her knowledge of the parent to put herself in the parent's shoes in order to consider the variety of ways the parent may perceive the conference. Such planning enables the teacher to "set the stage" for it.

Planning of this sort focuses on providing a comfortable setting for the conference. It is designed to keep the channels of communication open. The teacher, for example, avoids terms that may be technical jargon and incomprehensible to the parent.[31] Planning also involves presenting material in a way that will enable both partners in the conference to look at it without becoming defensive.

Planning should not be regarded as a strategy for interpersonal manipulation. When the teacher approaches the conference with fixed notions of what she is going to get the parent to do, little more than a sparring match may evolve. She may have a range of alternatives in mind, but the parent may come up with others. If the conference is effective, decisions are not made in advance but are arrived at through open discussion. The test of a good conference lies not only in the mutuality it engenders but also in the consequences it has for the child's learning and development.

---

[31] Delores Barnes, "Structuring Communication with Parents, Participation in Common Terms," ERIC document no. 071 180, 1972. Barnes found that parents from middle- and lower-class groups identified 1,265 terms they did not understand in the goal statements of elementary schools.

Observation and Participation

When parents "see with their own eyes," they can more readily understand how a program furthers, or perhaps hinders, their child's learning. The words the teacher uses take on added meaning when the parent's picture of the program in operation is based on observation or participation.

Opportunities for parent observation take many forms. They may be associated with, or separate from, participation. Many teachers are uncomfortable when they feel they are being observed. Likewise, many parents feel uncertain about the observer role. Both partners may feel more secure if the observation is given some focus. Printed observation guides may be used, or individual guidelines may be suggested, depending on the nature of the parent's interest or concern. For example, in an open classroom, a mother who wonders about the nature of the reading program might be asked to keep a list of the number of times the children spontaneously turn to books or need or receive help in reading and writing in the course of their activities.

Many parents (and teachers also) worry that the child will respond differently because of their presence. Often the children do just that. Open acknowledgment of the possibility and more frequent observations help to resolve a situation that must seem ambiguous to the child.

Participation gives the parent's presence added validity and may reduce self-consciousness on the part of all. The number of things that parents can do in early childhood programs runs from assisting in art activities or conducting a science experience to playing the zither. Many cooperative nursery school programs have been built around parent participation, and many kindergarten–first grade programs are richer because of this kind of parent involvement.

Like good conferences, good parent participation does not just happen. It has to be nurtured by a teacher who sees the possibilities in it. In one suburban community, for example, several kindergarten teachers remarked on the fact that each had a cluster of children who were keenly interested in beginning reading, along with other groups showing little or no interest. None wanted to impose a readiness program on the entire class. All lamented that their responsibilities for two classes, one in the morning and one in the afternoon, precluded the kind of individualized program they would like to have. Then one teacher, knowing that few of the mothers of her children were employed outside their homes, saw them as resources. With their help she transformed her classroom to a setting where those who were inclined could begin reading, and all had opportunities for highly individualized puppetry and film making as well as other creative activities and science and mathematics experiences.

Not all parents can give the extended time that these parents were able to contribute, but there are many meaningful ways that many parents, fathers as well as mothers, can participate.

Whether parents participate only occasionally or on a regular basis so that they become members of the teaching team, their participation needs to be planned with them, and also evaluated. In considering what they are to do with the children, and the children's probable reactions, and in going over the ways the plans worked out, they may learn new techniques and gain new insights. Working with children other than their own provides new perspectives for the parents both on children and on teaching them.

For the teacher, having the parent in a participatory role may illuminate many of the relationships involved in the parent-teacher-child triangle. It also leads the teacher to reflect on her teaching procedures and the rationale for them.

Home Visits

When the teacher goes to the child's home, the tables are, so to speak, turned on her. She may regard the classroom as *her* domain, but there can be no question about the home as the parents' domain. Seeing the child in his home may provide the teacher with deeper understanding of him. Her visit may also contribute to the child by providing a bridge between home and school or center; however, like the conference, it is a situation where she needs to consider her feelings if the roles were reversed. Will the parents regard her visit as a welcome sign of warmth and interest, or as an invasion of their privacy? When there is a valid and obvious reason for the visit, it should, if possible, be prearranged by phone call or note.

Many parents living in poverty welcome the friendly gesture of a teacher's visit, but the experience some of them have had leads them to be wary of any visitor who may be an investigator for a legal or welfare agency. It will be helpful for the teacher to be familiar with the cultural tradition of the families she visits. The point can be illustrated by an exchange that occurred when a group including Blacks, Mexican-Americans, and Asian-Americans planned the development of a child care center. One of the Black parents suggested that those who were already involved might invite other potentially interested parents to their homes for coffee and discussion. An Asian parent commented, "But *we* must know someone *very well* before we invite him to *our* homes."

The home visit may take several forms. At one level it is like any social call, but it may also take on some of the aspects of the conference. Since the child is apt to be present, and other members of the family as well, the constraints are different from those in the school or center.

The home visit may also be the occasion for teaching the mother, the child, or both. Since the most successful of the various innovative programs designed for the children of poverty included some sort of home intervention, interest in the development of home-based programs has spread.

Some of the home-based programs have focused on four-year-olds, others on infants and toddlers. In some programs a certified teacher is the home visitor. Other programs have trained community members as home visitors. This procedure may forestall problems related to cultural traditions and the conditions of poverty, but it still does not guarantee that all will go well in this kind of home visiting.

Lally[32] describes a number of problems. Some are specific to programs where teaching is involved, other are inherent in any kind of home visiting and in conferences as well.

Lally first notes that home visitors tend to prefer working with the child, thereby neglecting the teaching of the parent. This finding reinforces my contention that those who enjoy working with children do not necessarily enjoy working with adults, nor are they always successful with them.

People who prefer working with the child are likely to reinforce the child and neglect to make the experience equally enjoyable for the parent. When the home visitor teaches in such a way as to establish a pleasant interchange between parent and child, she sets up a reinforcing situation that can be recreated and expanded when she leaves.

Lally also notes that the home visitor is more effective when she recognizes and deals with many needs. As he puts it, "If there is a disaster of social and economic reality in a family which saps motivation and energy, you are not going to expect the mother to play with purple ovals when some matter of life and death is causing her not to focus on them."

Working with parents in this broader way often fosters dependency on the home visitor or teacher. Having someone to depend on is very gratifying to the parent and should enable her to develop greater strength. A problem arises, however, when the visitor is also gratified by the dependency and fails to see that her job is to encourage parental independence rather than continuing dependency.

Parent Meetings

"In union there is strength," and bringing parents together so that they share problems and solutions is one way to promote their independence.

Meetings take many forms, ranging from all the parents in the school, the center, or the school system gathering to see a film or hear a speaker, to the

[32] J. Ronald Lally, Presentation to Home Start Conference, St. Louis, April 3, 1972.

small group of parents who meet together to discuss problems of special interest to them. The kind of meeting parents find useful depends somewhat on their background. Some middle-class parents may derive support from the large meeting with an expert, but other parents may be quite disinterested. For them, something closer to their own concerns—coming together with other parents in their child's classroom, for example—may be more useful. Parents with little opportunity to socialize enjoy the meeting that is festive, with food, music, and perhaps dancing and games. Parents who are living in poverty are especially appreciative when meetings are planned in ways that provide for their children, of whatever ages, as well as themselves. For parents whose children are in day care centers the provision of a meal for the family is often the deciding factor in parent attendance.

Meetings of small groups of parents, extended over a number of sessions, are often productive of greater understanding of children, and sometimes of new skills as well. Leadership for such groups often emerges from within the group. However, skills and knowledge paralleling those required in the conference are usually needed to ensure that groups function effectively until the leadership emerges. Assistance may also be needed as groups redefine their purposes and need new kinds of information.

All the ways of working with parents so far described—informal contacts, reports, observation and participation, conferences, and parent meetings—provide opportunities for parent education, that is, for bringing to parents current knowledge about child development and the factors that support development. They may also provide an avenue for parent involvement in policy making.

PARENT EDUCATION PROGRAMS[33]

To what extent should parental knowledge about child development and learning involve changes in parental behavior? Is the focus of parent education to provide parents with information or is it to teach them new skills?

Many parent education programs, either explicitly or implicitly, teach middle-class child-rearing. Studies dating back to the 1940s and 1950s show that middle-class children pay a considerable price for the achievement striving so carefully inculcated in them and also that some parents believe that price is too high.[34] Nevertheless, these studies seem to have had little effect on most educators' ideas regarding proper child-rearing procedures.

---

[33] Evelyn Pickarts and Jean Fargo, *Parent Education toward Parental Competence* (New York: Appleton-Century-Crofts, 1971), provide a good statement of the work and methods of the parent educator.
[34] Davis and Havighurst, *Father of the Man,* 1947. Also Joseph Kahl, "Educational and Occupational Aspirations of 'Common-Man' Boys," *Harvard Educational Review,* 23:186–203, 1953.

The crucial issue for parent education is not the perpetuation of middle-class child-rearing. It is rather the identification of those practices that are most likely to ensure that the child's options on his future are not restricted before he enters elementary school.

Whether it is the parental child-rearing practices of poor people that have restricted their children's options, or whether the blame lies with the lack of options available to the parents themselves has been debated. Noteworthy, however, is the number of parents who, while living at a level of bare subsistance, have not only been willing to send their children to preschool programs but also to participate in them. Add to these parents those who have been willing to be taught at home and those who have actively involved themselves and their children in "Sesame Street." The interest in parent education seems clear.

Proportionally, however, the number of poor families that are reached by parent education programs remains relatively small. Assuming that all parents are in need of information about child development, the challenge to find ways of reaching those who do not readily respond is very great.

One early childhood educator suggests that short, snappy television "commercials" dealing with some aspect of child development might well be interspersed in those programs likely to be watched by these parents. Another possible setting for parent education programs is the supermarket[35] and the laundromat. It is dubious, however, that parent education programs will have great effect unless they are intermeshed in comprehensive services (health, nutritional, and psychological) accessible to families, beginning with prenatal care.

Another view is that parent education as currently conceived is not only too little but too late. It should begin in high school and be available to all young people *before* they become parents.[36]

Scheinfeld, whose work with poor families in some respects parallels the White and Watts study of competent children, cited earlier, argues that

> Parents cannot construe the child's relationship to the world in ways that are fundamentally different from the way they construe their own relationship to the world. Hence, to change child-rearing practices effectively, one must change the parent's own experience in the world.[37]

---

[35] Robert T. Filep, *Supermarket Discovery Center: Pilot Study* (El Segundo, Calif.: Institute for Educational Development, 1968).

[36] See, for example, *Children Today,* 2(2), March–April 1973.

[37] Daniel R. Scheinfeld, "On Developing Developmental Families," in Edith Grotberg, ed., *Critical Issues in Research Related to Disadvantaged Children* (Princeton: Educational Testing Service, September 1969, Fifth Seminar), p. 2.

Scheinfeld proposes that a *developmental* community is needed to sustain the changes in child-rearing that may be made in a single family. Thus, a parent education program involving poor families ought to be developed in such a way that the impact made on one family would spread to other families. It would also build "a system of community supports which will help sustain families in their growth over time."[38] In such a program parents are not merely educated; they assume responsibility for the education of others.

PARENTS AS POLICY MAKERS

Who determines the program of the early childhood school or center? The teachers? The parents? The local board of education? The state department of education or some other department? The federal government? These questions, many of them raised over and over again since public schooling began, assume new poignancy as the possibilities for enrolling younger and younger children, even including infants, grows.

Middle-class parents, when concerned about their schools, have always had some options. They go to see the principal, they activate the PTA, they form a committee, they elect a new board of education, or they send their children to private schools, or maneuver a transfer within the system. Their opportunities for direct control of the schools have, however, been limited by the educators' insistence on professional autonomy.

Poor parents, and especially those who are members of ethnic minorities, have lacked most of the options of more privileged parents. They have had no recourse but to accept the professional autonomy of school personnel.

The sense of constraint experienced by the poor and their aspirations for influencing their children's education are revealed in a comment made by a parent in the Child Development Group of Mississippi. This Head Start project, initiated in 1965, was one of the first to encourage poor parents to take responsibility for their own program—"to think what you want yourself and what you want for your children."[39] The parent said, reflecting on discussion in which parents had expressed views contrasting sharply with those of a professionally trained kindergarten teacher:

> This is a kindergarten, but the school people don't like it because they can't tell us what to do. Maybe they don't like us even a little worse because, maybe, we're going to do our kindergarten even a little better than them, since they never did one neither, and that's embarrassing to them. Besides, they're jealous. They thinks

---

[38] Scheinfeld, p. 6.
[39] Polly Greenberg, *The Devil Has Slippery Shoes* (Toronto: Macmillan Co., Copyright © 1969 by Polly Greenberg, Collier-Macmillan Canada Ltd.), p. 59.

they owns the childrens, and they hates to see the government admit we owns a piece of them too! They has never done very well raising citizens, look at our people in the past, have they been good citizens? We are going to do much better raising good citizens. I can tell just by listening to his talk here today. That's what the schools is jealous about.[40]

From the beginning of Head Start, parent advisory councils (later parent policy councils) have been mandatory for programs using federal funds. The question of their effectiveness has generated considerable debate. Much of this has had to do with whether parents judged ineffective in their child-rearing practices, and in need of intervention, should have responsibility for determining the nature of their children's education.[41]

In many communities professionals and politicians have manipulated opportunities for parent involvement at the policy level. When the educational experts think that they alone know best, there are many ways they can weaken parent advisory councils or prevent them from becoming strong. Greenwood and his colleagues note:

> Parents often need help in the beginning in: (1) overcoming their belief that the school personnel won't really involve them in decision-making; (2) building up their confidence and developing their skills in such activities as conducting business meetings, building budgets, analyzing curriculum, involving other parents, etc.[42]

When parents seek an equal partnership with professionals tension is often prevalent. Yet, as Knitzer notes, "parents tend to want the same things professionals want. Or if their wants do not coincide, parents tend to identify areas that should have been of concern to the profession."[43] She illustrates the point with a list of issues identified by parents at the Airlie House Conference on Child Development in 1970. Although the parents caucused apart from the professionals their lists were similar.

The fact that the goals for the children's development held by parents and by teachers may not be very different should be reassuring to those teachers who uneasily contemplate partnership with parents. It does not, however, relieve them from the responsibility of working with them openly and sensi-

---

[40] Greenberg, p. 78.

[41] Ira J. Gordon, *Parent Involvement in Compensatory Education* (Urbana: University of Illinois Press, 1970), pp. 72–74.

[42] Gorden E. Greenwood et al., "Some Promising Approaches to Parent Involvement," *Theory into Practice,* 11:183–189, June 1972.

[43] Jane Knitzer, "Parental Involvement: The Elixir of Change," in Dennis N. McFadden, ed., *Early Childhood Development Programs and Services: Planning for Action* (Washington: National Association for the Education of Young Children, 1972), p. 90.

tively and not manipulatively. Parents need time to think through the values they hold for their children. Their goals deserve careful, reflective consideration.

THE EARLY CHILDHOOD EDUCATOR'S ROLE

The present chapter has considered the role of the parent in the child's development and the ways the teacher and other staff members support the parental role. Just as the teacher may need help in developing and carrying through effective teaching strategies with the child, she may also require aid in working with parents.

The kind of help that is needed and the amount will vary with the situation and with the teacher's skills and interests. In situations where the number of children the teacher is responsible for is small, or where she has the assistance of aides, the teacher may also take responsibility for parent conferences, and for their observation and participation. With larger groups and less help, and when she does not feel comfortable working with parents, she may welcome an early childhood educator who can guide parents' observation, discuss aspects of their participation with them, and perhaps also work with them in groups.

In other circumstances the early childhood educator may serve more as a resource to the teacher, acting as a sounding board for the teacher's plans and for her interpretation of her work with the parents, and providing information about child development and community resources. The need for her role arises out of the increasing complexity of the teacher's role both in working with children and in working with parents.

In many instances, it appears that teachers will opt to have the early childhood educator serve as liaison person between them and the parent advisory board. When this is the case, she must remain in close touch with both the parents and the teachers.

The role of the early childhood educator in working with parents, accordingly, is prescribed by the particular needs of the teachers and the parents.

Chapter 9

Working with Other Adults

In life in general and in human life in particular, the vulnerability of being newly born and the meekness of innocent needfulness have a power all their own. Defenseless as babies are, they have mothers at their command, families to protect the mothers, societies to support the structure of families and traditions to give a cultural continuity to systems of tending and training. All of this, however, is necessary for the infant to evolve humanly, for his environment must provide that outer wholeness and continuity which, like a second womb, permits the child to develop his separate capacities in distinct steps, and to unify them in a series of psychosocial crises. [1]

To provide continuity and wholeness for children in a society that is complex, differentiated to the point of fragmentation, and changing rapidly is a major challenge to both parents and teachers. The agencies and institutions that have developed to protect the child and to further his health, education, and welfare do not always function in accord with one another. They are often unsuccessful

[1] Erik H. Erikson, *Insight and Responsibility* (New York: W. W. Norton, 1964), p. 114.

in maintaining the child's interests either against their own needs for self-perpetuation or against other more powerful interests in the society.

The teacher's role in whatever agency or institution she works is to support, complement, or supplement the role of the parent. The features of modern living that make fulfillment of the parental role difficult also impinge on the role of the teacher. She too needs certain kinds of support if she is to be effective.

In one center, for example, the teachers felt overwhelmed by the number of contacts, in addition to those with the parents, that were necessary to keep a full-day program in operation. They had to work with the nutritionist in making decisions about how meals were to be prepared, transported, and served. They went to the park commission to get a nearby park cleaned up and maintained so as to be safe for children. They had to deal with the church members in whose building the center was housed. It was not easy to respect their values while trying to maintain certain educational values that seemed not in accord with those of the church. The teachers also had to cope with strains that developed among the paraprofessionals regarding who could work in the classroom the most, who did the kitchen work, who got the early schedule, and so on. Besides all this, and the parents, they had to deal with representatives of funding agencies, neighbors to the center, public school administrators, and university staff and students.

One aspect of the role of the early childhood educator is to provide the support needed by the teacher. Another is to participate in the network of institutional relationships impinging on the child and his family. Her intent is to work toward institutional ways that further the child's development and his sense of wholeness and continuity.

In her participation in various organizations, the early childhood educator finds herself involved in two very different kinds of relationships. One kind may be described as hierarchical. She stands in subordinate relationship to someone in authority, and is in turn an authority to someone else. For example, as the director of an early childhood center in a public school system, she may be responsible to the superintendent of schools while she works with a staff that is responsible to her. In the other relationship, authority is, in a sense, shared. It is exemplified by the team, in which the members share responsibility, and decisions are reached through a pooling of talents and ideas from which an eventual consensus arises.

An understanding of the authority relationships, that is, of the way, "the right and power to command, enforce laws, exact obedience, determine or judge"[2] are established in a particular organization, should facilitate the early

[2] William Morris, ed., *American Heritage Dictionary of the English Language* (New York: American Heritage Publishing Co. and Houghton Mifflin Co., 1971), p. 89. Copyright © 1969, 1970, 1971, 1973 by

childhood educator's ability to work effectively with the adults involved in it. She also needs to recognize that the nature of the actual relationships often differs from that depicted in an organization chart.

There are two reasons for emphasizing the importance of an understanding of how organizations function. One has to do with the fact that getting things done for young children often involves going through organizational channels, ranging from the local fire department, to the state legislature, and on to federal funding agencies. The second is that the early childhood educator inevitably represents authority. She needs to understand its nature and the extent to which it will hamper or further her work for children.

Benne, in a discussion of authority in education, describes three kinds of authority.[3] The first is that of expertise. The early childhood educator, to the extent that she has a specialized knowledge of child development and of teaching strategies, has the authority of expertise. But it is a limited authority. It is limited in somewhat the way that the doctor's authority with his patient is limited. He can prescribe effectively only in relation to the diagnosed need of the patient. Similarly, the authority of the early childhood educator rests on her ability to match her expertise to the needs of the children and their parents.

A second kind of authority is that of rules. "The function of rules is to create a system of orderly transactions among participants in a joint action." And Benne further notes, "The authoritative character of rules and codes does not rest upon the 'original' legislation of founders or remote legislative bodies but upon re-legislation of the rules and codes through the decision by particular groups of people to act and interact through and in them."[4]

The authority of rules both constrains and protects the work of the early childhood educator. On the one hand, rules define the extent and the limits of her responsibility, but also assure her "due process" in the event of conflict. On the other hand, rules may reflect outmoded procedures for problems that no longer exist, and so restrict, for example, the availability of needed services for children. Rules can of course, be modified through legislation and through negotiation.

The third kind of authority is that which "operates as persons grow into membership in some more inclusive human community."[5] An individual becomes a bearer of such authority "by virtue of responsible efforts to mediate

---

American Heritage Publishing Co., Inc.; reprinted by permission from The American Heritage Dictionary of the English Language.

[3] Kenneth D. Benne, "Authority in Education," *Harvard Educational Review,* 40(3):385-410, August 1970.

[4] Benne, p. 398.

[5] Benne has coined the unwieldy term *anthropogogical* to refer to this kind of authority. In contrast to *pedagogical,* where the young are subjects and the old have the authority, it implies learning and reeducation for men and women of all ages.

between the present community involvements of those being educated and their expanding and deepening affiliations in the common life of a wider community."[6] To the extent that the early childhood educator is committed to and works for the kinds of institutions and education that support the human dignity of children and their parents, she shares in such authority.

The need for rational examination and reformulation of many organizational structures is apparent when the number of agencies involved in child care and education are considered.

Hierarchical Organization of Services

The varied settings and sponsorship for early childhood education and care that were described in Chapter 5 also represent a network of authority relationships.

At the local level, for example, the early childhood educator, as director of a child care center, has certain kinds of authority in relation to the center staff, but her authority is constrained by the board of the agency that assumes responsibility for the center. It in turn is constrained by regulations that stem from funding sources and from government-regulating agencies. If the early childhood educator works in a public school system, she is involved in a similar situation. She has some authority and she is subject to authority, but the sources of regulation differ. The local schools are subject to the authority of the state and, in certain respects, to that of the federal government.

Federal authority has many sources. According to Elliot Richardson:

> At the present time [September 1971], the Social Security Act, the Economic Opportunity Act, the Elementary and Secondary Education Act, and the Manpower Development and Training Act all contain child care or related provisions. Our intentions have been good and we have made some progress. But the scattered array of child-care authorities has often led to confusion, duplication and waste.[7]

In similar vein, Lazar[8] notes that the Appalachian Commission has identified over 200 federal programs whose provisions serve children under six years of age. Programs for young children are in every Cabinet department including Defense, State, Agriculture, Labor, Housing and Urban Development, and Commerce.

---

[6] Benne, p. 402.

[7] Statement of September 22, 1971, quoted in Policy Research Project Report, Child Development Policy for Texas, no. 2 (Austin: Lyndon B. Johnson School of Public Affairs, University of Texas).

[8] Irving Lazar, "On the Organization of Services to Children—Some Suggestions for Federal and State Action," in Dennis N. McFadden, ed., *Planning for Action* (Washington: National Association for the Education of Young Children, 1972).

In the 1960s many federal programs by-passed state administrations to deal more directly with local communities. The 1970s have seen a shift toward more centralized control at the state level. The Education Commission of the States, anticipating the passage of the Child Development Act of 1971 (later vetoed by President Nixon), appointed a task force to consider alternative plans. The task force report underscored "the duplication and competition caused by uncoordinated funding sources."[9]

At the state level, a Texas study noted the same problems but suggested that they are not unsurmountable:

> Ultimately, new legislation will be needed to firmly establish a comprehensive national effort for young children. However, much progress in this direction can be made in the meantime *on the basis of existing legislation.* By rethinking rules and regulations, by aggressively making use of federal funding opportunities and committing the required state matching funds, by consistently developing administrative mechanisms for bringing together services intended for the same client population, and by inter-facing child-care and child-development programs with social services provided for other age groups and functional needs—considerable headway can be made toward the development of integrated services that meet the several needs of young children.[10]

At the local level, the proliferation of programs funded in diverse ways and subject to different kinds of regulations has led to duplication of service while certain needs continue to be unmet. To some observers this fact indicates the need for more coordination of effort, perhaps through some central agency. Others think that major efforts should go into the establishment of services, with the problems of coordination being worked out as they arise. As they see it, time and money allocated for attempts at coordination from the top down are less effective than time and money put directly into services.[11] Obviously, those responsible for the services must also be alert to the possibilities for coordination.

The early childhood educator, regardless of the position she holds, is inextricably involved in a network of organizational structures. How she relates to these is in part determined by the nature of the role assigned to her. The role of early childhood educator may encompass several other roles. No

---

[9] Report of the Education Commission of the States Task Force on Early Childhood Education, *Early Childhood Development Alternatives for Program Implementation in the States* (Denver: The Commission, 1971), p. 71.

[10] Policy Research Project Report, *Child Development Policy for Texas,* p. 52.

[11] See, for example, Pat Bourne et al., *Day Care Nightmare,* Working Paper No. 5, Institute of Urban and Regional Development, University of California, Berkeley, February 1971; Kay L. Martin, "Planning for Day Care" (unpublished Master's thesis, University of California, Berkeley, 1972).

one person is likely to enact all those described here, but all are possibilities. Those described first—trainer, program advisor, or supervisor—focus on the provision of support to the teachers and other staff members involved in early childhood education and care. In the other roles, the emphasis shifts to the early childhood educator's participation in the network of institutions that impinge on the child and his family.

THE EARLY CHILDHOOD EDUCATOR AS TRAINER

The term "train" implies concentration on the particular skills needed to fit a person for a specified role. As trainer, the early childhood educator assumes responsibility for the preparation of competent workers for early childhood programs. As it is described here, the trainer role does not exclude approaches that are broadly educative as compared with those that are more narrowly focused.[12]

Like many other aspects of early childhood education, training for it is complicated by the number and diversity of programs and also by the different traditions related to the provision of care and the provision of education. Consideration of who is to be trained and where and when training is to take place precedes consideration of what the content of training is to be and how it is to be done.

Whom to Train

Parker and Dittman assert that everyone associated with day care programs needs training, beginning with national, state, and regional agencies, and including the trainers of trainers, program administrators, and staff developers as well as program staff.[13] The wisdom of their assertion cannot be refuted. In the present discussion, however, the focus is on training for those who are actually involved in services to the child—the family day care mother, the teacher, the teacher's aides and assistants, and such ancillary service personnel as the cook, the custodian, the bus driver, and the volunteer.

Although many programs require a nucleus of certified personnel, in whose training the early childhood educator is involved, other programs, particularly those involving day care, are staffed with paraprofessionals, individuals lacking training and experience in that field. Included among them

---

[12] The currently wide use of the term "training" as contrasted with the use of the term "education" in connection with early childhood programs probably stems from two sources. One is the application of behavior theory; the other is the increasing involvement of paraprofessionals.

[13] Ronald Parker and Laura Dittman, eds., *Staff Training* (Washington: U.S. Department of Health, Education, and Welfare, Office of Child Development, n.d.).

are indigenous persons who are familiar with the neighborhood and its people, college-trained persons who have been unable to secure teaching positions, and older persons who have had previous employment in some other field.[14] As Lally and his colleagues note, the involvement of "men and women, young people and old people, rich people and poor people, fat people and skinny people, students and professors, formally educated and practically educated people" for various roles in early childhood programs enables the children to "experience many different life styles, personalities and cultures."[15] In the public schools also, since the 1960s, the paraprofessional has made possible greater individualization of instruction and increased richness and variety in the curriculum.[16]

When programs are so largely dependent on staff who must to a large extent receive their training on the job, the recruitment and selection of suitable persons becomes extremely important. Likely prospects are those with demonstrated interest in children and their parents who have the basic qualities of warmth, openness, and energy that have been described as essential in teaching.[17] To the extent that they may be involved with the children, these same qualities are also important for ancillary staff. In a good program recruitment goes on continuously. The more a program becomes an integral part of the community, the more people know about it and suggest other individuals who may wish to participate in it.

Selection procedures vary. In some cases they precede an initial training experience. In others the training serves as part of the selection process. In either event, the trainee needs to be oriented to either the specific position for which he is being considered, or more generally to the kind of work for which the training may qualify him.

Experience with paraprofessionals in both schools and centers shows that many work their way up a career ladder that may lead to teacher certification or to positions such as center director, parent educator, or nutritionist. Experience also suggests that some individuals prefer to continue in the positions they fill originally, or may not qualify for further training. Still others would like to move but do not understand the kinds of knowledge and skills or the training needed for moving into new positions.

---

[14] Dorothy Haupt, "Personnel and Personnel Training," in Dennis N. McFadden, ed., *Early Childhood Development Programs and Services,* pp. 112, 113.

[15] J. Ronald Lally et al., "Training Paraprofessionals for Work with Infants and Toddlers," *Young Children,* 28(3):173–182, February 1973.

[16] Garda W. Bowman and Gordon J. Klopf, *New Careers and Roles in the American School* (New York: Bank Street College of Education, n.d.), recounts the experience of fifteen projects demonstrating the training and use of paraprofessionals in public school settings. *Aides to Teachers and Children* (Washington: Association for Childhood Education International, 1968), describes the recruitment and training of aides in a variety of settings.

[17] Parker and Dittman *(Staff Training)* suggest a number of selection procedures and outline competencies for both the entry and later levels.

Trainers carry great responsibility for helping paraprofessionals to appraise their own abilities and the job opportunities realistically. Workers who have been brought up in poverty often suffer from inadequate schooling and a consequent sense of uncertainty about their own capabilities. Their training must capitalize on their strengths and must also emphasize the skills that they need for success in the position they may hold next. The trainer contributes most to their development when she helps them to have confidence in themselves, but she does them no favor if she fails to differentiate between the skills they may have as they enter training, those they will need to succeed at the first job level, and those that are required to move on to another level.

An example of failure to communicate adequately regarding the different kinds of skills needed at different levels comes from a school program. In this program the teachers assessed the learning of the children and prescribed individual learning activities for them. The teaching needed for these activities was then carried out by both the aides and the teachers, while the teachers continued to reassess and make new prescriptions. The aides resented the fact that they and the teachers were teaching in the same ways, but that they received less recognition and less pay. Their training had focused too narrowly on the teaching without giving them an appreciation for the nature and complexity of the assessment and planning done by the teachers.

A similar example comes from the field of social work where the professionals serving as community workers were able to carry through many needed activities with families and children. However, they were not helped to think through the reason why one activity, in terms of long-term effects, might be preferable to another. In effect, their training failed to give them sufficient rationale for working beyond the most routine level.[18]

It takes a fine sense of a person's present knowledge as well as his skills and of the way these may develop for a trainer to properly match the training he provides to the needs of the trainee.

When to Train

One might infer from certification procedures that teachers accomplish their training *before* they begin services in the schools. On the other hand, the training of paraprofessionals is more likely to be an on-the-job matter. The assumption that training for the teacher can end when she is employed is obviously erroneous. Preservice education is essential if the teacher is to come to her job with a background of knowledge and an array of skills, but most

---

[18] Case Conference on the Neighborhood Subprofessional Worker, *Children,* 15(1):7–16, January-February 1968.

teacher educators would agree that the effectiveness of preservice training depends on the way it is sustained during the first years of teaching.

The experience of the various curriculum projects of the 1960s, as well as the theoretical analyses of the later development of teachers, also point to the necessity for inservice training that continues throughout the teacher's career. [19]

It also appears that just as inservice training may extend indefinitely, preservice training may begin long before an individual enters college. When elementary school children are involved in teaching other children, and in cross-age grouping, when older youngsters take parent education courses and participate in volunteer and field study programs, they formulate elementary notions of child development and of what teaching young children is like and begin to develop their own skills. [20]

Where to Train

Except for brief forays into the real world of the schools, training was once confined to the college. Now, however, the colleges, the schools and centers, and the community may all serve as sites where training occurs.

Recent proposals by Schwertfeger [21] and by Moore [22] illustrate some of the ways field-based programs may be implemented. Their proposals were made at the time passage of the Child Development Act of 1971 seemed imminent. Their plans include a number of features that are in at least partial operation in a number of colleges and universities across the country.

Moore describes a program for "qualified teachers who will be responsible for the care and education of groups of very young children." It is a two-year program and for those pursuing more advanced professional goals could be incorporated into a four-year B.A. or B.S. program. Throughout the program the students would spend about half their time in field settings, being directly involved in ongoing programs and participating in their weekly staff meetings. The remainder of their time would be divided between independent study assignments in the areas of child development and early education and participation in a professional seminar and a guest colloquium series. Moore also proposes that the program have at its disposal a resource center with library

[19] Frances F. Fuller, "Concerns of Teachers: A Developmental Conceptualization," *American Educational Research Journal*, 6(2):207–226 March 1969.

[20] Lilian G. Katz, "Developmental Stages of Preschool Teachers," *Elementary School Journal*, 73(1):-50–54, October 1972.

[21] Jane Schwertfeger, "Issues in Cooperative Training, The University and the Center," in McFadden, ed., *Planning for Action*, pp.101–109.

[22] Shirley Moore, "The Training of Day Care and Nursery-School Personnel," in McFadden, ed., *Planning for Action*, pp. 117–126.

and reading room, curriculum materials and film libraries, video-taping equipment, and a curriculum workshop.

Presumably, the resource center might or might not be located on the college campus. If not, the student could perhaps complete his two-year program with rare if any appearances on campus.

Schwertfeger similarly asserts that the training of caretakers must move out of the setting of the training institution (junior college, college, and university) into the day care center. She proposes a coordinated effort of two training groups, one from the training institution and the other from the day care center. The latter may involve the members of a single center staff or it may include others. She notes that "sessions should be held at the centers, at the university, in homes and in other schools."[23]

In Schwertfeger's plan, preservice and inservice training are amalgamated. Part of what is preservice for the students is inservice for the center staffs. Although there are advantages to training in the center where the practical realities are close at hand, something may also be said for the stimulation that may come from being in a new setting and with different people.

Haupt proposes a plan for training day care personnel that involves combining the resources of several centers. In this plan one center serves as model and resource center for several other centers.[24] Haupt sees considerable value, both to children and to parents, in keeping training closely tied to the center base.

Where a center's isolation makes sharing with other staffs difficult, stimulation can still be made available. For example, the trainer may serve as an itinerant teacher. Collins describes a program in which a teacher, equipped with a station wagon loaded with books, records, rhythm instruments, and other classroom materials, moved through a rural area of California, spending a week in each of several Head Start programs. "She saw herself as a teacher trainer with an obligation to upgrade the professional skills and the career potentials of the Head Start employees." She tried through observation to identify strengths and weaknesses and then to "provide a model through demonstrations to further strengthen the program.[25]

What Shall the Content Be?

What shall the content of training be? Chapter 6 has provided some indication of the knowledge and skills necessary for teachers. Not all the material appropriate for the teacher will be needed by the aide, and other staff members will need training along different lines.

[23] Schwertfeger, p. 106.
[24] Haupt, pp. 113–115.
[25] Camilla Collins, "The Itinerant Teacher," *Young Children,* 27(6):374–379, August 1972.

According to Spodek, the content for teachers "needs to be determined by its relevancy to the teaching act. No course content should be included ... simply because it is significant child development knowledge or important historical fact."[26]

The better the trainer knows the realities of the school or center, the more obvious the needs for training are, but sometimes what seems to be obvious needs for acquiring certain skills also reflect the need for more knowledge. It is not easy to draw a fine line between content that is sure to have classroom application and that which may only be needed as the problems faced become more complex.

The current emphasis on "competency-based" training has several sources, including the concern that content be relevant to teaching. The application of behavior theory to problems of classroom interaction and management has also been influential. Perhaps also the number of studies that have analyzed teaching behaviors have contributed. Competency-based training stresses "the ability to do" in contrast to more traditional emphases on "the ability to demonstrate knowledge."[27]

The competencies to which training is to be directed vary in their explicitness. For example, McNeil's statement of behavioral objectives for a student teacher in the area of assessment describes the behavior the student is expected to exhibit quite specifically:

> The student teacher will be able to diagnose an individual learner's deficiencies in a particular content area. The standard of performance in diagnosis demands that the student (a) prepare a task analysis of an instructional objective by which entry or prerequisite skills are identified; (b) select and develop measures for assessing the pupil's status with respect to these prerequisites; and (c) use these measures in assessing the pupil's status and from the data collected formulate objectives that promise to "close the gaps" identified.[28]

In more global terms, Parker and Dittman describe the competencies that day care workers should have and suggest the kind of evidence needed to demonstrate the competency. They note, for example, that at the "middle level" of performance, the worker should be able to "plan and carry out at least one learning activity with children" and "should show an understanding of the differences between individual children." Evidence that the worker has these

---

[26] Bernard Spodek, "Constructing a Model for a Teacher Education Program in Early Childhood Education," *Contemporary Education,* 40:145–149, 1969.

[27] W. Robert Houston and Robert B. Howsam, *Competency-based Teacher Education* (Chicago: Science Research Associates, Inc., 1972), p. 3.

[28] John D. McNeil, *Toward Accountable Teachers* (New York: Holt, Rinehart and Winston, 1971), p. 117.

particular competencies comes from the observation that the children assigned to a worker "usually respond and stay with an activity," and that the worker "reacts positively but differently to different children in the same situation."[29]

The differences in explicitness of these competency statements reflect the differences between expectations for two different age levels, and also the difference in expertise to be expected from personnel whose primary function is education as compared with those whose primary function is care. The differences may also reflect different orientations with regard to teaching behavior.

How fine-grained an analysis of teaching behavior is useful for training purposes? Are the competencies most effectively taught as a sequence of component parts, or can the trainee, given more general statements of the anticipated competencies, work out his own ways of developing them? What competencies are generally agreed upon and which are specific to specific programs? How do the competencies relate to the behavior of the children and to their longer-term development? These are questions that research has only begun to consider. As the discussion in Chapter 6 implied, much is yet to be learned about teaching, and consequently, about the most effective ways of training teachers.

Without question, the movement to competency-based instruction has had some salutary effects. Many trainers who have been teaching early childhood courses, or directing workshops, have had to rethink their procedures when confronted with a requirement to specify outcomes in the behavior of the students. Experienced teachers have had to analyze their own teaching and become more explicit about their expectations for student teachers. In all probability trainees in competency-based programs and other programs as well have received a clearer picture of what their trainers expected from them.

Nevertheless, limitation of the content of a training program to instruction in specific competencies may be stultifying. The trainee may learn each of the sets of behaviors specified in the program without becoming an accomplished teacher. Effective teaching involves more than a repertory of teaching strategies. It requires analysis, judgment, and artistry in application. What strategy should be used for what child at what time and in which setting? Or is it more appropriate at this point to refrain from teaching? These kinds of decisions require the teacher to integrate what she knows about the child, the situation, and the available strategies in a way that is right for her as well as for the child.

Combs, in a critique of competency-based instruction, notes that "good

---

[29] Parker and Dittman, eds., *Staff Training,* p. 16.

teaching is a highly personal matter." He compares teaching to other professions that deal with human problems and observes that

> The effective professional worker in medicine, social work, clinical psychology, guidance or nursing is no longer seen as a technician applying methods in more or less mechanical fashion the way he has been taught. We now understand him as an intelligent human being using himself, his knowledge and the resources at hand to solve the problems for which he is responsible. He is a person who has learned to use himself as an effective instrument.[30]

Is the teacher's use of herself as an instrument for teaching proper content for training? Or, to put it another way, shall training ignore or capitalize on the fact of human indivduality?

To introduce into training a concern for the individual, to incorporate into it the different ways the trainees view the world, their fears, anxieties, and hostilities, as well as their joys and triumphs, is to complicate enormously the work of the trainer.

Such introduction involves inevitable risks, including the disruption of personal defenses, objectivity replaced by subjectivity, and loss of sight of the essential work of the teacher to assist children in their development and learning. These are risks that must be taken, however, and taken knowingly, for the risks of training that denies or merely tries to engineer the human factors are equally great.

How to Train

Students often complain that their teachers do not teach them as they are expected to teach children. When they mean that teachers fail to respect their individuality, provide more negative than positive reinforcement, talk over their heads, or use a very limited number of teacher strategies, their grievance seems justified.

On the other hand, adults are not children, and neither their experience nor their ways of thinking are as limited. Accordingly, the trainer who works with adults may appropriately use some teaching strategies that cannot be used with children.

Just as the teacher of young children needs time for planning, the "preactive" phase of teaching is equally as important for the teacher who works with adults. In that period the early childhood educator, as trainer, considers the nature of her relationship to and knowledge of the trainees.

---

[30] Arthur W. Combs, "The Personal Approach to Good Teaching," in Ronald T. Hyman, ed., *Contemporary Thought on Teaching* (Englewood Cliffs, N.J.: Prentice-Hall, 1971), p. 261.

They may, for example, be students in an ongoing program for certification or members of a program in which she is director or supervisor, or they may be members of a group with whom she has had no previous association, and whom she may or may not continue to meet. In any event, her knowledge and experience of the trainees, together with her knowledge of the goals of the program, determine the training strategies she uses. She considers whether these are best accomplished in a group or whether individuals can work independently. The following are strategies that are frequently used.

Lecture   This strategy is in bad repute, and with good reason, for it is probably the most overworked of all strategies available for teaching adults. However, the lecture may be appropriate when there is need to present material in an organized fashion, and particularly when such material cannot be made available through reading. The trainer needs to know the reading habits and inclinations of the trainees and to what extent she can rely on reading as a useful way for them to acquire information or to expand their understanding. She may also ask whether the material she proposes to deliver in a lecture might more appropriately be presented in the form of programmed learning.

The lecturer can adapt to the needs of trainees with limited backgrounds by the use of many concrete examples. Indeed, concrete illustrations make the lecture more meaningful to any audience. Lally shows how questions may be used to stimulate the trainees to clarify their ideas and become more involved in the training topic. For example, in a lecture on language development, the lecturer might ask: "What kinds of ways *besides* the use of words can babies let us know what they want or need?" or "What could a baby be doing that would make you decide that it was a good time to teach him the word 'cookie'?"[31]

Discussion   This is another hard-worked strategy. It is also an integral part of most of the other strategies. Its success is partly dependent on the size of the group. When more than fifteen people are involved, it often deteriorates into either a question and answer session (sometimes necessary to clarify information) or a series of monologues.

The success of the discussion also depends on the leader's ability to stimulate participation (sometimes by establishing subgroups), to ask appropriate questions, to follow the thread of the discussion, and to keep it in focus. Discussions may serve a variety of purposes: to "brainstorm" an idea; to solve a problem; to clarify ideas and feelings. It is important for the group to

[31] Lally et al., "Training Paraprofessionals for Working with Infants and Toddlers," p. 178.

understand the purpose of the discussion, and where groups continue over a period of several sessions, to see how they as members can make the group more productive.

When the leader of the group is open in her expression of feeling and encourages the members of the group to express both thought and feeling, the potential for meaningful experience is greatly increased. The early childhood educator needs to be aware of this, but she must also be sensitive to the possibility of unleashing feelings that go deeper than she realizes. Brown cautions that one of the unfortunate concomitants of current interest in group techniques and affective education is the appearance of "instant" leaders. "Persons who have attended only one or two workshops in such growth approaches as encounter groups, sensitivity groups, or sensory awakening want and feel competent to lead groups themselves." He suggests that they ask themselves, "What does it do for me to be a leader?" In other words, they "need to face the question of whether the intent is to teach or to manipulate." Moreover, the rule in all groups should be that "no one should be coerced to do what he does not want to do."[32]

Trainers of teachers for at least a quarter of a century have explored the dynamics of groups as a means of initiating and supporting change in their students. Certainly, the fact that the students will in their turn be group leaders gives validity to their study of group dynamics, but the question of whether the qualities of good human relationships can be taught, or engineered, is still open.[33] Apple's comment on teacher education models that attempt to break such a phenomenon as empathy into its component behaviors suggests the dilemma that is faced: "The conscious articulation of the 'skills' of empathy, etc. may open people to the possibility of greater interpersonal involvement, but, at the same time, it may destroy the very quality of humaneness that makes such encounters worthwhile."[34]

---

[32] George Isaac Brown, *Human Teaching for Human Learning* (New York: Viking Press, 1971), pp. 240–241.

[33] For an analysis of the origins of the study of group dynamics and the evolution of encounter and sensitivity groups, together with an appraisal of the evidence on their effectiveness, see Kurt W. Back, *Beyond Words: The Story of Sensitivity Training and the Encounter Movement* (New York: Russell Sage Foundation, 1972). One chapter deals with "Teachers and Change Agents."

[34] Michael Apple, "Behaviorism and Conservatism," in Bruce Joyce and Marsha Weil, eds., *Perspectives for Reform in Teacher Education* (Englewood Cliffs, N.J.: Prentice-Hall, 1972), pp. 260–261. In this connection Truax and Mitchell report that "within 100 hours of training personnel such as hospital aides can be brought to levels of accurate empathy, warmth and genuineness usually offered by professional therapists." They suggest that the inference from this finding can either be that the empathic skills are relatively superficial and can be learned rather quickly, or that they are learned early in development and the training merely capitalizes on the early learning. See Charles B. Truax and Kevin M. Mitchell, "Research on Certain Therapist Interpersonal Skills in Relation to Process and Outcome," in A. E. Bergin and Sol L. Garfield, eds., *Handbook of Psychotherapy and Behavior Change: An Empirical Analysis* (New York: John Wiley & Sons, 1971).

Films, Video Tapes, and Recordings   Next to being in the classroom with the trainees, audiovisual materials and equipment provide the trainer with the best opportunity to help trainees understand children and appropriate ways of working with them.

Films and video tapes are particularly useful in training for observational and recording skills. When an episode can be repeated, the observer can check his initial perceptions and broaden his ability to take in and record information.

The video tape is also a powerful tool when the trainee herself is taped, but the experience has potential for being disruptive. Fuller and Manning, following a comprehensive review of the use of video tapes in both therapy and education, remark that such self-confrontation "now seems to us more promising than we had hoped and more dangerous than we knew to fear."[35]

Fuller and Manning emphasize the need for more research on the nature of the process involved when the trainee sees herself on tape. They suggest that the procedure works best when the trainee has concerns or goals for her own performance, when she is taped in a familiar situation, and when she can identify before the playback the deficiencies in her performance as she was aware of them. Playback should occur as soon after performance as possible.

Focus should be provided for the playback and should be on the accomplishment of previously agreed upon goals. Such focus may be provided by various interaction schemes, described in a later section. The trainee may be concerned about her appearance or something that she regards as blemish or defect. However, the focus is on an aspect of the performance that can be improved, such as her questioning strategies. Greatest progress is likely to be made when discrepancies in the various perspectives (hers and her trainer's, before and after the performance, for example) that may be brought to bear on the observed performance are moderate rather than large or small.[36]

Video tapes can also be used in the inservice education of teachers. Experience indicates that the procedure carries with it promises and dangers similar to those at the preservice level. Its use may be especially effective when the teacher has developed confidence in her own ability to work with a group of children and she begins to be interested in new techniques and different ways of doing things.

Audio-taping carries some of the same qualities of self-confrontation but seems less powerful. It is very useful for training for interviewing or for other questioning strategies.

---

[35] Frances F. Fuller and Brad A. Manning, "Self-Confrontation Reviewed: A Conceptualization for Video Playback in Teacher Education," *Review of Educational Research,* 43(4):469–528, Fall 1973.
[36] Fuller and Manning, p. 509.

Microteaching In microteaching, as it was originally developed, the trainee presents a brief lesson to a group of three or four upper elementary or high school youths, who afterward use a brief questionnaire to critique the lesson. Since very young children cannot respond in this fashion, the procedure is modified for them.

Where video-tape equipment is available, the teacher or trainee works out a procedure that she wishes to use with a particular child or children, and tapes it.[37] In one training program, video-taping equipment was loaned to teachers in several remote areas. Each teacher taught and retaught a lesson as often as she wished before sending the final tape back to the trainer.[38]

Taping is not essential for microteaching. Within any group of young children several can usually be found who will be willing to participate in a brief session with the trainee-teacher. Often the effectiveness of her procedures is directly obvious, since younger children are usually quite open in their expressions of interest or boredom.

Direct Observation Direct involvement in a teaching situation gives the trainer many opportunities to influence the teaching of the trainee. She may demonstrate with the trainee observing, or she may observe the trainee in operation. In either event, a mutually agreed upon scheme for focusing the observation lends objectivity to the situation.

The number of observational systems or instruments for categorizing behavior and events in classrooms runs over a hundred.[39] However, not all these are suitable for use at the early childhood level,[40] and many of them are too complex to be used without a considerable amount of special training. In some instances coding must be done after the observation has been taped, and in some instances tapes must be transcribed.

Some systems, many of which are derived from an interaction analysis scheme devised by Flanders, can be learned fairly quickly and may be used by both trainers and trainees.[41] Rosenshine notes that there are eleven systems that have been used specifically for teacher training.[42]

---

[37] For an example of the use of this technique in training teachers to work with handicapped children, see interview with Jasper Harvey, "Development of a Staff Training Prototype for Early Childhood Centers," *Exceptional Children,* 37:670, 672–675, May 1971.

[38] John Meier and Gerald Brudenell, "Remote Training of Early Childhood Educators" (Greeley, Co.: Institute for Child Study, Colorado State College, 1968). ERIC document no. 027 262.

[39] Barak Rosenshine and Norma Furst, "The Use of Direct Observation to Study Teaching," in Robert M. W. Travers, ed., *Second Handbook of Research in Teaching* (Chicago: Rand McNally, 1973), p. 132.

[40] For a collection of instruments appropriate for use at the early childhood education level, see Alan R. Coller, *Systems for the Observation of Classroom Behavior in Early Childhood Education* (Urbana, Ill.: ERIC Clearinghouse on Early Childhood Education, April 1972).

[41] N. A. Flanders, *Analyzing Teacher Behavior* (Reading, Mass.: Addison-Wesley, 1970).

[42] Rosenshine and Furst, pp. 160–161.

At least two cautions should be considered in using any of these schemes. One is that the connections between the behaviors they isolate and the learning of the children have been established in very few instances. The other is that most of the devices, while explicitly descriptive, become prescriptive in use. Although the trainer can be expected to have biases as to what *should* be revealed in the trainee's teaching behavior, the use of a single observation instrument may lead to an overemphasis on some behaviors and the neglect of others.

Role Playing   When children are not available, teaching strategies may be enacted with students taking the roles of the children. Many adults find it difficult to follow the role of the young child in appropriate detail, however, and such role playing may accordingly deteriorate into unproductive comedy. Preliminary observation of children focused on the kinds of responses they make in similar situations may be useful. The trainer may also provide trainees with a set of typical responses to give more validity to the episode.

Role playing has particular value in preparing trainees for situations that will involve adults, such as conferring with a parent or a principal, teaching another adult, or leading a discussion. It has been effectively used to prepare parents, inexperienced with parliamentary procedures or in dealing with bureaucracies, to get their points across.

Role playing complements discussion. It may be used to concretize issues, to practice discussion skills, and to clarify feelings. When it is used to deal with issues, trainees need to have information so that they can adequately present a point of view. The need for information sometimes becomes evident as the playing proceeds or may be anticipated by the trainer.

In discussion, a skillful trainer, noting that the discussion is not going well, may ask the group to shift to a role-playing situation in which such problems as failure to listen to another's point of view, failure to clarify an important point, and so on can be examined. Role playing can also be used to identify the feelings that may lie under the discussion, with individuals playing their roles differently in accord with different emotions.

The effectiveness of role playing as a strategy seems to depend on the trainer's ability to make its purposes clear to the group and to keep it and the related discussion moving.

Games   Another simulation strategy is that of the game. This may take a variety of forms, serving purposes similar to those described in relation to encounter groups and sensitivity awareness,[43] or it may be directed toward

---

[43] See, for example, Carl Weinberg, "Problems in the Presentation of the Real Self," in Bruce Joyce and Marsha Weil, eds., *Perspectives for Reform in Teacher Education,* pp. 86, 87.

cognitive ends such as understanding the structure of a bureaucracy.[44]

Current enthusiasm for the use of games in the education of adults is apparent in a statement by Avedon and Sutton-Smith. "After business and industry started using games for in-service education, the more formal pre-service university programs followed suit." At present research and development of games with simulated environments is being carried out in six major research centers.[45] Games designed to teach problem solving and decision making in the context of parent-family relationships may be useful to early childhood educators. The early childhood educator may also design her own games for training.[46]

Avedon and Sutton-Smith comment that the values attributed to games by their designers and by those who use them are "endless. Only one of these supposed values is substantiated by research evidence. That is, games do attract and hold student interest and attention."[47]

Workshops For many years early childhood educators have relied on the workshop as a training strategy. The essence of the workshop is "learning by doing." In addition to whatever the trainee may learn directly from participation, she may also learn from the organization of the workshop ways of organizing a classroom for children's work and play.

The range of activities that can be included in workshops is endless. Trainees may construct equipment for children, engage themselves in movement and dance, paint or sculpt, experiment with science materials, design and use puppets, explore materials that are new to them, and so on.

Often a major purpose of the workshop is to help trainees see the possibilities in materials that children use, or to experience the use of materials in the fresh way that children do. Another purpose is to understand how their own attitudes and ways of relating to materials may hamper or facilitate the children's experience with them.

Baker and his colleagues, who have served as facilitators in a Creative Environment Workshop, also note that the workshop provides adults with a setting where they can plan, direct, and value their own work.[48] This is an experience that has been missing from the education of many.

---

[44] For example, Dennie L. Smith, *WEB, A Simulation of Working in an Educational Bureaucracy* (Lakeside, Calif.: INTERACT, 1973).

[45] Elliot M. Avedon and Brian Sutton-Smith, *The Study of Games* (New York: John Wiley & Sons, 1971), p. 319.

[46] William France and John McClure, "Building a Child Care Staff Learning Game," *Child Care Quarterly,* 2(3):192–203, Fall 1973.

[47] Avedon and Sutton-Smith, p. 321. See also James S. Coleman et al., "The Hopkins Games Program: Conclusions from Seven Years of Research," *Educational Researcher,* 2(8), August 1973.

[48] William E. Baker et al., "The Creative Environment Workshop," *Young Children,* 26(4), March 1971.

Field Trips   Just as the workshop helps the trainee understand important elements in a classroom environment for children, so field trips may help them see ways of extending that environment. Like workshops, field trips can cover a wide range of experience.

At the simplest level, trainees explore a given area to exploit its possibilities for child learning. At more complex levels, they visit a setting that would not be appropriate for young children but that may provide insight into the way children integrate new experience, or into forces that impinge on children's lives. Thus, a group might go together to an art gallery, sharing their impressions and feelings, or they might visit Family or Children's Court to get a firsthand view of the judicial process.

The effectiveness of the field trip depends in large part on the trainer's ability to help the participants articulate their experience in some way and to relate it to their work with the children.

Conferences   The early childhood educator as trainer accomplishes much of her work in conferences with the trainees. The conference provides an opportunity to get to know the trainee as an individual, to assess the trainee's view of her own progress, and to plan with her. The conference also serves as a setting for continuing evaluation. The conference may involve other individuals, such as the teacher in whose class the trainee may work, or the director or supervisor of a program.

Effective conferences with trainees call for abilities similar to those involved in conferences with parents. Chief among these are a willingness to listen and to sense the other's concern, along with an ability to keep focus on the essential intent of the conference—to support the trainee in achieving the goal of training.

Evaluation   The early childhood educator's role as trainer covers many areas of knowledge and skills as they relate to both direct and ancillary services to children. She can use many different training strategies. How does she determine which ones are effective for her use, and how does she appraise the impact of the training experiences on the trainees?

The first answer to such questions is, of course, that "how" depends on "what" and also on "when" and "where." The evaluation procedures must be appropriate to the content of training and to the goals set for the training. Procedures appropriate for preservice training may differ from those to be used at inservice levels. The "one-shot" training session associated with an ongoing center program has different requirements from those in a continuing inservice program or in the year-long college or university-based program. The questions the early childhood educator asks about the strategies she uses are not the same as her questions about their effects.

When instruction is competency-based, and particularly when competencies are stated as behavioral objectives, the criteria for evaluation are clearly shared by trainer and trainee. The evaluation of both trainer and trainee is, in a sense, built into the training. If the trainee accomplishes the behavioral objectives, both she and the trainer have succeeded. If, on the other hand, the trainer takes the more developmental, long-term view that has been emphasized throughout this book, the answers to questions of evaluation are not so clear-cut.

From the standpoint of the trainer, something more than the accomplishment of the objectives is required. Has the strategy she has chosen also given her satisfaction? Was she challenged and stimulated in the process of using it? Or may the very fact of its apparent success suggest the need to try something else lest repetition become boring?

As far as the effects on trainees are concerned, the critical questions also go beyond the accomplishment of a particular objective or the arrival at a mutually agreed upon goal. Such questions are especially important when the trainee is enrolled in a teacher preparation program. They include: Is the individual developing a teaching style that is appropriate to her personally and effective with children? Is her knowledge of children expanding so that she adapts what she does with individuals in the light of that knowledge? Does she recognize when her own knowledge and skills are insufficient and know where to go for help?

Evidence to answer these kinds of questions is not as easily acquired as answers to such questions as "Does the trainee use positive reinforcement?" Nevertheless, these questions relate to areas that are likely to have considerable import for the trainee's eventual and continued effectiveness as a teacher.

The suggestion that evaluation not be limited to the immediate and directly observable is not intended to underestimate the importance of the collection of that kind of evidence. For example, the trainer may have considerable evidence that indicates the trainee is becoming a resourceful, self-reliant, and adaptable teacher. This should not preclude her insistence that the trainee should, for example, demonstrate several strategies for the teaching of beginning reading.

Evaluation, from the viewpoints of both the trainer and the trainee, is a matter of building into the training strategies some means of obtaining evidence on their immediate effects. It is also a matter of asking the harder questions of their eventual consequences. Many techniques are available for answering questions related to the immediate effects, but others are only beginning to be investigated. Investigators are just beginning to consider effects that are mediated through the personality of the teacher throughout the training period and into her later teaching.

In summary, the early childhood educator's role as trainer of adults in some ways parallels her role as teacher of children. It requires the use of some strategies that are similar to those she uses as a teacher of children and others that are different. The need for evaluation and the problems related to developmental consequences for trainees are in many respects similar to those that arise in the teaching of children.

THE EARLY CHILDHOOD EDUCATOR AS PROGRAM ADVISOR

The role of program advisor was created in several Follow Through models as a means of providing direct support to the teachers who were implementing the models. In certain respects the role in some of the models closely resembles that just described for the trainer involved in an inservice program.

In the Responsive Program the functions of the advisor are to make frequent visits to demonstrate classroom procedures; to make systematic observation; to give feedback to the teachers; to conduct workshops and seminars based upon material supplied by the developers of the Responsive Program and also upon material from classroom observations.[49] The advisor is appointed by the community and trained in a series of seminars provided by the Responsive Program.

In the Tucson Early Education Model, the role of "program assistant" is described as providing "ongoing training" to the local programs.[50]

In the Education Development Center's Open Education Model, program advisors, who are usually experienced teachers, have a facilitative role.[51] Advisors are described as playing a highly supportive role, nondirective and nonevaluative; they are in no way supervisors. Ideally, advisors should offer assistance only at the request of a teacher. Advisors are not expected to evaluate, criticize, or tell the teacher what to do, except at the teacher's request. Their role is to listen to the teacher's needs and problems and assist in whatever way is needed.

Amarel and her colleagues studied the advisor role in the Education Development Center and other open models as the teachers who were advised perceived it.[52] On the basis of in-depth interviews with the teachers they categorized the teachers' reports of the ways the advisors functioned and also

[49] *Early Childhood Information Unit: Resource Manual and Program Descriptions* (New York: Educational Products Information Exchange, 1973), Responsive Model, p. 96.
[50] Ibid., Tucson Early Education Model, p. 65.
[51] Ibid., Education Development Center: Open Education Model, p. 51.
[52] Marianne Amarel et al., "Teacher Perspective on Change to an Open Approach," presented at the Annual Meeting of the American Educational Research Association, New Orleans, Mar. 1, 1973.

how they felt about them. The study suggests that the teacher's perception depends on her frame of reference. Some teachers see the improvement of their teaching largely as a matter of "method," that is, varying their strategies and using new materials. Others assume that they need to match a certain "model" classroom. Still others have a more abstract frame of reference and are guided by certain assumptions and values regarding the nature of the teaching/learning process.

The *intent* of the advisors is *not* to impose either new methods or a particular model, but rather to stimulate the teachers to consider more thoughtfully the relationships between teaching and learning and actively to exploit their own resources and potential, while also drawing more actively on the resources of other adults.

Nevertheless, some teachers tend to take a very passive stance toward the advisor. They describe her as someone who renders a service, such as bringing or ordering materials; or as one who provides an extra pair of hands. Alternatively, they may see her as someone who demonstrates ways of working with children, or as one who gives advice on what to do about certain specific problems.

Other teachers report that the advisor in various ways encourages their own activity. She suggests alternatives, but the teacher makes the judgment as to which is appropriate for her classroom. The advisor explicates theoretical principles so that the teacher can also apply them. She discusses and analyzes situations and raises questions in ways that help the teacher to make her own analyses. The advisor's ways of interacting with the children and with other adults suggest how the teacher might also interact.

Just as teachers differ in their perception of what the advisor does, they also vary in the way they regard the emotional support the advisor gives. Some emphasize the reinforcement and praise she provides and her sympathy and "caring." Others find support in the advisor's respect for their own individuality and professional integrity.

Many early childhood educators function in roles that differ in certain respects from the role described here. Nevertheless, the Amarel study throws into clear detail a way of collaborating with other adults that is equally appropriate in many of the other roles the early childhood educator may hold. It also illustrates the important point that teachers, and other adults, when they share the same early childhood educator, will inevitably see her role in different ways.

THE EARLY CHILDHOOD EDUCATOR AS SUPERVISOR

In her role as supervisor the early childhood educator may or may not have a position that carries that title. She may be called a coordinator, or a director, or a specialist, but when she has direct influence on the maintenance and improvement of the education and care of the children in any program, her function is essentially supervisory. Her influence operates through the staff members who teach or care for the children and possibly also through those who supply ancillary services.

The supervisory function calls on many procedures that have been outlined or suggested in the discussion of the roles of trainer and program advisor. The essential elements of supervision seem to be observation, evaluation, individual or group conferences, and the choice and implementation of various strategies for change.

The supervisor can have little effect without adequate knowledge of the goals of the program and of the ways it operates. Staff members need to be observed often enough and with sufficient regularity so that the supervisor maintains a continuous and accurate sense of their concerns, triumphs, and disasters.

The goals of the program, shared by all staff members, give direction to the goals set for a particular aspect of the program or for a particular staff member. For example, in the infant program described by Lally,[53] one of the goals was to provide appropriate matches between the behavior of the babies and the responses of the caretakers. Such matches were discussed, demonstrated, and practiced in the training period. The program supervisor's observation of the caretaker in the ongoing program compares the caretaker's performance with that prescribed in training, a simple form of evaluation.

The next step in the supervisory process is to check the caretaker's perception of his interactions with the babies. This may be done in an individual conference, or it may be handled in discussion with several staff members. Finally, where change is needed the supervisor, caretaker, and perhaps the other staff members as well, settle on a plan of action—the training strategies to be used to help the caretaker become more effective.

This illustration, an extrapolation from Lally's report, shows the continuity between supervision and training. It may also be used to make the point that good supervision has consequences. As Lally puts it, speaking of paraprofessional caretakers:

> As a result of such training endeavors, program directors will find that they have *forwardly mobile* people in their employment. With a minimum amount of encouragement, such as released time for community college work . . . paraprofessionals will move on in their own learning careers.[54]

---

[53] Lally et al., "Training Paraprofessionals for Work with Infants and Toddlers."
[54] Lally et al., p. 181 (Italics added.)

Good supervision emphasizes the positive. The supervisor's empathetic ability to place herself in the role of the staff member, and her ability to establish constructive team relationships contribute to the picture of supervision as a process that releases capabilities and talents.

But such a picture tends to gloss over those situations where the training strategies do not work and a particular staff member does not or cannot effectively realize the program goals. These are instances where the supervisor's responsibility to the program and most especially to the children requires her to take a firm stand. Unfortunately, in too many cases where the supervisor reaches an impasse that can only be resolved by reassignment or dismissal, the signals of ineptitude appeared long before they were accepted as such. Good supervision comes to terms with problems as they arise.

THE EARLY CHILDHOOD EDUCATOR IN AN INTERDISCIPLINARY TEAM

The early childhood educator tries to promote team relationships when she works with staff members in a school or center. She may also be involved in team relationships that include members of other disciplines and professions. Such a team, perhaps involving pediatrician and psychiatrist, may function in relation to several schools or centers.[55] It may also involve psychologists, social workers, and community members. In such team relationships the authority of expertise is shared as a variety of problems, ranging from the need for comprehensive services to specific recommendations for an individual child, are examined and solutions proposed. More early childhood educators may expect to find themselves in such teams as health and social services are integrated into more early childhood programs and also as programs expand to include children with handicaps.[56]

THE EARLY CHILDHOOD EDUCATOR AS CONSULTANT

The expanding need for day care and the extension of public schooling downward, coupled with a shortage in personnel with knowledge of child development, early education and care, have created another role for the early childhood educator—that of consultant. In this role she may work with groups or individuals who want to start programs for young children, or with those who are already operating programs but wish to change or strengthen them.

[55] See, for example, Harvey P. Katz et al., "Pediatric-Child Psychiatry in a Community Early Childhood Education Center," *Young Children,* 28(4):237–243, April 1973.
[56] Interview with Jasper Harvey, *Exceptional Children,* May 1971.

The old joke that the consultant is one who blows in, blows off, and blows out is not an accurate description of the consultant role. It does, however, touch on an important aspect of the role, namely, its temporary quality. Kiester thinks that this aspect is most important to clarify with the client.[57] The consultant comes at the invitation of the client, and only for as long as the relationship is productive to both. The consultant's major function is to clarify problems, that is, to diagnose the situation and then to help find alternative solutions. Which ones are chosen is up to the client.

When the clients are inexperienced, as those who want to start programs often are, considerable time may be needed for the establishment of mutual respect. The consultant must be sensitive to the concerns of the client and begin with those rather than with her own ideas of how the center might run. She does not, of course, withhold her knowledge, but rather considers how it can be adapted to a particular context.

The consultant role draws on the knowledge and skills of the early childhood educator in much the same way as the role of program advisor. However, the consultant role places somewhat more emphasis on the use of the authority of expertise. It may terminate with the finding of solutions to agreed upon problems, whereas the advisor is contracted for a specific period of time.

THE EARLY CHILDHOOD EDUCATOR AS CODE-ENFORCER

Concern over the quality of programs for young children leads to insistence that they be regulated in some fashion. Morgan reviews the major forms of regulation,[58] including administrative self-monitoring by public institutions; guidelines and accounting systems; federal interagency requirements applicable to any program using federal funds; zoning, fire, safety, and sanitation requirements; requirements for incorporation; Internal Revenue Service requirements for tax exemption; state transportation laws; staff credentialing and its relation to adult-child ratio; and licensing.

Morgan suggests that licensing is not the appropriate means to raise the quality of programs. Rather, education of the public, staff training, increased commitment of funds, and voluntary accreditation must precede the raising of quality through licensing requirements. Nevertheless, licensing is the basic and essential tool in maintaining a specific level of quality.[59]

Prescott and Jones's study of day care centers, nurseries, and nursery

---

[57] Dorothy J. Kiester, *Consultation: Day Care* (Chapel Hill: University of North Carolina, 1969).
[58] Gwen G. Morgan, *Regulation of Early Childhood Programs* (rev. ed.; Washington: Day Care and Child Development Council of America, January 1973).
[59] Morgan, p. 47.

schools in California[60] substantiates Morgan's view. It also provides a picture of the complexities involved in enforcing the codes that apply to a particular institution. The problem is that, although in some respects, the work of the code-enforcer is comparable to that of the consultant, the code-enforcer also serves as policeman. Accordingly, her attempts to establish a good working relationship with the operators of centers or of day care homes may be regarded with suspicion. They are afraid that they cannot trust her advice. A suggestion may mean that the regulations are to be changed, or that failure to follow it will result in a loss of the license. Many representatives of licensing agencies work through these problems with their clients and serve them very much as a consultant would, but they establish firmly in their own minds, and in the minds of their clients, the fact that any advice they offer is advice and nothing more.

THE EARLY CHILDHOOD EDUCATOR AS NEGOTIATOR

Trends toward the unionization of teachers and child care workers, and the need for change in the functioning in certain agencies, may bring the early childhood educator into the role of negotiator.

In some situations the early childhood educator, because of the position she holds, may participate in the negotiation team that represents the "establishment." As the director of a child care center she may meet with representatives of a union for city employees or for child care workers. In other instances she may be involved with parents and colleagues in efforts to secure change in other parts of the establishment. Such change may involve such matters as the reinterpretation of existing codes so as to open more facilities for children and their parents or the modification of policies regarding eligibility.

Among other things, this role calls for a clear knowledge of the authority relationships that may be involved. What are the established prerogatives for each of the negotiating organizations? Each negotiator also needs to be in command of the relevant facts. In the case of negotiations relating to salary and the conditions of work, what is the situation for workers of equivalent training and experience in other agencies, both locally and elsewhere? Tolerance, patience, and the ability to suspend judgment until all the evidence is in are also important qualities for the negotiator.[61]

[60] Elizabeth Prescott and Elizabeth Jones, *The Politics of Day Care* (Washington: National Association for Education of Young Children, 1972).
[61] Edmund B. Shils and C. Taylor Whittier, *Teachers, Administrators and Collective Bargaining* (New York: T. Y. Crowell, 1968), describe one type of negotiation in considerable detail.

THE EARLY CHILDHOOD EDUCATOR AS CHILD ADVOCATE

Child advocacy, recently given considerable publicity and also special recognition by the federal government,[62] has a history that goes back at least to the first White House Conference on Children in 1909. Kahn and his colleagues, after studying recent developments in child advocacy at federal, state, and local levels, define it as "intervention on behalf of children in relation to those services and institutions that impinge on their lives."[63]

Child advocacy takes different forms. Case advocacy occurs when a worker in some program finds that services or benefits that are supposed to be available to a child and his family do not materialize. Assuming that the worker can speak for them, and that the agency responsible for the service or benefit has had ample opportunity to produce it, the worker enters into the situation to correct it.

Class advocacy is directed toward the prevention of problems and is a kind of "wholesale" intervention on behalf of people who are having difficulty in relation to the variety of agencies that have been set up to serve them. Such advocacy may focus on policy or administrative procedures or budget, and occasionally on specific personnel, and it may concern itself with laws and with political action.

The early childhood educator may participate in child advocacy by becoming a member of any of the organizations that have been established for class or policy advocacy. She has a particularly important role with regard to case advocacy. As Kahn notes, such advocacy may require little more than a telephone call or a letter. "If staff in traditional agencies, e.g. teachers, nurses, recreational leaders, assumed responsibility for case advocacy on behalf of the children for whom they work, the need for specialized case advocates would be greatly reduced."[64]

THE EARLY CHILDHOOD EDUCATOR AS INSTITUTION BUILDER

The need in education for institutions that change, that are adaptive to the changing needs of society, has become a truism. Janowitz, in an analysis of

---

[62] The Office of Child Development established a Center for Child Advocacy in 1971.

[63] Alfred J. Kahn et al., *Child Advocacy, Report of a National Baseline Study* [U.S. Department of Health, Education and Welfare, Office of Child Development, DHEW (OCD), Publication No. 73-18].

[64] Kahn et al., p. 136.

urban education, has proposed a new model for building such institutions.[65] The model includes such elements as decentralized policy making with more autonomy for the teacher as a professional, more emphasis on a team approach, including subprofessionals and volunteers, and closer involvement of the staff in the community.

In both early childhood education and child care, existing institutions also require change, and others must be built from scratch. The early childhood educator can hardly escape the role of institution builder.

The functions of the role have been described as developing the mission of the school, center, or program, and the means to accomplish the mission; developing the social system and the technical support system that will make realization of the goals possible. These functions clearly overlap with other roles of the early childhood educator.[66]

There are two reasons for identifying the role of institution builder. The first is that merely bringing the role into the conscious awareness of the early childhood educator may set off a new and helpful perception of the nature of her work. The second reason is that too often in the past the role of the teacher and others involved in the education and care of young children has been seen as that of *preserving* institutions rather than as assisting in their dynamic adaptation to the needs of children and families.

SUMMARY

Parent educator, trainer, supervisor, consultant, code-enforcer, advocate, institution builder—all these are roles[67] that may be encompassed in the role of the early childhood educator. Each of these roles involves collaboration with other adults. Each requires certain kinds of competence that are not inherent in the role of the teacher. Yet, in a sense, the most important contribution the early childhood educator makes in any of her additional responsibilities stems from her knowledge of children's development and learning. In that area she is a specialist. She can bring her specialization to bear most effectively in these other roles when she is not only a good teacher but also a person who enjoys and is good at working with other adults. Then she can indeed promote the continuity and wholeness for children that Erikson sees as essential in our fragmented society.

---

[65] Morris Janowitz, *Institution Building in Urban Education* (New York: Russell Sage Foundation, 1969), pp. 35–60.

[66] Bruce Joyce, "The Teacher-Innovator, A Program for Preparing Educators," in Joyce and Weil, *Perspectives for Reform in Teacher Education,* pp. 10, 11.

[67] These are not the only roles, as Chapters 7, 10, and 11 show. However, I think effective realization of these roles is most dependent on the ability to work with adults.

Chapter 10

Assessing Development and Learning

To a large extent, each child's development is a mystery story whose outcome we cannot really predict. The complexity of the developmental process with the emerging capacities, drives, investments, conflicts, is still far beyond our complete comprehension, at our present primitive stage of understanding.[1]

When a school, center, or other program takes the facilitation of the child's development as an aim, it commits itself to the assessment of development. In effect, it says to parents and to the community, "Children who come here develop more fully and are more adequate persons because of their participation here." But it is not only the inevitable "How can you tell?" asked by parents and community that propels the program toward assessment. The concept of development implies that qualitative changes will be appraised.

It is one thing to be committed to the assessment of development, quite

---

[1] Lois Barclay Murphy, "The Stranglehold of Norms on the Individual Child," *Childhood Education,* 49(7):344, April 1973.

another to do it well. Murphy points to one source of difficulty—insufficient knowledge of the process of development. Another is the limited number of individuals who have a grasp of what is currently known about development. Still another is the quantity of data needed for adequate documentation of developmental change. Consequently, those who propose to assess development had best anticipate limited or modest success.

CRITERIA FOR DEVELOPMENT

The reader may recall that the discussion in Chapter 6 suggested some criteria for development. These are clearer for the physical and cognitive aspects of development than for the social and personality aspects.

One criterion relates to the direction of development. As Werner describes it, "Wherever development occurs it proceeds from a state of relative globality and lack of differentiation to a state of increasing differentiation, articulation, and hierarchic integration."[2] Kohlberg adds that "developmental behavior change is also irreversible."[3]

The work of Kohlberg[4] and also of Turiel[5] provides some criteria for moral development. In the period of early childhood, however, relatively little research has been done, and criteria for stages of moral development must be largely inferred from what is known about personality and social development.

In the area of personality development, Erikson's work on the growth of the ego[6] has given guidance to some programs that have been interested in assessing development. Others have found Anna Freud's work on the assessment of development helpful.[7] At infancy level, DeCarie's empirical work[8] shows the close correspondence between sensorimotor development as described by Piaget and affective development as described by psychoanalytic ego psychology. As suggested earlier, Loevinger's[9] approach to ego development provides a close parallel to the cognitive stages of Piaget's theory. Harvey,

[2] Heinz Werner, "The Concept of Development from a Comparative and Organismic Point of View," in Dale Harris, ed., *The Concept of Development* (Minneapolis: University of Minnesota Press, 1957), p. 126.

[3] Lawrence Kohlberg and Rochelle Mayer, "Development as the Aim of Education," *Harvard Educational Review,* 42(4), November 1972.

[4] Lawrence Kohlberg, "Stage and Sequence: The Developmental Approach to Socialization," in David A. Goslin, ed., *Handbook of Socialization Theory and Research* (Chicago: Rand McNally, 1969), pp. 347–480.

[5] Elliot Turiel, "Stage Transition in Moral Development," in Robert M. W. Travers, ed., *Second Handbook of Research on Teaching* (Chicago: Rand McNally, 1973), pp. 732–758.

[6] Erik H. Erikson, *Childhood and Society* (2d ed.; New York: E. P. Dutton & Co., 1963).

[7] Anna Freud, *Normality and Pathology in Childhood* (New York: International Universities Press, 1965).

[8] Therese Gouin DeCarie, *Intelligence and Affectivity in Early Childhood* (New York: International Universities Press, 1965).

[9] Jane Loevinger and Ruth Wessler, *Measuring Ego Development,* vol. 1 (San Francisco: Jossey-Bass, 1970).

Hunt, and Schroder[10] also provide an integrated description of cognitive and personality development. None of these approaches, however, provides a method of assessment that can be used with young children.

Information regarding the sequences of development provides a necessary framework for appraising the progress a child is making, but it is not sufficient to account for that progress or its absence. One must know more about the child as an individual—his physical characteristics, strengths, and vulnerabilities, the kinds of protection and care he has had, the expectations others have had for him, and so on, before one can appraise how his development is going.

Lawrence K. Frank, long an advocate of an interdisciplinary approach to the study of child development, and for many years committed to development as the aim of education, shortly before his death outlined the information needed to study the effects a particular program might have on a child.[11] Baseline data should include "somatic observations such as height, weight, various physiological functions and capacities"; "the various motor capacities and performances including manual skills"; "nutritional condition"; "tests of sensory acuities"; "kinesthetic awareness"; "standardized neurological tests"; "ability to speak, to listen and interpret language and to communicate by language"; "cognitive style (some children learn and have a preference for visual experiences, others for auditory experiences and later for reading, and then there are those who prefer and learn through tactile and haptic contacts)"; "the individual child's image of himself, composed of the symbols by which the child gives meaning to the words *I, me, my, mine,* in terms of which most of his contacts and interpersonal relations with others are carried on." Frank proposed that measures of the child's position with regard to these and other dimensions could be plotted on polar coordinates. (A polar coordinate is a graphic device showing a circle with 360 radii which can be divided into segments.) Such plotting would, Frank thought, be a useful and dynamic way to show gains for each individual child.

Not many programs in the immediate future are likely to be able to secure baseline data in anything like the detail Frank thought necessary. That reality need not deter them from appraising development, however, so long as they recognize the limitations of their knowledge and respect the individuality of the children.

---

[10] O. J. Harvey et al., *Conceptual Systems and Personality Organization* (New York: John Wiley & Sons, 1961).

[11] Lawrence K. Frank, "Evaluation of Educational Programs," *Young Children,* 24(3):167–174.

THE ROLE OF THE EARLY CHILDHOOD EDUCATOR

One aspect of the early childhood educator's role in assessment is to keep it honest. She contributes to honesty in several ways. Her knowledge of child development and the complexities of individuality give her a perspective which she shares with teachers and parents. She knows the expectations that are reasonable for children of a given age, and also the many factors that may detract from their reasonableness for a particular child.

She is sophisticated about assessment procedures. She knows a variety of instruments that may be used with young children, but she also knows what each is designed to do and what its limitations may be. She values the information that can be collected in the classroom or by the teacher, but she is aware of the biases that may affect such information. She is less concerned with single incidents or the results of one test than she is with the patterns that emerge when information accumulated over time from several sources is examined.

Another aspect of the role of the early childhood educator in relation to assessment is to serve as clarifier for parents and teachers. When the goals for a program or for a particular child are formulated, she helps make distinctions between long- and short-term expectations. She provides information about the assessment process and the ways information derived from assessment is used to modify programs and teaching procedures.

The early childhood educator also provides support to the teachers in developing, or deciding upon, and using assessment procedures. She respects the teachers' knowledge of children and helps them make it more explicit, more influential in their own teaching procedures, and more available to other members of the staff and to the parents.

Assessment, when used to facilitate children's development and learning, becomes part of a continuing process. It begins, although not always formally, in the first contacts the child and his parents have with the program.

GATHERING INITIAL INFORMATION ABOUT THE CHILD

Children come to early childhood programs at different ages. Some may become involved in day care or in other programs for infants early in their first year. Others have no such contacts until they enter kindergarten or first grade. In either case, those taking responsibility for the child's care and education need to have information about him in order to plan appropriately for him.

There are two major sources of information about the child—his parents and the observations made by the teacher or, in some programs, a social worker. In addition, the child should have a physical examination and some form of developmental screening.

Parent Information

In most instances, no one knows the child as well as the parent, or is as well qualified to describe the child's developmental history. Most parents understand the need for certain kinds of information, particularly if the child is an infant or preschooler. They are not surprised to be asked about the child's ways of making his wants known, his schedule of eating and resting, his favorite activities, his experience with children and adults, and any possible fears he may have.

Those who gather information from the parents should understand the pressures that may inhibit them from responding freely. When the number of places for children is limited and parental desire or need to enroll the child is very great, the parent is likely to present the child in a way calculated to secure his acceptance. Sometimes feelings of which the parent is not consciously aware color what the parent tells about the child. For example, the mother of a young infant, despite a desperate need for care, may feel that she should not be separated from the child. She may accordingly distort the picture of his activities and development.

The kinds of information that relate to the child's developmental history, that illuminate his present status and provide a backdrop to his future development, may, for a number of reasons, not be readily available, especially when the child is no longer an infant. Was he an active, vigorous infant, eager to get at the world, or was he more passive, perhaps needing special stimulation? Did his mother regard him as easy to handle or fussy and demanding? How has he been trained for independence and for control of aggression? What have been important influences in his life—illness, hospitalization, accidents, brothers and sisters, grandparents, changes of residence? Questions such as these may seem an invasion of privacy. They may have been asked, in one form or another, in so many programs and agencies that the parent has lost all sense of their possible relevance. Many parents also know that the information collected by schools and other agencies does not always remain confidential and is sometimes given out without the parent's permission.[12]

Against this background the parent's lack of trust is reasonable. Only when she completely understands the purposes of the program and the way all information about the child is used will she enter fully into shared planning. Accordingly, many programs will find that they must rely heavily on their own observations of the child.

---

[12] Diane Divoky, "Cumulative Records: Assault on Privacy," *Learning,* 2(1):18–23, September 1973.

Observation of the Child

Any break in his usual routine, or any new situation, provides the observer of the young child with clues to the ways he copes with the world. Thus, a child's first visit to a program or, in the case of the home-based program, his reactions to the home visitor can be observed for tentative information on such matters as his attention and interest in new situations, his motor and language skills, his ways of relating to strange adults and possibly to other children. Such initial observations may or may not conform to the picture given by the parent, and they may or may not conform to the way the child will later adapt to the program. They do give the astute teacher a basis on which to plan the child's first experiences in the program.

Developmental Screening

Developmental screening procedures are, in a sense, an extension of the less-structured observations described above. They supplement the medical history and examination and serve several purposes. They provide clues to the child's needs for periodic health care, identify developmental delays, and can serve as a guide to the appropriate individualization of the child's curriculum.

Developmental appraisal of this sort was once done only by pediatricians or by individuals with a Ph.D. in developmental psychology. Recently, however, some developmental inventories [13] have become available that may be used by teachers or other staff members who have had special training. Such training includes supervised practice under the close supervision of a pediatrician or developmental psychologist. Ongoing supervision is also essential.

SETTING GOALS FOR INDIVIDUAL CHILDREN

There would be little point in gathering information about the child if it were not to be used in planning for him.

At the infancy level, particularly when the baby is to be separated from the mother, as in day care, the appropriate use of developmental information is essential if the child is to thrive. For example, the infant's attachment to his mother should be supported. [14] At around 10 to 12 weeks the baby begins cooing and smiling and reaching out to his mother. Whatever arrangements are made for the baby's care should be so timed and organized that this important process of attachment is not disrupted.

---

[13] For example, The Denver Developmental Screening Test, described in the *Journal of Pediatrics,* 71:191, August 1971; and A Developmental Screening Inventory for Infants, developed by Knobloch, Pasamanick, and Sherard, described in *Pediatrics,* 38, December 1966.

[14] T. Berry Brazelton, "Working with the Family," in Laura L. Dittmann, ed., *The Infants We Care For* (Washington: National Association for the Education of Young Children, 1973).

A suitable goal for one baby may be to eat finger foods independently, for another to begin the transition from bottle to cup. In this connection, White and Huntington[15] cite an example of planning that disregarded developmental needs. A day care mother, more concerned with her own convenience than with the growth of the children, gave toddlers their orange juice in bottles though several had already achieved independence in drinking from a cup.

At still older levels, goals must also be set in the light of developmental information, and programs should be planned accordingly. A general initial goal may be for the child to enjoy his participation. Beyond that, one child may need encouragement into movement activities designed to improve his coordination, another into play with a single companion to advance his social development, while still a third may be engaged in make-believe games with the teacher to enhance his ability to represent absent objects and events mentally.[16]

Individualization in the light of developmental information is no less important for children in kindergarten and first grade. The fact that children have had preschool experience provides no guarantee that all are similarly ready for beginning reading instruction. As I suggested in earlier chapters, it takes both experience *and* maturation to bring the child to the point where he can easily begin integrating the bits of information that are essential to the reading process. Kagan concurs, saying that if the child isn't doing this, "it may be wise to wait, for he is likely to reach this maturational point in six months to a year."[17] Kagan's statement, based in part on his studies of the development of children in other countries, supports pre-1960 views about the nature of reading readiness. Waiting, however, need not mean doing nothing. The teacher's assessment of the child's interests as well as his general level of development should suggest activities to further the child's development and build toward his eventual interest in reading.

The goals for children's development are, of course, always multiple, and much that goes on in a program may facilitate children's development in a general way. Different goals take priority for different children at different times.

---

[15] Burton White and Dorothy Huntington, "Our Goals for the Infant and His Family," in Laura L. Dittmann, ed.

[16] Some of the preschool programs established for disadvantaged children in the 1960s emphasized planning for children on the basis of individual assessment. The program developed by Kamii is noteworthy because of its concern with the thought processes of children. For a comprehensive description of the assessment procedures used in that program, and also in other preschool programs, see Constance K. Kamii, "Evaluation of Learning in Pre-school Education: Socio-emotional, Perceptual-motor, Cognitive Development," in Benjamin S. Bloom et al., *Handbook on Formative and Summative Evaluation of Student Learning* (New York: McGraw-Hill, 1971), pp. 281–344.

[17] Jerome Kagan, "Late Starts Are Not Lost Starts," a talk with Ruth Mehrtens Galvin, *Learning,* 1:82, September 1973.

CONTINUING ASSESSMENT

Assessment continues as the child continues in the program. Various techniques are used to secure information about the child and the effects the program has on him. From a practical viewpoint, assessment is continuous to the extent that the staff members are constantly alert to the child's behavior and development. However, few programs have the staff or the resources for continuous monitoring of development—nor is it certain that such would be desirable. As has been suggested earlier, children need time to *be,* as well as to *become.*

Information from the initial assessment guides the initial expectations of the child. Continuing observations then provide evidence regarding both the validity of the initial assessment and subsequent changes in the child.

Unfortunately, assessment procedures are not always used for the child but rather place him in a "pigeonhole" from which he cannot escape. Accordingly, some educators and parents, particularly those in minority groups, regard assessment procedures of any kind with skepticism if not outright hostility. For example, in one state a committee of educators advising on state programs for four-year-olds hesitated to specifically recommend developmental screening. They feared that poor children might be classified as "slow-learning" or "language-handicapped." So categorized, they might be deprived of the rich variety of experience planned for other four-year-olds and receive instead routine drill to "correct their deficits."

Such concerns reflect the fact that school programs are often nonadaptive and some teachers unresponsive to children who differ from the norm. Unless the information from assessment procedures is used in ways that help children to participate in and enjoy the varied aspects of the program, unless it helps teachers to capitalize on children's strengths and support their weaknesses, such procedures had better be abandoned.

When a program is genuinely committed to assessment as a means of facilitating children's development and learning, numerous procedures can be used to assess each child's progress and to provide "feedback" on the effectiveness of the program for him.

Observation

No program can be responsive to the individual needs of children without a staff skilled in observation. Observation is the primary means of assessment at the early childhood level.

The early childhood educator works with staff members to sharpen their observation skills and to help them find efficient ways of recording their observations. Records have value only to the extent that the staff puts them to use in guiding and instructing the children.

In addition to the observations that are only recorded in the teacher's head, [18] different kinds of observational records can be made. [19] The diary, time sample, or specimen record [20] attempts to capture all that a particular child does in a specified time period. The anecdotal record reports briefly on an observed incident involving the child. Or an observation may be structured in advance and note only the occurrence of certain specified behaviors, using a checklist or code.

Diary records are cumbersome and time-consuming, but they have some special values. They are useful in training staff members. When two individuals record the behavior of the same child, the reality of different perceptions of the same behavior becomes readily apparent. Such recording also expands the individual's ability to perceive the finer details of behavior.

Diary records are sometimes essential in clarifying what is happening to a child. For example, careful and extended observation of a child with a learning disability reveals not only the sources of frustration but also areas of competence and satisfaction.

In an "open" program where children customarily engage in activities of their own choosing, systematic observation of individual children over a period of time provides a more accurate picture of the experience each child is having than can be obtained from the impressions of the teacher. [21]

Anecdotal records are less precise and more selective than diary records. Their usefulness lies in the way they recapture significant occurrences and events in the child's development and learning. Unless some system is set up to regularize their collection they may overemphasize problems and difficulties or focus on children whose characteristics make them more visible to the teachers than others.

Observations that are structured by a category system [22] require less writing effort on the part of the observer than do diary or anecdotal records. However, those using such systems need special training to ensure that they

---

[18] For an example of the ways an effective teacher keeps her observations in her head and translates them into action, see Ann Cook and Herbert Mack, "The Teacher as Observer," in Charles E. Silberman, ed., *The Open Classroom Reader* (New York: Vintage Books, 1973), pp. 240–245.

[19] Some books that include observational techniques are: Millie Almy, *Ways of Studying Children* (New York: Teachers College Press, 1959). This book is directed to teachers in service. Ann Boehm and Richard Weinberg, *The Classroom Observer: A Guide for Developing Observational Skills* (New York: Teachers College Press, in press). Dorothy Cohen and Virginia Stern, *Observing and Recording the Behavior of Young Children* (New York: Teachers College Press, 1958), particularly useful for preschool and kindergarten teachers. Betty Rowen, *The Children We See* (New York: Holt, Rinehart and Winston, 1973). This book, intended for preservice students, includes observations from infancy through elementary school, as well as other assessment procedures.

[20] Herbert F. Wright, *Recording and Analyzing Child Behavior* (New York: Harper & Row, 1967).

[21] Susan S. Stodolsky, "Defining Treatment and Outcome in Early Childhood Education," in Herbert J. Walberg and Andrew T. Kopan, eds., *Rethinking Urban Education* (San Francisco: Jossey-Bass, 1972).

[22] Alan R. Coller, *Systems for the Observation of Classroom Behavior in Early Childhood Education,* (Urbana, Ill.: ERIC Clearinghouse on Early Childhood Education, April 1972).

record only the behaviors that are agreed to represent the established categories. The information obtained is limited to those categories.

Direct, hand-recorded observation can be supplemented by filming and video- or audio-taping. Like hand-recorded observations, these are useful only when the information derived from them is organized and related to the goals for the program or to goals for individual children.

Informal or Situational Tests

Another way of focusing observation to assess the child's progress is to set up a situation in which he can demonstrate what he knows or can do. For example, at the infancy level, the teacher may hide an object in front of the baby and observe his strategies for retrieving it. The teacher of older children may set up an "obstacle course" designed to reveal both general coordination and such specific skills as walking on balancing boards of different widths and at different heights, hopping, and jumping.[23]

Structured situations are advantageous when the teacher wishes to assess behavior that may not appear spontaneously. For example, as Cazden notes, the child in situations where he can respond to clues other than the words does not clearly reveal his level of comprehension of language per se.[24] The child who correctly brings two pencils when the teacher requests him to "bring the pencils" may understand the plural s, or he may simply see no reason to leave one of the two pencils behind; or perhaps he responds to the tone of command and the direction of her glance rather than to the words.

The work of Piaget has provided inspiration for any number of structured situations from which the teacher may, with proper questioning, deduce something of the level and stability of the child's concepts. Such situations may be incorporated into the ongoing curriculum so that assessment and teaching are essentially combined. The preschool curriculum developed by Kamii[25] provides one example of this blend. The materials and activities provided in "Let's Look at Children"[26] are also illustrative.

Informal tasks can be used to assess many aspects of the child's thinking. The level of the child's concepts is not the only aspect of his thinking to be considered. How does the child bring his thinking to bear on a problem? For example, does he have a repertory of varied actions for exploring an object? In interviewing four- and five-year-olds in certain schools, I have been im-

---

[23] Laurel Hodgden et al., *School before Six, A Diagnostic Approach* (Ithaca: Cornell University, 1969).
[24] Courtney B. Cazden, "Evaluation of Learning in Preschool Education: Early Language Development," in Bloom et al., *Handbook on Formative and Summative Evaluation of Student Learning* (New York: McGraw-Hill, 1971), pp. 345–398.
[25] Kamii, in Benjamin S. Bloom et al., eds.
[26] "Let's Look at Children" (Princeton: Educational Testing Service, in press).

pressed with children who give immediate (although not always correct) verbal responses to my queries, but who will not manipulate an object put in front of them. When specifically requested to so so they make only brief investigations. Perhaps their lack of activity reveals as much about the school as it does about their thinking. Bussis and Chittenden[27] have made similar observations with regard to older children. Some, they note, reveal thinking that seems bound to a two-dimensional, paper-and-pencil world. They can write in their workbooks $4 \times 3 = 12$, but when they are confronted with the problem of the total number of legs three chairs have, they resort to counting one by one.

Informal tasks can also be used to appraise the range of the child's ideas and associations. One teacher used a version of the "close your eyes—hold out your hands—guess what's in your hands" game as an informal test. Using such objects as a piece of corrugated foam rubber, a glass telephone insulator, and a piece of shale rock, she assessed individual children's language, their ways of handling materials, and their ingenuity in suggesting possible uses.[28]

Teachers have always used paper-and-pencil tests to assess aspects of children's learning. With younger children these are impractical. But even when children are competent readers, informal or situational tests appraise certain important dimensions of the child's development more effectively than many paper-and-pencil tests.

Checklists and Rating Scales

Most teachers, even when they do little in the way of recording observations or setting up informal tests, know a great deal about many aspects of the child's behavior and development. Considerable evidence attests to the fact that their judgments of children in need of psychological assistance corresponds quite well to the independent appraisals made by psychologists and psychiatrists.[29]

One way to bring the teacher's knowledge of the child into his assessment is to ask her to rate his behavior or personality traits on certain specified dimensions. Such a procedure may involve indicating how frequently a child engages in a particular behavior, or it may involve indicating whether he is like a child described, for example, as "easily distracted." Certain tendencies of raters, including those of consistently rating high or low, or failing to use the extremes of the scale, or rating globally in terms of the general qualities of the

[27] Anne Bussis and Edward Chittenden, "The Horizontal Dimension of Learning," in *Evaluation Reconsidered* (New York: Workshop for Open Education, City College, May 1973).
[28] E. Paul Torrance and R. E. Myers, *Creative Learning and Teaching* (New York: Dodd, Mead, 1972), p. 128.
[29] Nadine M. Lambert, *The Development and Validation of a Process for Screening Emotionally Handicapped Children in School,* U.S. Office of Education, Cooperative Research Project No. 1186 (Sacramento: California State Department of Education, 1963).

individual rather than in terms of specific characteristics, may vitiate the ratings. Training in their use helps to correct such tendencies.

The Children's Products

As the child grows older, his own products provide considerable evidence of his development. The scribbles of the toddler are gradually replaced by recognizable drawings and legible writing. Experimentation with color in painting moves forward into interesting designs and clearer representations of reality. Dictated stories and poems change themes, grow more complex, and finally are written by the child himself. What better evidence of the child's increasing ability to cope with the mysteries of the printed word than his own list of the books he had read for enjoyment and interest?

In this connection, the question of the child's involvement in his own assessment may be raised. When families lived in the same house year after year, most children derived considerable satisfaction from seeing their changing height marked, birthday by birthday, on a convenient door jamb. Schools and centers can also provide children and their parents with an objective record of their development, and the children can contribute to the record. Children, in our age-graded society, have a keen sense of the importance of being bigger and older, but do we help them understand the ways *they* change as they develop? Sometimes such understanding comes by chance, as when a child who has recently come to understand that the number of a set of objects does not change when the objects are rearranged encounters a child who lacks that insight. We continually nudge children to move forward, to be bigger, to think and do better. Perhaps they also need the opportunity to reflect on their changes.

Respect for individuality enhances the appreciation of change. One beautifully coordinated child quickly masters the "obstacle course" described earlier; another goes through a series of exercises for a long time before he masters the course, and his performance is far from smooth. One child comes to school speaking standard English; another speaks Black English at home; and still another speaks Spanish. From the narrow and ethnocentric view that too often pervades the thinking of the school, the first child is advanced over the other two. More realistically, as the latter begin to learn standard English, they move ahead of their monolingual peer.[30] They are acquiring a bilingual facility that he lacks. From a developmental view, comparisons of the performances of different children tend to be invidious. Comparing the performance

---

[30] The school or center for the young child whose language background is not standard English should include staff members who speak and understand his language.

of a child at one time with his performance at an earlier time puts the focus on his accomplishment.

Obviously, the program carries responsibility for seeing that accomplishment does occur. Glaser, discussing the place of individual differences in subject matter instruction, notes that ways can be found to ensure that most children learn to read competently. Responsible instruction maximizes the ways in which the child can progress rather than assuming deficiencies in the child. "What is emphasized is not the discrepancy between potential and accomplishment; rather, *accomplishment,* not potential, *is viewed and valued in its own right.*"[31]

The kind of continuing assessment so far proposed relies heavily on the abilities of the teachers to grasp the nature of the child's individuality and to plan his program in the light of that understanding. Such understanding is guided by the results of the initial assessment and by information from selected assessment devices (including some to be considered in a later section of this chapter), but it is most influenced by observation of the child as he functions in the program. This kind of assessment may be seen as a process in which the teacher confronts the mind of the child and learns therefrom.

If this kind of assessment results in a program that is adaptive to individuals, so that all make progress developmentally, differentiating skills, learning new ones, acquiring knowledge and integrating it, the assessment procedures may be regarded as satisfactory.

Record Keeping

The question of how much information should be recorded and how such recordings are to be organized so as to be most useful to the teacher is difficult to answer. Many programs struggle with this question.

Some may elect to turn to computers. Some data-processing systems can handle anecdotal annotation. For example, Lambert and her colleagues studied classroom observations, teacher reports, principal contacts, parent reports, and other incidental information[32] that had been collected in several school districts. They analyzed 10,000 free observations of more than 2,000 children in 75 classrooms in 10 schools and developed a "Lexicon of School Observations." The use of the lexicon makes possible the efficient storage and retrieval of a great deal of material relevant to the child's development. Obviously, the observations must be translated into the lexicon, and there must be agreement as to what is to be stored and how it is to be used.

[31] Robert Glaser, "Educational Psychology and Education," *American Psychologist,* July 1973, p. 563. (Italics added.)
[32] Nadine M. Lambert et al., "APPLE, An Annotated Pupil Information System," n.d. (Mimeographed.)

Some programs try to represent the events of the child's development and the events in the program by case studies of the children and documentation of the curriculum.[33] The aim is to maintain the integrity of the children's experiences without merely reproducing them. The procedures are biographical and historical rather than evaluative.[34] The records are used for ongoing examination and interpretation of the mental processes of development and learning.

STANDARDIZED TESTING

To what extent does the assessment of development and learning in early childhood rely on standardized tests? McClelland, in an article criticizing the use of intelligence and aptitude tests in American education, says ironically, "It is a sign of backwardness not to have test scores in the school records of children."[35]

Very young children must be tested individually and by a skilled examiner. He must be sure that he has the attention and interest of the child and that the child understands what he is supposed to do and wants to do it. The child's performance often varies from one day to the next. Tests given in the early childhood years are not very good predictors of the child's later status. For example, MacFarlane reports on the results of eight mental tests given a group of youngsters during the years from six to eighteen.[36] For three-fourths of the group the *average* change from test to test was less than 10 IQ points. However, for 58 percent of the children the *range* of IQ points was 15 or more. Bayley, commenting on a sample of 248 children between the ages of 21 months and 18 years who were given mental tests, cautions, "Whereas the results for the group suggest mental test stability between 6 and 18 years, the observed fluctuations in the scores of individual children indicate the need for the utmost caution in the predictive use of a single test score, or even two such scores."[37]

Considering the problems involved in testing young children and the difficulties in interpreting the results, one might expect that few tests appropriate for them would be available. This is not the case, although some tests, such as the Stanford-Binet, have been used more than others.

Dyer[38] writes that the Head Start Test Collection, a cooperative venture

---

[33] Patricia F. Carini, "Documentation: An Alternative Approach to Accountability," in *Evaluation Reconsidered* (New York: Workshop Center for Open Education, City College, May 1973).

[34] For a discussion of the usefulness of these kinds of materials, see Donald F. Spence, "Analog and Digital Descriptions of Behavior," *American Psychologist,* June 1973, pp. 479–488.

[35] David C. McClelland, "Testing for Competence rather than for Intelligence," *American Psychologist,* January 1973, p. 1.

[36] Jean Walker MacFarlane, "From Infancy to Adulthood," in M. C. Jones et al., *The Course of Human Development* (Waltham, Mass.: Xerox College Publishing Co., 1971), pp. 406–410.

[37] Nancy Bayley et al., "The Stability of Mental Test Performance between Two and Eighteen Years," in Jones et al., *The Course of Human Development,* pp. 117–123.

[38] Henry S. Dyer, "Testing Little Children: Some Old Problems in New Settings," *Childhood Education,*

between the U.S. Office of Education and Educational Testing Service, contains 908 different tests, with an additional 2,199 research instruments waiting to qualify for inclusion. The variety of the tests and measurements that are being used is suggested by another collection of *unpublished* instruments[39] for use with children from birth to twelve years. This collection includes measures of cognition, personality and emotional characteristics, perceptions of environment, self-concept, motor skills, sensory perception, and social behavior.

The present situation with regard to testing in early childhood education is easily summarized. There are too many tests. Many of the tests are poor tests. Some of the better tests are often used inappropriately. As Dyer says, "Some are psychometrically respectable; some are trying to become respectable; and some are innocent of any psychometric properties whatsoever."[40]

Of the available tests for young children, those most widely used are intelligence and language tests, and readiness and achievement tests. Tests to measure self-concept are currently receiving considerable interest.

The misuse of older tests and the inundation of new tests have led some people to demand the elimination of all tests.

The classification of children as "slow," "average," or "fast" on the basis of group intelligence tests given as early as first grade has doomed large numbers of children to perpetual failure. In too many schools the implicit assumption that both intelligence and competence can be well represented in a group test went unchallenged until recently. Just as some schools used intelligence tests to lock children into ability tracks, they also used achievement and readiness tests to freeze the curriculum.

To some extent the programs designed for preschool children in poverty areas have also been oriented more to tests than to the development of the children. With these younger children, the Stanford-Binet individual test frequently served as the measure of the program's effectiveness. The curriculum included practices of the abilities required in the test. Some programs emphasized the abilities tested in the reading-readiness test.

It seems clear that neither intelligence nor achievement tests should domi-

April 1973, pp. 362–367. The Head Start Test Collection is located at the Educational Testing Service, Princeton, N.J. From time to time annotated bibliographies regarding specific kinds of tests are prepared. The Center for the Study of Evaluation and the Early Childhood Research Center at the University of California, Los Angeles, has prepared a monograph listing over one hundred tests for preschool and kindergarten. Tests are evaluated for validity, appropriateness, ease of administration and interpretation, and normed technical excellence.

[39] Orval G. Johnson and James W. Bommarito, *Tests and Measurements in Child Development* (San Francisco: Jossey-Bass, 1971).

[40] Dyer, p. 362.

nate the curriculum or determine the nature of the child's school experience. However, complete elimination of all these tests at the present time seems unlikely and perhaps unwise. Both kinds of tests provide an objective means of assessment to supplement teacher judgment.

The individual intelligence test in the hands of a qualified examiner can provide much useful information about the child's functioning. Some such appraisal along with the use of other diagnostic instruments seems helpful if programs are to be adequately individualized.

Achievement tests, and perhaps certain readiness tests that are in effect achievement tests, would not need to be ruled out in an assessment program if those who used them recognized their limitations. The tests do provide a means of comparing the child's performance at one time with his performance at a later time. They permit the performance of a class and of individuals to be viewed against the performance of other youngsters of similar age. When the test norms are based on children of similar backgrounds, which is often not the case, such comparisons need not be invidious.

Unfortunately, the content of the tests that are given often bears little resemblance to the curriculum the children have had. Worse, in some schools the curriculum represents little more than what is covered in the achievement test.[41] Current tests do not encompass the variety of skills and knowledge children acquire in a rich and individualized curriculum.[42]

In some states achievement testing required by the state is done on the basis of random samples. The tests are broken into several parts, and no child takes all parts. The results give a good picture of the level of performance of children in a particular community, but children and their classrooms are not identified.

If achievement tests are given, teachers, having recorded the scores, might well look beyond the scores to see the kinds of errors a child makes, and whether there may be a pattern in them. The test may also be reviewed with the child. Such review may reveal instances where the child misunderstood the directions, rushed or dawdled, gave wrong answers for a good reason, or perhaps right answers for a poor reason.

When testing has been mandated, there seems to be no good reason why children, even those in first and second grade, should not be helped to take a reasonable and constructive attitude toward them. The child should know that the test has been put together for large groups of children, and may contain

---

[41] Margaret de Rivera, "Academic Achievement Tests and the Survival of Open Education," a paper prepared for EDC Follow Through, Philadelphia School System Follow Through Program, Apr. 1, 1972, shows how a citywide testing program can disrupt and constrain programs focused on development.
[42] Deborah Meier, "The Fatal Defects of Reading Tests," in Charles E. Silberman, *The Open Classroom Reader* (New York: Vintage Books, 1973), pp. 587–598.

items with which he is unfamiliar. If he can approach it as a challenge for which he has some resources, he can learn something from his own performance. But such a test represents only a small part of what he knows, and the skills he has, and only a small part of what is important for him to know and do.

The early childhood educator may not be able to eliminate testing, but she can demand more appropriate tests and teach teachers and other staff, including administrators, the uses and the limitations of tests, especially for young children. If every teacher understood these and knew how to examine tests with proper regard for their reliability and validity and the adequacy and appropriateness of the norms, they might be able to loosen the stranglehold testing now has on schools.

Some indication of the current lack of sophistication about testing among many teachers and other educators is revealed in the eager search for tests dealing with dimensions of development and learning other than intelligence or achievement. Assuming that good early childhood education should influence the child's competence in solving many kinds of problems, enhance his creativity, and maintain or improve his sense of self-worth, how do you measure such effects? Just as educators in the past have turned to standardized tests to provide an appraisal of achievement other than that which is derived from the judgment of teachers, now they are looking for measures of self-concept and creativity. In some instances, ironically, those who would do away with achievement tests are joining the search for an objective measure of self-concept.

The issues having to do with measures of the self are even more complicated than those having to do with intelligence. Coller, reviewing and analyzing some fifty available iinstruments purporting to assess the self-concept of the young child, notes that "the bulk of currently available self-concept tests are not likely to be of significant value to the educator concerned either with the development or modification of specific educational programs." For such needs he recommends the development of criterion-referenced tests. [43]

Criterion-referenced tests are tests in which scores are translated into statements about the behavior to be expected of a person with that score. [44] Dyer foresees that the further development of criterion-referenced tests will serve to dissociate the selecting and classifying functions of testing from the diagnosing and feedback functions. [45]

[43] Alan R. Coller, "The Assessment of Self-Concept," in *Early Childhood Education*, ERIC Clearinghouse on Early Childhood Education, Urbana, Ill., July 1971.

[44] Lee J. Cronbach, *Essentials of Psychological Testing* (New York: Harper & Row, 1970), p. 847. For an analysis of differences between criterion- and norm-referenced tests, and their use by teachers, see Ann E. Boehm, "Criterion-Referenced Assessment for the Teacher," *Teachers College Record*, 75(1):117–126, 1973.

[45] Dyer, "Testing Little Children."

One example of a criterion-referenced test that can be used at the early childhood level is the Boehm Test of Basic Concepts.[46] In this test each of the several areas tested is broken down into levels of difficulty. For example, with regard to color, at the first and most difficult level, the child is asked to identify a specific color—"What color is this dress?" If he has difficulty the examiner moves to a question such as "Show me the dress that is red"; if that is too difficult, she moves to a matching task—"Find another one like this."

Hunt has recently developed criteron-referenced tests of semantic mastery in school readiness. Color, position, shape, and number are included. The tests begin with perceptual identification (imitating the action of the examiner in matching colors), move to spoken identification (naming the indicated color), and then to listening identification (pointing to the spoken color). The tests have an interesting final section in which two children are involved, one in the role of speaker and the other in the role of listener, each with an examiner. A visual barrier between the two children necessitates that they communicate by spoken language. Although this latter procedure seems somewhat cumbersome, it gets at an important dimension of representational competence. Those who can describe objects and tell the other child what to do with them have the appropriate vocabulary and can also conceive what the other child needs to know. With regard to the criterion-reference aspects of the test, Hunt notes that the assessment is limited to "that information and those information-processing abilities and strategies present or absent at the age at which the child is examined."[47] Unlike norm-referenced tests, these tests "imply nothing about the general learning ability of those tested and nothing about what their achievements in the distant future may be." Rather they are designed to assure a proper match between the school learning situation and what the children already know and can do.

Glaser, discussing individuals and learning, describes how "open testing and behaviorally indexed assessment" will play their part in educational environments that are more adaptive than our present schools. As he sees it, current research on cognitive processes will lead to better identification of the basic aptitudes of individuals; part of their education will then encourage and extend those basic abilities. He goes on to say:

> Tests will be designed to provide information directly to the learner and the teacher to guide further learning. These tests will have an intrinsic character of openness in that they will serve as a display of the competencies to be acquired,

---

[46] Ann E. Boehm, *Boehm Test of Basic Concepts: Grades K-2* (New York: Psychological Corporation, 1969).

[47] J. McV. Hunt and Girvin Kirk, "Criterion-Referenced Tests of Semantic Mastery in School Readiness: A Paradigm with Illustrations," May 1973, p. 23. (Mimeographed.)

and the results will be open to the student who can use this knowledge of his performance as a yardstick of his developing ability. These tests will also assess more than the narrow band of traditional academic outcomes. Measures of process and style, of cognitive and non-cognitive development, and of performance in more natural settings than exist in the traditional school will be required.[48]

BEHAVIORAL OBJECTIVES

Most of the preceding discussion has assumed that the early childhood programs in which assessment goes on have chosen the children's development as their aim. It has spoken of the goals of the program and of the parents and also of goals for children based in part on an appraisal of their development. These goals have only been described in general terms.

It is obviously important that goals be specified in such a way as to make the nature of acceptable evidence regarding their achievement clear. At the present time many educators believe that the best way to accomplish this is to specify objectives in behavioral terms.

Vance, following Mager,[49] writes:

> Instructional objectives that are stated in vague, abstract terms make it impossible to measure effectiveness of instruction. When an instructional objective does not state a specific, observable child activity, it is not a behavioral objective. Many instructional objectives, sometimes referred to as educational goals, are stated in nebulous terms.[50]

She notes that such words as "know," "feel," "appreciate," "comprehend" are inappropriate for writing objectives unless they specify observable behavior. Using a classification system derived from the work of Gagné and Merrill, Vance describes the writing of behavioral objectives for psychomotor, cognitive, and affective behavior at different levels of complexity. She gives an example of an objective for complex cognitive behavior exemplifying rule learning:

> Given a board placed on an inclined plane and several objects of different shapes, including three toy wheels, he will correctly select the wheels and roll them down the plane when the teacher says, "Show me wheels roll."[51]

---

[48] Robert Glaser, "Individuals and Learning: The New Aptitudes," *Educational Researcher,* 1(6):12, June 1972. Copyright by American Educational Research Association, Washington, D.C.

[49] Robert F. Mager, *Preparing Instructional Objectives* (Palo Alto: Fearon Publishers, 1962).

[50] Barbara Vance, *Teaching the Prekindergarten Child: Instructional Design and Curriculum* (Monterey, Calif.: Brooks/Cole Publishing Co., 1973).

[51] Vance, p. 69.

An example of an expressive problem-solving behavioral objective is the following:

> Each child will create an original easel painting about things he likes to do with other children using easel paper, paints in each of the primary colors, and a brush 3/4" wide.[52]

Affective behavior can be observed only in a free-choice situation. For example:

> Each child . . . will resolve conflict situations with other children verbally rather than physically and without the aid of an adult.[53]

The statement of the objectives specifies the nature of the evidence needed to validate its accomplishment. The test, which is criterion-referenced, Vance notes, may come at any of several points. It may come during the "apply" step of the show-discuss-apply-reinforce sequence of teaching-learning activities. It may come in a review session of the "apply" step. Or, it may be part of a periodic posttesting session. In any event, if the objective is not demonstrated, it is retaught.[54]

The clarity with which behavioral objectives can be stated and communicated, and the specificity they give to teaching and assessment, have great appeal. In many early childhood programs, teachers and curriculum consultants are writing behavioral objectives and designing strategies for teaching them, but other teachers are not so beguiled by what has become extremely fashionable. They ask many questions.

One question has to do with the criteria for selecting objectives. No one need be at a loss for possibilities. If the *Taxonomies of Educational Objectives*[55] are insufficient, the Center for the Study of Evaluation at Los Angeles can provide charts of hierarchical objectives for twenty-one goal areas ranging from personality and social development through cognitive functioning and creativity to health, safety, and social studies.[56] Nevertheless, any one of those objectives must be translated into more specific behavioral terms, stating the observable behavior, the circumstances under which it is to be emitted, and

---

[52] Vance, p. 70.
[53] Vance, p. 74.
[54] Vance, pp. 194–198.
[55] Benjamin S. Bloom, ed., *Taxonomy of Educational Objectives. Handbook I: Cognitive Domain* (New York: David McKay, 1956), and David R. Kratwohl et al., *Taxonomy of Educational Objectives. Handbook II: Affective Domain* (New York: David McKay, 1964).
[56] Preschool/Kindergarten Hierarchical Objectives Charts, Center for the Study of Evaluation, Los Angeles, n.d.

how well it must be done to count as successful. How does one know the behavior one has chosen is appropriate?

Baer confronts the problem when he writes in the foreword to Vance's book:

> To make a potential benefit into an actual one, it will be necessary to choose correctly from all the behavior changes possible in our classrooms and playground. . . . The proof that a given behavior change will actually be to a measurable advantage of the child in whom it is made is simply not available in the typical case, even if we agree on how to define advantage.[57]

The possibility that many of the behavioral objectives may have dubious value is not lessened by the requirement that knowledge be expressed in behavior. Just as the child's competence in language may not be expressed in his performance, so the child may also know or understand or appreciate without telling, pointing, or choosing. Conversely, the child may say the expected response without grasping its meaning.

The problem when objectives must be stated in terms of behavior rather than knowledge is nicely revealed in Kamii's examination of children taught by Engelmann. Kamii comments:

> The six-year-old children who took part in the experiment were taught to conserve weight and volume and to explain specific gravity. In the post-test they were often found to give the correct answers, but usually in a sing-song fashion, as if they did not understand what they were saying. Teaching methods that are rooted in the child's entire cognitive framework, which is in turn rooted all the way back to sensori-motor intelligence, must encourage him to express *exactly* what he experiences and *exactly* what he believes.[58]

Programs using behavioral objectives do not necessarily discount the importance of the child's experience. Vance, for example, emphasizes that children should have direct contact with actual objects, people, places, and events. Firsthand experiences should not be limited to vision alone. "The child's concepts can then be built on reality, not error."[59]

From the viewpoint of cognitive-developmental theory, however, "error" is inherent in the process of knowledge construction. "Error" may occur when new information is assimilated to existing cognitive structures. It may not be corrected until a considerable amount of experience makes the child aware of the discrepancy between his views and actuality or the views of others.

---

[57] Vance, p. viii.
[58] Constance Kamii, "Pedagogical Principles from Piaget's Theory," in Milton Schwebel and Jane Raph, eds., *Piaget in the Classroom* (New York: Basic Books, 1973), p. 212.
[59] Vance, p. 93.

Inherent in much of the discussion of those who espouse the behavioral objectives approach is the notion that the teacher is in command of the learning process. If the children go through the steps she lays out for them, they will learn, even though it may be necessary to reteach some of the steps.

At a more sophisticated level, behavior theorists recognize that the child is not completely malleable, and some are interested in knowledge-behavior relationships.

From a practical point of view, and certainly for the immediate future, there is, as Simons' analysis of behavioral objectives concludes, "No compelling reason for using behavioral objectives. The behavioral evidence of knowledge can be described and measured through the traditional means—standardized tests, subjective judgments, rating scales, teacher-made tests."[60]

ACCOUNTABILITY

Assessment procedures serve a variety of purposes. As much of the preceding discussion has emphasized, they inform the teacher of the progress the child is making and lead to modifications in the curriculum or the teaching strategies or both. Used in this way they contribute to what Scriven describes as *formative* evaluation.[61] Some of the assessment procedures are also appropriate for *summative* evaluation, in which the effectiveness of the curriculum and the teaching is of concern.

Since the resources for education and care are finite, questions of effectiveness are inevitably related to questions of cost. For the amount of time and effort involved, do the children benefit sufficiently? If not, where does the responsibility lie?

To answer these knotty questions of accountability, many school systems have turned to the behavioral objectives approach. The teachers, or the curriculum committee, outline the behavioral objectives for a particular grade. Objectives may be set for individual children, but, perhaps more commonly, a prediction is made as to the percent of children who are expected to achieve each objective. (What happens to the 10 to 20 percent who cannot reach the objective is not specified.) The teacher's competence is then judged on the basis of the extent to which the performance of the children corresponds to the projected accomplishment of objectives.[62]

[60] Herbert Simons, "Behavioral Objectives: A False Hope for Education," *Elementary School Journal,* 73(4):173–181, January 1973.
[61] Michael Scriven, "The Methodology of Evaluation," *Perspectives of Curriculum Evaluation* (Chicago: Rand McNally, 1967), pp. 39–93.
[62] George D. Redfern, "Legally Mandated Evaluation," *The National Elementary Principal,* 53(5): 45–50, February 1973.

At first glance this way of measuring teacher competence appears to be a good way to guarantee accomplishment for a majority of youngsters. In schools where the rates of failure, even when children are promoted regularly, are excessive, this form of evaluation appears to assure better achievement. Examined more closely, it seems no more promising than more traditional procedures. It provides no assurance that the behaviors the children will exhibit are important, nor that they are undergirded with solid knowledge and understanding. Furthermore, it is doubtful that the average teacher will be challenged to set objectives that she and the children can reach only by strenuous effort. Thus, the curriculum may sink to a level of mediocrity where most children can succeed, but in tasks that are insignificant from the long-term view.

As Carini notes, evaluation of this sort reflects "a pragmatic orientation in which efficiency is the covert, if not overt, standard of judgment."[63] Concern is with the end-products, not the processes of learning and thinking. For example, early word recognition is valued with little questioning as to the child's probable involvement or skill in reading at a later time. Nor is consideration given "the meaning of reading in relation to language as an organic and innate human process."

Carini proposes an alternative to accountability based on a narrow or short-term view of child achievement. She follows Whitehead's dictum that the schools and not the scholars should be inspected.[64] What is most important about a school is its ability to reflect on what it is about. Thus, its "potential for ongoingness, continuity, and renewal" must rank with its current accomplishment. It cannot be judged according to isolated elements, nor can the children or teachers be so judged. Accordingly, what goes on in the school must be documented:

> The documentation or description of the program, reflecting its continuity and interrelatedness can be the basis for evaluation, according to any standard that the evaluator wishes to apply. Such evaluation stands in relation to the totality of the program rather than as an absolute judgment rendered in isolation.[65]

Documentation derives from such diverse sources as the children's work, the teacher's journals, weekly records, their assessment of children's work in reading and math activities, their reports to parents, classroom observations, sociograms, and "curriculum trees" (records showing how the activities in which the children engage originate and evolve, how they are interrelated and how they tie into the development of the children).

---

[63] Carini, *Evaluation Reconsidered,* p. 15.
[64] Carini, *The Prospect School; Taking Account of Process,* p. 352.
[65] Carini, *Evaluation Reconsidered,* p. 16.

The behavioral objectives and the Carini approaches represent two extremes for dealing with the issue of accountability. If development is taken as the aim of education, it appears that assessment of the sort described by Carini is more likely to be appropriate.

SUMMARY

Perhaps no aspect of the early childhood educator's work provides greater challenge than that of assessing development and learning. If she takes development as the aim of education and care, she will need to find and develop new modes of assessment, new ways of looking at children. She will always run the risk of subjectivity and poorly documented proof of progress. She will need to defend her position against those who take a narrower view and look for more immediate and directly observable results. Nevertheless, an increasing number of educators and other professionals and parents are dissatisfied with present ways of assessing children and evaluating programs. The early childhood educator will not be alone in her search for better ways.

Chapter 11

Researching Early Childhood Education

Emphasis on humanistic criteria does not imply a retreat from science; rather it points to the need for an enlargement and a rededication of the scientific enterprise. Scientists must give greater prominence to large human concerns when choosing their problems and formulating their results. In addition to the science of things, they must create a science of humanity, if they want the intellectual implications and practical applications of their efforts to be successfully woven into the fabric of modern life. [1]

Dubos, concerned lest our urbanization and technology destroy our humanness, observes that orthodox experimental methods need to be supplemented by others that better approximate the ways human beings experience reality. He notes, and regrets, that the study of the parts of living organisms has not been "sufficiently complemented by ecological studies of systems functioning as integrated wholes." [2]

[1] René Dubos, *So Human an Animal* (New York: Charles Scribner's Sons, 1968), p. 247.
[2] Dubos, p. 242.

The early childhood educator soon learns that much of the research that is relevant to her field deals with limited aspects of children's functioning. Too seldom is that functioning viewed in the context of the child's total experience.

This statement is true despite the fact that the period of early childhood has, in the last decade, received unprecedented attention from both psychologists and educators. The research reports from hundreds of experimental studies, and demonstration projects focusing on the development and learning of young children can probably be weighed by the ton.

RESEARCH IN THE PAST DECADE[3]

Early childhood research encompasses both the basic psychological research related to development and learning and that dealing more specifically with the child in the educational setting. Previous chapters have emphasized how the former provides a base for educational programs. This chapter gives major attention to the latter and suggests the contribution that the early childhood educator has to make to it. First, however, it considers some of the characteristics of the research of the last decade. That research has in certain ways affected the schools and the communities in which it was done. It has engendered attitudes toward research, especially as it focuses on the children of the poor, that current researchers must take into account.

Basic Psychological Research

As Bettye Caldwell[4] notes, the initiation of Project Head Start in 1965 gave instant status to a field (early childhood education) that had long been a stepchild of both education and psychology. The politics of the time provided many psychologists the opportunity to validate certain aspects of developmental and learning theory in natural settings, such as Head Start, and more importantly in experimental programs where closer monitoring was possible.

New avenues of inquiry opened as three-, four-, and five-year-olds of widely differing backgrounds became readily available for the research of psychologists who had previously worked with older children or with middle-class nursery school and kindergarten youngsters. Initially, it is true, they tended to treat the cultural differences they found as deficits. Gradually, however, many have moved toward the view that learning and thinking cannot be adequately understood apart from their cultural context. Certainly, if devel-

---

[3] Portions of the sections that follow were prepared under contract with the Educational Research Information Center for Early Childhood Education, Urbana, Ill.

[4] Bettye M. Caldwell, "Introduction: Period of Consolidation," in Jerome Hellmuth, ed., *Disadvantaged Child*, vol. 3. *Compensatory Education, A National Debate* (New York: Brunner/Mazel, 1970), pp. v–vii.

opmental psychology is more comprehensive and less ethnocentric than a decade ago, the researchers' experiences with Head Start and other innovative early childhood programs have contributed to the change.

Researchers are no longer limiting their interest to the readily accessible three- and four-year-olds but are also studying infants and beginning to devote attention to the toddlers. The knowledge base on which early childhood education can be built is expanding and undergoing revision.

Educational Research

Much of the research related to early childhood education in the past decade deals with the effects of some kind of educational intervention in the lives of preschool children living in poverty areas. In general the strategy of the researchers was to specify a curriculum. A model for the content of the program, the teacher's interaction with the children, and the children's behavior was prescribed. Those concerned with the training of the teachers tried to ensure that the teachers followed the model rather than their own inclination for responding to the child. (This statement applies more to some programs than to others.) The content of the curriculum was very similar from program to program and tended to be derived more often from an analysis of the deficiencies in the academic performance of first graders than from an analysis of how the knowledge and skills manifested in competent intellectual performance usually developed. By the end of 1971 the available evidence from a number of evaluative and comparative studies of Head Start and other experimental programs had been reviewed several times.[5] The research problems were given major prominence in Volume 3 of *The Disadvantaged Child,* edited by Hellmuth, and also in the 1972 Yearbook of the National Society for the Study of Education.[6]

Stearns, in a report to the Office of Child Development,[7] summarizes the evidence succinctly. She notes that, over the short run, public preschool programs have been successful in changing the intellectual and social behavior of disadvantaged children in positive directions. In small-scale, expertly staffed experimental programs, the improvements in measured intellectual abilities

---

[5] Lois-Ellen Datta, "A Report on Evaluation Studies of Project Head Start," *International Journal of Early Childhood Education,* 3:58–69, 1971; Dennis N. McFadden, *Final Report on Preschool Education to Ohio Department of Education* (Columbus: Battelle Memorial Institute, September 1969); James O. Miller, *Early Childhood Education and Research Support Literature—A State of the Art Review* (St. Louis: Central Midwestern Regional Educational Laboratory, March 1972).

[6] Ira J. Gordon, ed., *Early Childhood Education,* Seventy-first Yearbook of the National Society for the Study of Education, Part II (Chicago: University of Chicago Press, 1972).

[7] Marian S. Stearns, *Report on Preschool Programs. The Effects of Preschool Programs on Disadvantaged Children and Their Families* (Washington: Department of Health, Education, and Welfare, Office of Child Development, 1971).

have been even more striking. Nevertheless, after several years the children who have had the preschool experience show no advantage as far as school achievement is concerned over those who did not have it.

When the circumstances that surrounded many of the intervention programs are considered, the evidence gathered appears not insubstantial. Consider that most programs were planned and researched under the pressure of time, without a well-developed and specifically elaborated theoretical base. Very few measures of intellectual skills, other than those represented in the intelligence tests, were available. For other variables, especially those related to self-concept and motivation, the lack of appropriate instruments for use in large-scale studies was even greater. Comparison groups—children of similar age and background who were not involved in a program—were often difficult to locate. Moreover, in too few instances was sufficient consideration given the intricate kinds of relationships that can affect the results and that need to be anticipated when the research is planned.

A major point to be made is that the researcher, as Dubos implies, needs to be concerned not only with the variables in his intended treatment and its expected outcomes. He must consider those intervening variables that may affect the results and also the possible side effects of the treatment. Messick and Barrows, discussing strategies for research and evaluation in early education, list over fifty variables that can affect or be affected by the intervention. As they note, early childhood education deals with a "complicated system"— "a set of multifaceted organisms changing over time in interaction with diverse environmental influences." Furthermore, this system also involves overlapping subsystems—"the child, the family, the community and various peer groups as the school, the teachers and the programs."[8] A number of variables were largely neglected in much of the intervention research.

Health and Nutritional Factors   The bulk of the intervention research focused on children older than three years. As Chapter 6 emphasized, inadequate nutrition and the associated physiological and health factors, prenatally and in the first months of life, greatly restrict the child's development and learning. The question of whether massive pediatric and nutritional intervention in the infancy period might have substantially altered the findings of the educational intervention is unanswered.

Socioeconomic Factors   Also unanswered is the question of the effects that a direct attack on socioeconomic factors related to educational disadvan-

---

[8] Samuel Messick and Thomas H. Barrows, "Strategies for Research and Evaluation in Early Childhood Education," in Gordon, ed., *Early Childhood Education,* p. 262.

tage might have had. From the point of view of research, however, the lesson is that "socioeconomic status" measured by such indices as income and place of residence, masks a number of other factors, such as the adult's perception of his ability to control his environment, that are very influential in the development of the child. Furthermore, members of ethnic minorities are the target of racist attitudes that shape and limit their expectations for both themselves and their children.

Timing of the Intervention   Assuming that an educational intervention is an appropriate strategy, there is considerable question about its timing. Sigel's[9] analysis of the relevance of development to early intervention called attention to the fact that the human organism is made up of a variety of subsystems—perceptual, cognitive, language, sensorimotor, and so on. The relationships among these systems appear to differ at different stages of development, and instruction related to a particular subsystem may have different effects on other subsystems at different points in time. The cumulative effects of instruction in one subsystem may also depend on the nature of the contexts for learning at succeeding stages of development.

White has outlined the matrix of developmental changes that occur between five and seven years.[10] His evidence, drawn from many different fields, highlights the many respects in which the preschooler thinks, learns, and generally responds differently from the older child. The significance of the developmental characteristics of the three- and four-year-old, however, was not very deeply explored by the program developers and educational researchers.[11] They rarely acknowledged that "the child's developmental stage is an important determination in his ability to understand a new cognitive unit."[12]

Only a few programs have taken a view of cognition broad enough to include attention to other than directed thinking processes. Yet it may be that, from a developmental standpoint, the fantasy and spontaneous play that characterize this period and the opportunities provided for them may have as much bearing on later development as does instruction in directed thinking.

In this connection it is interesting to note that Vygotsky, who in general saw the necessity for instruction to be paced a bit ahead of development, considered play in the preschool period "to provide a background for changes

---

[9] Irving E. Sigel, "Developmental Theory: Its Place and Relevance in Early Intervention Programs," *Young Children,* 27(6):364–372, August 1972.

[10] Sheldon White, "Some General Outlines of the Matrix of Developmental Changes between Five and Seven Years," *Bulletin of the Orton Society,* 1970.

[11] In fairness, the fact that research dealing with cognitive processes at these ages was sparse should be noted. The bulk of Piaget's work, for example, included few three- and four-year-olds.

[12] Jerome Kagan, "Cognitive Development and Programs for Day Care," in Edith H. Grotberg, ed., *Day Care: Resources for Decisions* (Office of Economic Opportunity, 1971), pp. 135–152.

in needs and in consciousness of a much wider nature than instruction." In this period, he believed, "Play is the source of development and creates the zone of proximal development."[13]

Evidence that the improved functioning in the intelligence test that characterized many programs may be better attributed to motivational factors than to instruction comes from a program that made ample provision for play. Zigler and Butterfield compared poor children who attended a nursery school with those who did not.[14] The nursery school program, in addition to providing time for free play, included directed musical activities, the reading of stories, occasional excursions, and emphasized pleasant and positive experiences among the children and with the adults.

Zigler and Butterfield also compared the performances of the children when standardized procedures for intelligence testing were used with their performances three weeks later when procedures designed to optimize performance were used. At this point one group had had three weeks of nursery school, the other had not. Both groups performed better in the test using optimized procedures. However, the children who had had the nursery school experience did better than those who had not. The same standard-followed-by-optimized-testing procedures were used after the nursery school group had had seven months in the program. Again, all the children performed better when optimized-testing procedures were used, and again, the nursery school children's performance was significantly better than that of their counterparts who did not attend. Zigler and Butterfield note that "the primary benefit accruing to the children" appears to be "not an increase in their rates of formal cognitive development, but rather that . . . they were better able to use their intelligence in a standard testing situation."[15]

Several other investigators have questioned the developmental appropriateness of formal instruction in the preschool years. Elkind suggests the hypothesis that "the longer we delay formal instruction up to certain limits, the greater the period of plasticity and the higher the ultimate level of achievement."[16] Noting that there is no evidence for either advantaged or disadvantaged children of the *long-term* effects of either instruction or enrichment, Elkind does, however, believe that the nursery school experience has value for children. Such value lies in the way it promotes enjoyment of the immediate world and the opportunity to develop social skills.

Rohwer takes a similar stand.[17] His view is particularly interesting be-

[13] L. S. Vygotsky, *Thought and Language* (Cambridge, Mass.: M.I.T. Press, 1962), p. 104.

[14] Edward Zigler and Earl C. Butterfield, "Motivational Aspects of Changes in IQ Test Performance of Culturally Deprived Nursery School Children," *Child Development,* 39(1):1–26, March 1968.

[15] Zigler and Butterfield, p. 10.

[16] David Elkind, *Children and Adolescents, Interpretive Essays on Piaget* (New York: Oxford University Press, 1970), p. 129.

[17] William D. Rohwer, Jr., "Prime Time for Education: Early Childhood or Adolescence?" *Harvard*

cause it stems from research based on verbal learning rather than from developmental theory. Rohwer's research dealt with tasks involving paired associate learning. In these tasks the researcher presents the learner with a list of word pairs. Later he tests the learner's ability to recall one word from each pair when given the other word as a clue. Research indicates that successful learners mentally elaborate the association between the pairs, either verbally or pictorially. Older learners (age twelve or more) appear to elaborate without being instructed to do so. Younger learners do not appear to elaborate spontaneously, but their performance improves when the conditions of the initial presentation of the pairs provides elaboration (they are associated in sentences or in pictures, for example). When the researchers attempted to *train* the children to elaborate, however, rather than providing the associations for them, the training had small effects for second graders and no effects for kindergartners and preschoolers. The samples in these studies included both white children of high socioeconomic status and Black children of low socioeconomic status. Rohwer's extension of his studies to children in first, third, sixth, eighth, and eleventh grades in school districts serving white children, one with a high socioeconomic population, the other with a low, leads him to propose a hypothesis similar to that of Elkind. This is that the "prime time" for the training of intellectual skills is not the preschool period or even the elementary school years, but rather the point at which in Piaget's terms formal operations begin to emerge—the beginning of adolescence. Intellectual activity is not ruled out for the earlier years. Instead, "the guiding principle of early education (preschool and elementary) should be to provide the child with repeated experiences of gratification resulting from intellectual activity." He adds, "mastery would not be required at a particular early age, rather at the time the child can acquire the skills (and prerequisite subskills) readily and successfully."[18]

Influence of the Research on Practice It is difficult, and perhaps too soon, to estimate the effect that the intervention research has had on classroom practice. That the curricula emphasized cognition is clear, and that teachers increased the amount of direct instruction they gave seems probable, but whether the quality of teaching improved, outside of the closely supervised and well-supported experimental programs, is questionable.

In 1967, in a period that had been noteworthy for the number of research and demonstration programs, many related to early childhood, Goodlad[19] and

Educational Review, 41(3):316–341, 1971.

[18] Rohwer, p. 338.

[19] John Goodlad et al., *Behind the Classroom Door* (Worthington, Ohio: Charles A. Jones Publishing Co., 1970).

a group of associates visited and observed in some 150 kindergarten and primary classrooms across the country. They sought evidence as to how the reforms implicit in the research and demonstration efforts were reflected in the classrooms. They found little. A later study of nursery schools brought equally dreary results.[20] My own informal observations on two coasts have pinpointed some classrooms that clearly do reflect what has been going on in research and in innovative programs in the last decade. But they have not led me to believe that their effects are more widespread than Goodlad found.

New Strategies for Research

If the intervention research was not strikingly successful, it has led to thoughtful reappraisal and to suggestions for new directions to be taken. Science, it may be noted, moves ahead not only through its successes, but also through its failures.

Bereiter, noting that "existing technology already enables us to teach young children far more than they can benefit from," suggests that what we need to do is to "construct articulated educational programs that permit us to teach in the preschool what will be of use later and to teach later what builds upon what was taught in the preschool."[21] He thinks there is little to be gained in research limited to the preschool level. Rather, preschool research should now be incorporated into the programs of research at the elementary school level.

Rohwer,[22] drawing on his own research in verbal learning, proposes a strategy for establishing how and when a particular skill or particular content can be learned with ease. The strategy involves cumulative research using tasks that tap a psychological process involved in school learning. The learning of paired associates, as in his own research, is an example of such a task.[23] These tasks, which should resemble but also differ from typical school tasks, are then to be applied over as wide a developmental range as possible to determine possible developmental shifts. Experimentation is necessary to find the conditions for optimal performance at different ages and with different kinds of children. Instruction can then be planned in accordance with the findings.

Bussis and her colleagues[24] propose a departure from the experimental

---

[20] John Goodlad et al., *Early Schooling in the United States* (New York: McGraw-Hill, 1973).

[21] Carl Bereiter, "An Academic Preschool for Disadvantaged Children: Conclusion from Evaluation Studies," in Julian C. Stanley, ed., *Preschool Programs for the Disadvantaged* (Baltimore: The Johns Hopkins University Press, 1972), p. 16.

[22] William Rohwer, "Decisive Research: A Means for Answering Fundamental Questions about Instruction," *Educational Researcher*, 1(7):5–11, July 1972.

[23] In many respects Olson's examination of the child's acquisition of diagonality, referred to in Chapter 6, represents a similar research strategy.

[24] Anne M. Bussis et al., Draft of a position statement on *Methodology in Educational Evaluation and*

tradition that has been influential in recent early childhood education research. The methodology for research and evaluation they propose stems from the phenomenological tradition in psychology. This tradition is concerned with the belief systems of the individual. It provides constructs that the researcher might use to examine educational programs.

Starting with a finding from much of the intervention research—the teacher, not the curriculum model, makes the important difference in programs—the researcher, for example, asks what the "frame of reference" of the teacher is. What are her assumptions about the nature of the child, his individuality, his ways of learning, his motivation? What does she believe is important to learn? Teachers who have different values as reflected in their reference systems may be expected to teach differently, even within the same curriculum model.

A phenomenological approach also looks at children not as emitters of behavior but rather as individuals with resources and capabilities for intelligent effort, responsibility, and concern for others. Whether such capabilities are realized depends on the extent to which the environment calls for and appreciates them.

In terms of evaluation and research, the phenomenological approach looks for evidence that is based on "standards of quality" rather than specific behavioral objectives. Such standards relate to both the process of learning and its content, and also to the context in which it occurs. In the process aspects of learning, the researcher might look for evidence of responsibility, purposeful effort, and originality on the part of the learner. In the content aspects he might be concerned with the "powerfulness" of the concepts the child acquires. A powerful concept is one that most people would agree is important and central. It also facilitates the attainment of a number of other important concepts.[25] In the area of science, for example, children in early childhood programs often have a variety of experiences with animals. Evidence that these experiences are being so assimilated that the children are developing some understanding of the interdependence of the animals and their environment would suggest that the intended learning involves a powerful concept. With regard to the context of learning, the researcher would look for evidence regarding desired qualities in the relationships among the children and between children and adults. Such qualities might include, for example, respect for an individual's effort and his feelings.

Bussis and her colleagues are concerned, as is Dubos, that we find ways

---

Research, Educational Testing Service, Princeton, N.J., March 1973.

[25] See John Flavell, "Concept Development," in Paul H. Mussen, ed., *Carmichael's Manual of Child Psychology* (New York: John Wiley & Sons, 1970), pp. 988–989.

to encompass in educational research and evaluation more of the reality that confronts teachers and children in the process of education. Their concern is timely. Research following the approach they propose should help to clarify some of the essential ingredients in the education for development recommended in this book.

Although we know a great deal about how children develop and learn as revealed in interviews and laboratory experiments, we have relatively little information on the ways they function in the natural setting of the classroom.

Studies of this aspect of early childhood education are needed, including those that are purely descriptive, if the field is to move ahead into exploratory and hypothesis-generating studies. It seems essential to build a backlog of knowledge, comparable to that which has accrued in psychological studies of learning and development, before attempting major experimental manipulations.

The suggestion that descriptive and explorative studies should take precedence over experimental studies imposes a heavy burden on the researcher. In such investigation the researcher must impose his own conceptual rigor, unaided by the logic of experimental design.

The phenomenological approach proposed by Bussis and her colleagues does not eliminate the necessity for well-conceived procedures, although they are different from those used in experimental investigations. For example, the teacher's "frame of reference" may be determined by interview, but the interviewers must cover the same areas with each teacher, and in approximately similar fashion, if they are to derive any information about similarities and differences among the teachers. Similarly, when naturalistic observations of the classroom are made, the researchers must reach some agreement, either prior to observation or after study of the recorded observations, as to what constitutes quality. Under what circumstances, for example, does a child's effort meet the criterion of "purposeful"? Knowledge of the child, as well as knowledge of the context for the incident, may be required.

THE EARLY CHILDHOOD EDUCATOR AS RESEARCHER

The early childhood educator as described in this book has great potential for initiating and perhaps conducting the kind of research that is currently needed in early childhood education. She knows the realities of the classroom, the interests and capabilities of the children, and the concerns of the teachers and parents. She has the inquiring mind that raises the kinds of questions on which evidence should be brought to bear.

Obviously, if the early childhood educator is carrying responsibility for some teaching of the children, for working with parents, for training and supervising staff, and for administration, she is unlikely to have either the time or the energy to become a researcher as well. On the other hand, if her work can be arranged so that she has some time for reflection, she can contribute a great deal to the research enterprise, even if she does not take major responsibility for it.

If the early childhood educator understands how research is done (her training should certainly involve participation in research), she is in a good position to serve as a bridge person between the researchers and the intended consumers of research. She can serve as a corrective against a tendency for the researcher and his research to become increasingly remote from the actualities he is researching. Modern technology makes it quite possible to collect and analyze data relating to a multiplicity of variables in quantities unthinkable a decade or two ago. The data and their analysis appear to take on a reality and meaning of their own, quite apart from the educational situations and problems they represent. The distance between the researchers and the researched widens. The possible significance of the research in human terms often is overlooked. Skepticism, and even hostility toward research, is engendered, and these attitudes are not directed only toward educational research.

Kass, in an issue of *Science,* writes: "We are witnessing the erosion, perhaps the final erosion, of the idea of man as something splendid or divine and the replacement with a view that sees man no less than nature as simply more raw material for manipulation and homogenization." Hope, he thinks, "lies only in education, in a public educated about the ways and limits of science and enlightened in its use of technology."[26] Further, he suggests that the current lack of money for research gives time to rethink and reorder our priorities.

The situation with regard to early childhood education research seems not dissimilar to that Kass describes for biological research. Funding is likely to be relatively limited. We too need time to rethink and reorder our priorities, keeping in mind our concern for maintaining our humanness.

The early childhood educator may be in a strategic position to shift some of the focus toward research that has clearer relevance to the teachers and to the parents. This may well mean involving them more as participants than as "subjects" in research that they can understand.[27]

The "action research" that was popular in the early 1950s may provide some clues for what is needed, but circumstances then differed in many respects from those of today. The notion behind this kind of research was that

---

[26] Leon R. Kass, "The New Biology: What Price Relieving Man's Estate?" *Science,* Nov. 19, 1971, pp. 779–788.
[27] For an example of such involvement, see Betty Van Wyck, "Research for Understanding," *Young Children,* 27(2):93–96, December 1971.

teachers identified the problems for which they felt they needed answers. They developed hunches about the causes of the problems and also about how they might be solved. Then they collected evidence regarding causes and possible solutions and eventually tried the hunch (which might have been reformulated following the initial collection of evidence) in action.

This way of working takes into account the fact that each classroom situation is different. What works in one may not work in another. If it is to advance understanding of the educational process, however, it needs to move beyond the individual classroom. Unless it involves some individuals who can relate it to the growing body of knowledge in education and to the variety of research strategies, it may become extremely parochial. The need for the early childhood educator to be informed about the research in the field, and about research methodology, seems obvious.

At this point, the reader may find it profitable to turn back to some of the earlier chapters to consider the kinds of questions that have been raised, which ones are appropriate for research by the early childhood educator, and what research strategies might be most appropriate.

NEEDED RESEARCH

What kinds of steps might be taken to provide greater involvement of parents and teachers and more obviously relevant research? In each of what Messick and Barrows have identified as domains of largely unmeasured variables there are many questions that researchers, together with parents and teachers, might investigate.

The Child and His Family

Consider first the child and his family. There should be no need to belabor the ethnocentric assumptions in much recent early childhood research and in many programs. With increasing awareness of the stereotyping implicit in the notion of cultural deprivation, it may be possible to come to terms with the *realities* faced by parents in different groups and the *specific* nature of their strengths, their concerns and aspirations for their children as well as the *specific* nature of their relationships with them. How do these affect what they want for their children and their expectations for the classroom?

In the last decade many measures of cognition, many ways of looking at cognitive processes in young children, have been developed. It seems time to examine more closely how such processes are reflected in the social-emotional behavior of the individual child as well as in his school tasks. What is a reasonable balance between time given to assessment, time given to instruction, and time for the child to proceed on his own? Currently, at least in some parts of the country, and even as early as kindergarten, as much or more time is spent in assessment as in instruction, with little if any time left for the child's autonomous investigation and learning—for him to find out who he is.

Although one finds in the current literature of early childhood education, and in the research related to it, considerable emphasis on individualization, case studies of young children revealing the nature of their individuality and its significance for their education, are rarely encountered. Do we not need in the 1970s researchers who will work with parents, teachers, and children to show how young Black, Chicano, Asian, native American, and other children from varying backgrounds cope with their widening world, much as Murphy described Topeka children in the 1950s?[28]

Better ways also need to be found to get at the children's perceptions of what goes on in the classroom. It is too easy to assume that their performance reveals all they know or feel. How many times, for example, have children presented a facade to the teachers such as that recently reported by an anthropological observer.[29] A group of Spanish-surname six-year-olds were being taught English in a behavior modification program. They were not responding appropriately, and were giving the teacher, for example, an orange when she asked for an apple. Once the teacher left the room, however, the children with roars of laughter, began an elaborate mimicry of the earlier task, first giving the *correct* response to each object, and then chanting every possible wrong name.

The Classroom and the Teaching

The classroom and the teaching each represent additional domains for investigation. Work on the early childhood education classroom as an activity setting, in the ecological tradition of Barker and Wright discussed in Chapter 7, promises to be especially fruitful. Kounin and his colleagues[30] video-taped 600 lessons chosen and planned by student teachers for small groups of nursery school children. They also taped 37 two-hour sessions of free play in the same racially and socioeconomically mixed nursery school. Their analyses of the tapes have provided information about the properties of the lessons as related to the way children behave. Within the same lessons they have also studied the incidence of glee on the part of the children. In the free-play setting they

---

[28] Lois B. Murphy, *The Widening World of Childhood* (New York: Basic Books, 1962).

[29] Henry G. Burger, "Behavior Modification and Operant Psychology: An Anthropological Critique," *American Educational Research Journal,* 9(3):343–360, Summer 1972.

[30] Jacob S. Kounin et al., Papers presented at the meetings of the American Psychological Association, Montreal, Canada, 1973.

studied the holding power of various parts of the setting and also the nature of the children's interpersonal conflicts.

This kind of research falls in the descriptive, hypothesis-generating rather than hypothesis-testing category. As one of the investigators points out, the nursery school teacher has long been involved in creating settings for children's learning and development. Yet most research has focused on the child rather than the ecological context. The fact that many of the findings from the ecological studies show that the behavior of a child may be predicted more accurately on the basis of *where* he is rather than *who* he is underscores the importance of this line of investigation.

In much recent research, as has been emphasized, the curriculum model in use has received major attention. There is some evidence that the curriculum, to some extent, influences the teaching. The Soars[31] applied interaction analysis, adapted to identify both affective and cognitive aspects of learning and the sequences of teacher and pupil talk, to classrooms representing eight curriculum models. They were able to identify three groups of classrooms within which the differences were not significant, although the differences between the groups were significant. It should be noted, however, that the variability within the classrooms representing a single curriculum model was greater than the differences from model to model.

The classroom processes revealed by the analysis were found to relate to the cognitive growth of the children. Greater teacher direction increased simple-concrete learning but at the expense of complex-abstract growth. The Soars, however, note that there are limits with respect to the amounts of pupil freedom, interaction, and self-direction that are functional.

This study, taken in conjunction with Gordon's[32] analysis of the instructional theory underlying the various curriculum models, raises a number of questions about curriculum, more about teaching.

Aside from the differing reliance they place on workbooks, many of the curriculum models look surprisingly alike when seen in operation. Each has a similar array of toys, games, and audiovisual equipment, plus the paint, clay, blocks, and in some instances housekeeping equipment that has been standard in the nursery school for years. Does this seemingly infinite variety of materials and equipment really enhance the children's learning? Or does it merely reflect the American propensity for conspicuous consumption? Clearly the teacher is under less pressure to intervene in the children's activities if there are enough, or more than enough, materials to keep them busy on their own. How do the

---

[31] Soar and Soar, "An Empirical Analysis of Selected Follow Through Programs," in Gordon, ed., *Early Childhood Education,* 1972.

[32] Gordon, "An Instructional Theory Approach to the Analysis of Selected Early Childhood Programs," in *Early Childhood Education,* 1972.

children use the materials? What ones are essential? What is gained by adding others? Is it possible to have so many materials as to detract from both the social and the cognitive interaction of the children? May the teacher become so involved in the acquisition and upkeep and storage of curriculum materials as to lose sight of their essential purpose?

As Weikart has commented,[33] the curriculum is for the teacher more than for the children. It may be useful to examine the elements of the curriculum that further the fulfillment of the teaching role as contrasted with those that may actually impede it. For it is the role of the teacher and the support she has that make for the major differences among curriculum models.

Especially in programs that focus on the development of the individual child, we need to know much more about the range of behaviors that are initated by the children, and also about the variety of responses teachers make to such initiations. What is the nature of teaching in classrooms where the children have a high degree of autonomy? Observational studies will be helpful in this regard but may not be sufficient. Ways need to be found to reveal more than the teacher's behavior. Are her responses to the children merely intuitive, or are they guided by theoretical knowledge? As Jackson suggests,[34] the ongoing demands of the classroom are too intense for on-the-spot reflection, but this need not preclude an analysis of the teacher's preplanning in relation to what actually occurred, nor perhaps more importantly an analysis of her reflections on those occurrences. Such an analysis might be related to the frame-of-reference approach suggested by Bussis.

Other questions need to be asked. For example, how does the teaching done by parent participants, volunteers, or paraprofessionals differ from that done by the professionally trained teacher? Or *does* it differ initially and then come to resemble the teacher's? Insistence that at least one member of the team needs professional training seems reasonable, but where are the data to show what the professional does differently from the less well-trained? Are the differences important to the child's thinking and learning, or may they merely reflect cultural differences in child-rearing practices that have no necessary consequence to the child's eventual development? Obviously, questions such as these cannot be easily or quickly answered, but it is clear that we need to look closely and carefully at the variety of strategies adults have for teaching the young child, and give consideration to their effects on him.

The fact that programs for three- and four-year-olds, and to a growing extent those for five- and six-year-olds, increasingly involve the operation of

---

[33] David Weikart, "Relationship of Curriculum, Teaching, and Learning in Preschool Education," in Stanley, ed., *Preschool Programs for the Disadvantaged,* 1972.
[34] Philip W. Jackson, *Life in Classrooms* (New York: Holt, Rinehart and Winston, 1968).

a team raises additional questions about the teacher's role. How much of her time is spent in interaction, not with children but with other adults, and what goes on in those interactions? What effect does this changing and expansion of the teacher's role have on her effectiveness with children and on satisfactions she derives from it?

In the past it appeared that many individuals who elected to teach at the earliest levels did so because they preferred working with children to working with adults. Is this true at the present time?

What if the teacher is a man? The increasing involvement of men in early childhood programs provides an excellent opportunity to examine some of the assumptions that have dominated teaching at this level. Has it been dominated by feminine conceptions and goals? Do those who are consciously aware of sex stereotyping teach differently from those who are more traditionally oriented?

The Institutional Setting

Investigation of teaching should also raise questions about another set of variables, those having to do with the institutional setting. Preschool programs are now to be found in many public schools, but they are also affiliated with a variety of community agencies, and in some instances are relatively autonomous. Does the setting affect the teaching and the program, and in what ways? The younger the children, the less amenable they are to the kinds of regulations that have come to characterize many elementary schools. Are programs in schools more constricted than those in other settings? What is the nature of the interaction between the teachers and the administration? Does the prekindergarten program tend to become isolated as it appears the kindergarten did earlier, or is it incorporated into the totality of the school?

Evidence related to questions such as these is particularly important at this time when many people find persuasive the argument that extension of public education downward can only result in the same kind of bureaucratization that pervades elementary and secondary education.

Research and the Researcher

If bureaucracy is inherent in the public school system, it is also an inevitable concomitant of large-scale research. Many of the questions that I have raised here could be incorporated in a grand design, involving many schools and centers, many children, and many, many teachers in many parts of the country. We may be in a position to ask different and better questions, however, if the questions are pursued in smaller ways with the participation, not merely the cooperation, of parents and teachers. When they are involved from the beginning, helping to formulate the purposes of the research, considering the evidence to be gathered, how it is to be validated, and how it is to be used, research should take on new meaning, not as something esoteric but as a means to an end. That end is improved practice, and fuller realization of the human potential of the children, the teachers, and the parents.

Chapter 12

The Work of the Early Childhood Educator: A Personal View

To feel for *others (as distinguished from going through the motions of* doing *for others),* to feel with *others (as distinguished from going through motions of* cooperating *with them), it is essential that the teacher draw upon his own capacity for feeling. And he can do this only if he respects his feelings and is at home with them, if he accepts them as part of himself. This means self-acceptance, which involves compassion for oneself.*[1]

In this book I have proposed a new role in early childhood education. Building on the role of the teacher, it extends beyond the classroom, to provide support to teachers and to parents in the education and care of young children.

I can identify many individuals whose work corresponds in fact to the work involved in the role that I have termed "early childhood educator." Their titles vary. Some are classroom teachers, but teachers with profound knowledge of children and deep respect for parents, and skill in working with other

---

[1] Arthur T. Jersild, *When Teachers Face Themselves* (New York: Bureau of Publications, Teachers College, Columbia University, 1955), p. 133.

adults. Others are known as directors, consultants, or coordinators. Titles do not matter. What does matter is that there should be a sufficient number of them to ensure that the education and care of young children, whether in school or center or home-based programs, is of good quality.

"Quality" has become a slogan for programs that are more than custodial, a euphemism for programs that cost more—but quality, when it comes to children, is less a matter of money than it is of people. This is not to say that good early childhood programs are not expensive. They are. I see no reason why those who choose to work with children and are effective should not be paid on a scale commensurate with that of other comparably skilled workers. Many are clearly underpaid.

The effectiveness of people, however, seems not a matter of what they are paid, but rather of the depth of their insight and the breadth of their knowledge. I have tried to show the complexity of factors that are involved in providing adequately for the development and learning of young children in a society already beset by "future shock." I do not contend that all who work with young children need grasp this complexity, but I do maintain that every program needs direct access to a person who does, and who also knows the children and their parents as persons, not merely as statistics. I do not think that it is sufficient to have such a person available in an administrative office comfortably removed from the action that is inherent in any good program for children. Obviously, however, I hope those in the upper echelons of whatever bureaucratic structures are inevitable will be equally knowledgeable.

RETROSPECT

In the presentation of the case for and the description of the work of the early childhood educator certain themes have recurred. I shall emphasize some of them again.

Individuality

Each child, each parent, each teacher is unique. Each has potential for development. The aim of programs for young children should be to foster the fullest development of the child in ways that also allow for the development of parents and teachers.

The fact of individuality means that what enhances development for one child may be less effective for another. Each child's concerns, interests, style of learning, and level of development needs consideration if the program is to provide an appropriate match to his developing abilities.

The "Whole" Child in Context

We never deal with children who are other than whole, but children learn, remarkably soon, to fit the context that is provided for them. If the situation demands that they function like disembodied intellects, they make a good pretense of being just that. They can also conform to a regime that treats them as though they are mindless.

Older children align themselves with their peers and develop their own defenses against adults who make provisions inadequate to their needs. Young children are more vulnerable and need more protection from programs that exploit one aspect of their development at the expense of another. This matters even more when, as seems to happen more and more often, the child spends the major part of his waking hours in a program.

Concern for the whole child and for his unique abilities implies regard for his competence. Promoting the development of skills that enable him to cope with an increasing array of problems seems a sensible way to ensure his ability to adapt to a changing world. Filling him with facts or teaching him to deal only with problems that are important in school, but not elsewhere, is not.

Cognition and Affect

Writing this book in the years when preoccupation with cognition, often to the exclusion of other aspects of development and learning, is beginning to abate, I have nonetheless written more about intellectual development than about the emotional, physical, or social aspects of development. The emphasis is deliberate. In part it reflects an assumption that the primary concern in most schools and many centers continues to focus on the cognitive. This appears to be true even though many of the researchers who initiated that emphasis are now counseling caution as they turn their attention to other related aspects of development and as they become more involved in cross-cultural investigation.

My emphasis on intelligence also anticipates a trend already in evidence. This is represented in programs where the major focus is on experiencing and enjoying, perhaps one might say more on "being" than on "becoming."

The proponents of many such programs, profoundly dissatisfied with a society that categorizes and manipulates people with little regard for human and existential meanings, take an essentially anti-intellectual stance. Although their critique of modern society seems valid, the implicit assumption that emotion somehow outranks intellect in human value seems dubious. The human animal is at once intellectual and emotional.

Having a good recollection of certain programs in the 1950s that were so oriented to social-emotional development as to preclude something for the minds of the children, I cannot support programs that emphasize cognition but not affect, nor programs that emphasize affect but not cognition. I have tried to show that there are many ways of knowing and that feeling and thought are necessarily intertwined.

The Wise Use of Technology

A return to a simpler, more natural environment both for living and for education is appealing, but the chances that today's children will grow to adulthood in a world bereft of technology seem too slight to orient their education around that possibility. It does seem important, however, to consider carefully the long-term as well as the short-term consequences involved in the technology that is used in early education.

BECOMING AN EARLY CHILDHOOD EDUCATOR

The themes that characterize the approach to early childhood education and care taken in this book are equally applicable in the education of the early childhood educator. As I have indicated, however, the early childhood educator, as an adult with an adult intelligence, can also acquire information and knowledge in ways that are not appropriate for the young child.

I shall not reiterate themes already reviewed. Rather, I turn to the kinds of personal demands and rewards the individual can expect as she (or he) works as an early childhood educator.

Prospect

Some people are pushed into the role of early childhood educator. The setting in which they are working, usually as a teacher, has need for someone who can carry out certain additional functions, and they are chosen. Other people, an increasing number if early childhood education continues to expand, choose the role and plan their careers with that focus.

Whether choosing or chosen, individuals looking toward the role as their life work need to face very seriously two questions. One has to do with their working relationships with other adults. Do adult relationships afford them satisfactions equivalent to those derived from working with children? What additional satisfactions are anticipated or fantasized for the new role? Being known and liked by more people? Power? Superiority? Pleasure in sacrifice for the good of others? No one can expect to be free of such motivations, but no one can function effectively to promote the development of others unless he or she is aware of and in command of them and of other more constructive motivations. Thus, it seems, the early childhood educator, both in preparation for and occupation of this role, needs the kind of open exchange with some other adults that keeps him in touch with the reality of his own feelings.

The other question the prospective early childhood educator ought to face has to do with an interest in solving problems by bringing knowledge to bear on them. Neither the individual who takes little pleasure in exploring ideas and their consequences nor the one who plunges ahead on each new idea, seeing no necessity for either reflection or the marshalling of evidence, seems appropriate for the role.

A Person, Not a Paragon

In trying to depict the many functions that may be encompassed in the role of the early childhood educator and some of the essential requirements for effective functioning, I may have created the impression that only a paragon, not an ordinary human being, can fill the role.

No one person is expected to carry out all the functions that have been described. Furthermore, each person will do some things better and more happily than other things. Pressures to be "all things to all people" can, however, be expected, and must, if the individual is to maintain integrity, be resisted.

I believe that the role is best filled by the person who, in addition to his (or her) knowledge of children, interest in them, in adults, and in problem solving, has a strong sense of self. With awareness of one's own frailties and one's own strengths, one is likely to have the basic regard and compassion for other human beings that are essential.

Index